I dedicate this book to all the people I met during my years as a Xamarin developer that never believed in Xamarin. If you read this book, you will hopefully understand how great Xamarin is!

– Daniel Hindrikes

This book is dedicated to the spider in my basement that motivated me to write a book thick enough to finally kill him with.

– Johan Karlsson

`mapt.io`

Mapt is an online digital library that gives you full access to over 5,000 books and videos, as well as industry leading tools to help you plan your personal development and advance your career. For more information, please visit our website.

Why subscribe?

- Spend less time learning and more time coding with practical eBooks and videos from over 4,000 industry professionals

- Improve your learning with Skill Plans built especially for you

- Get a free eBook or video every month

- Mapt is fully searchable

- Copy and paste, print, and bookmark content

Packt.com

Did you know that Packt offers eBook versions of every book published, with PDF and ePub files available? You can upgrade to the eBook version at `www.packt.com` and as a print book customer, you are entitled to a discount on the eBook copy. Get in touch with us at `customercare@packtpub.com` for more details.

At `www.packt.com`, you can also read a collection of free technical articles, sign up for a range of free newsletters, and receive exclusive discounts and offers on Packt books and eBooks.

Foreword

Xamarin.Forms was launched 6 years ago with the humble intention of being a simple tool for creating simple apps. In the years since then, the toolkit has grown considerably, becoming more capable and more complex. To my astonishment, a community sprung up around this little project, and before we knew it there were thousands of early adopters. It turns out there was a real call for bringing a XAML-style framework to mobile application development.

The journey to today has not been without mistakes. At times, things have become more complicated or less clear than they ought to have been. With the public release of version 1.0, there were many problems with the toolkit, and it took a lot of work, along with help from the community, to get most of them ironed out. I tell you this not to turn you away from using Xamarin.Forms—quite the opposite—it has had its trial by fire. I tell you this because having a guide who has seen where the traps and pitfalls are can save you time and anguish.

Johan Karlsson and Daniel Hindrikes have proven with this book that they not only understand how to use the tool we created, but they understand the vision of where we are trying to go. Their knowledge and expertise will help you to have a more complete understanding of the toolkit, as well as letting you navigate its ups and downs. This book will walk you through the most basic aspects of Xamarin.Forms through to some of the most complicated, and takes in some interesting side-streets along the way.

Jason Smith

Xamarin.Forms co-creator

Contributors

About the authors

Johan Karlsson has been working with Xamarin since the days of MonoTouch and Mono for Android, and it all started with writing a game. He is a full-stack developer, currently focusing on mobile applications using Xamarin. But he has, in the past, worked a lot with ASP.NET MVC, Visual Basic.NET, and C#. He has also created a whole bunch of databases in SQL Server over the years.

Johan works at tretton37 in Sweden and has about 20 years experience in the trade of assembling ones and zeros.

I want to send a special thanks to my ex-wife, Jenny, for allowing me to pursue my coding interest by letting me fly around the world at the most inconvenient times! (Honey, I'm heading to The United States tomorrow. Please feed the cat and pick our kids up from daycare, etc.) And, of course, to my children, Ville and Lisa, for being an inspiration in life!

Also, thanks to Packt and our tech reviewer, Jimmy Engström, who has nitpicked our applications, and made us sit up late at night correcting the code. (Smiles...)

Xamarin.Forms Projects

Build seven real-world cross-platform mobile apps with C# and Xamarin.Forms

Johan Karlsson
Daniel Hindrikes

BIRMINGHAM - MUMBAI

Xamarin.Forms Projects

Commissioning Editor: Pavan Ramchandani
Acquisition Editor: Trusha Shriyan
Content Development Editor: Pranay Fereira
Technical Editor: Aishwarya More
Copy Editor: Safis Editing
Project Coordinator: Pragati Shukla
Proofreader: Safis Editing
Indexer: Priyanka Dhadke
Graphics: Alishon Mendonsa
Production Coordinator: Shraddha Falebhai

First published: December 2018

Production reference: 1261218

Published by Packt Publishing Ltd.
Livery Place
35 Livery Street
Birmingham
B3 2PB, UK.

ISBN 978-1-78953-750-5

www.packtpub.com

Daniel Hindrikes is a developer and architect whose passion is for developing mobile apps powered by the cloud. Daniel fell in love with Xamarin in its early days, when he realized that he could use C# even for iOS and Android apps, and that he could share code with the Windows applications he was building. But Daniel started to build mobile applications long before that: he built Android applications with Java and even Java ME applications (a long, long time ago).

Daniel enjoys sharing his knowledge, for example, by speaking at conferences, blogging, and recording the podcast The Code Behind.

Daniel works at tretton37 in Sweden and has experience of working with both local and global customers.

My special thanks to my family; my wife, Anna-Karin; and our twins, Ella and Willner. They've supported me during the writing process.

Also, I would like to say thanks to the fantastic team at Packt and our technical reviewer, Jimmy Engström, who has reviewed the content and helped us make it better.

About the reviewer

Jimmy Engstrom wrote his first line of code when he was 7 years old, and it has been his greatest passion. It is a passion since that day that has made him the developer he is today and that has taken him around the world, spreading his knowledge. It has given him awards such as second place in Dice's worldwide game developer competition, a place in the top ten best developers in Sweden, five Microsoft MVP awards in Windows development, not to mention Geek of the year. When he is not out spreading his knowledge, he is working as a web developer, trying out the latest tech, or reading up on the latest framework.

Jimmy also runs his own company, called Azm Dev, with his wife, where they focus on *future tech* such as AI, bots, and holographic computing, but also on teaching UX and presentation skills.

He is the co-host of a podcast called *Coding After Work*.

> *A big thank you to my wife, Jessica, who has been picking up my slack while reviewing this book.*
> *Love you!*

Packt is searching for authors like you

If you're interested in becoming an author for Packt, please visit `authors.packtpub.com` and apply today. We have worked with thousands of developers and tech professionals, just like you, to help them share their insight with the global tech community. You can make a general application, apply for a specific hot topic that we are recruiting an author for, or submit your own idea.

Table of Contents

Preface

Xamarin.Forms Projects is a hands-on book in which you get to create seven applications from the ground up. You will gain the fundamental skills you need in order to set up your environment, and we will explain what Xamarin is before we transition into Xamarin.Forms to really take advantage of truly native cross-platform code.

After reading this book, you will have a real-life understanding of what it takes to create an app that you can build on and that stands the test of time.

We will cover, among other things, animations, augmented reality, consuming REST interfaces, real-time chat using SignalR, and location tracking using a device's GPS. There is also room for machine learning and the must-have to-do list.

Happy coding!

Who this book is for

This book is for developers who know their way around C# and Visual Studio. You don't have to be a professional programmer, but you should have basic knowledge of object-oriented programming using .NET and C#. The typical reader would be someone who wants to explore how you can use Xamarin, and specifically Xamarin.Forms, to create applications using .NET and C#.

No knowledge of Xamarin is required ahead of time, but it would be a great help if you've worked in traditional Xamarin and want to take the step toward Xamarin.Forms.

What this book covers

Chapter 1, *Introduction to Xamarin*, explains the basic concepts of Xamarin and Xamarin.Forms. It helps you understand the building blocks of how to create a true cross-platform app. It's the only theoretical chapter of the book and it will help you get started and set up your development environment.

Chapter 2, *Building Our First Xamarin.Forms App*, guides you through the concepts of Model-View-ViewModel and explains how to use Inversion of Control to simplify the creation of Views and ViewModels. We will create a to-do app that supports navigation, filtering, and the adding of to-do items to a list, and will also render a user interface that takes advantage of the powerful data-binding mechanisms in Xamarin.Forms.

Chapter 3, *A Matchmaking App with a Rich UX Using Animations*, lets you dive deeper into how to define a richer user interface with animations and content placement. It also covers the concept of custom controls to encapsulate the user interface into components that are self-contained.

Chapter 4, *Building a Location-Tracking App Using GPS and Maps*, taps into using geolocation data from the device's GPS and how to plot this data on a layer on a map. It also explains how to use background services to keep tracking the location over a long period of time to create a heat map of where you spend your time.

Chapter 5, *Building a Weather App for Multiple Form Factors*, is all about consuming a third-party REST interface and displaying the data in a user-friendly way. We will hook up to a weather service to get the forecast for the current location you are in and display the results in a list.

Chapter 6, *Setting up a Backend for a Chat App Using Azure Services*, is the first of a two-part chapter in which we'll set up as a chat app. This chapter explains how to use Azure Services to create a backend that exposes functionality through SignalR to set up a real-time communication channel between apps.

Chapter 7, *Building a Real-Time Chat Application*, follows on from the previous chapter and covers the frontend of the app, in this case, a Xamarin.Forms app that connects to the backend that relays messages between users. The chapter focuses on setting up SignalR on the client side and explains how to create a service model that abstracts this communication through messages and events.

Chapter 8, *Creating an Augmented Reality Game*, ties the two different AR APIs into a single UrhoSharp solution. Android uses ARCore to handle augmented reality, and iOS uses ARKit to do the same. We will drop down into platform-specific APIs through custom renderers and expose the result as a common API for the Xamarin.Forms app to consume.

Chapter 9, *Hot Dog or Not Hot Dog Using Machine Learning*, covers the creation of an app that uses machine learning to identify whether an image contains a hot dog or not.

To get the most out of this book

We recommend that you read the first chapter to make sure that you are up to speed with the basic concepts of Xamarin in general. After that, you could pretty much pick any chapter you like to learn more about. Each chapter is standalone but the chapters are ordered by complexity; the further you are into the book, the more complex the app is.

The apps are adapted for real-world use but some parts are left out, such as proper error handling and analytics, since they are out of the scope of the book. You should, however, get a good grasp of the building blocks of how to create an app.

Having said that, it does help if you have been a C# and .NET developer for a while, since many of the concepts are not really app-specific but are good practice in general, such as Model-View-ViewModel and Inversion of Control.

But, most of all, it's a book you can use to kick-start your Xamarin.Forms development learning curve by focusing on what chapters interest you the most.

Download the example code files

The code bundle for the book is also hosted on GitHub at `https://github.com/PacktPublishing/Xamarin.Forms-Projects`. In case there's an update to the code, it will be updated on the existing GitHub repository.

We also have other code bundles from our rich catalog of books and videos available at `https://github.com/PacktPublishing/`. Check them out!

Download the color images

We also provide a PDF file that has color images of the screenshots/diagrams used in this book. You can download it here: `https://www.packtpub.com/sites/default/files/downloads/9781789537505_ColorImages.pdf`.

Conventions used

There are a number of text conventions used throughout this book.

`CodeInText`: Indicates code words in text, database table names, folder names, filenames, file extensions, pathnames, dummy URLs, user input, and Twitter handles. Here is an example: "Open the `DescriptionGenerator.cs` file and add a constructor, as shown in the following code."

A block of code is set as follows:

```
public class DescriptionGenerator
{
  private string[] _adjectives = { "nice", "horrible", "great",
                                 "terribly old", "brand new" };
  private string[] _other = { "picture of grandpa", "car", "photo
                            of a forest", "duck" };
  private static Random random = new Random();
  public string Generate()
{
  var a = _adjectives[random.Next(_adjectives.Count())];
  var b = _other[random.Next(_other.Count())];
  return $"A {a} {b}";
}
}
```

When we wish to draw your attention to a particular part of a code block, the relevant lines or items are set in bold:

```
{
    TabLayoutResource = Resource.Layout.Tabbar;
    ToolbarResource = Resource.Layout.Toolbar;

    base.OnCreate(savedInstanceState);
    global::Xamarin.Forms.Forms.Init(this, savedInstanceState);
    Xamarin.Essentials.Platform.Init(this, savedInstanceState);
    LoadApplication(new App());
}
```

Bold: Indicates a new term, an important word, or words that you see onscreen. For example, words in menus or dialog boxes appear in the text like this. Here is an example: "Select **System info** from the **Administration** panel."

 Warnings or important notes appear like this.

 Tips and tricks appear like this.

Get in touch

Feedback from our readers is always welcome.

General feedback: If you have questions about any aspect of this book, mention the book title in the subject of your message and email us at customercare@packtpub.com.

Errata: Although we have taken every care to ensure the accuracy of our content, mistakes do happen. If you have found a mistake in this book, we would be grateful if you would report this to us. Please visit www.packt.com/submit-errata, selecting your book, clicking on the Errata Submission Form link, and entering the details.

Piracy: If you come across any illegal copies of our works in any form on the Internet, we would be grateful if you would provide us with the location address or website name. Please contact us at copyright@packt.com with a link to the material.

If you are interested in becoming an author: If there is a topic that you have expertise in and you are interested in either writing or contributing to a book, please visit authors.packtpub.com.

Reviews

Please leave a review. Once you have read and used this book, why not leave a review on the site that you purchased it from? Potential readers can then see and use your unbiased opinion to make purchase decisions, we at Packt can understand what you think about our products, and our authors can see your feedback on their book. Thank you!

For more information about Packt, please visit packt.com.

Introduction to Xamarin

1

This chapter is all about getting to know what Xamarin is and what to expect from it. It is the only chapter that is a pure theory chapter; all the others will cover hands-on projects. You're not expected to write any code at this point, but instead, simply read through the chapter to develop a high-level understanding of what Xamarin is and how Xamarin.Forms are related to Xamarin.

We will start by defining what a native application is and what .NET as a technology brings to the table. After that, we will look at how Xamarin.Forms fit into the bigger picture and

learn when it is appropriate to use traditional Xamarin and Xamarin.Forms. We often use the term *traditional Xamarin* to describe applications that don't use Xamarin.Forms, even though Xamarin.Forms applications are bootstrapped through a traditional Xamarin application.

In this chapter, we will be covering the following topics:

- Native applications
- Xamarin and Mono
- Xamarin.Forms
- Setting up a development machine

Let's get started!

Native applications

The term **native application** means different things to different people. For some people, it is an application that is developed using the tools specified by the creator of the platform, such as an application developed for iOS with Objective-C or Swift, an Android app developed with Java or Kotlin, or a Windows app developed with .NET. Other people use the term *native application* to refer to applications that are compiled to machine code that is native. In this book, we will define a native application as one that has a native user interface, performance, and API access. The following list explains these three concepts in greater detail:

- **Native user interface**: Applications built with Xamarin use the standard controls for each platform. This means, for example, that an iOS app built with Xamarin will look and behave as an iOS user would expect, and an Android app built with Xamarin will look and behave as an Android user would expect.

- **Native performance**: Applications built with Xamarin are compiled for native performance and could use platform-specific hardware acceleration.

- **Native API access:** Native API access means that applications built with Xamarin could use everything that the target platforms and devices offer to developers.

Xamarin and Mono

Xamarin is a developer platform that is used for developing native applications for iOS (Xamarin.iOS), Android (Xamarin.Android), and macOS (Xamarin.Mac). It is technically a binding layer on top of these platforms. Binding to platform APIs enables .NET developers to use C# (and F#) to develop native applications with the full capacity of each platform. The C# APIs we use when we develop applications with Xamarin are more or less identical to the platform APIs, but they are *.NETified*. For example, APIs are often customized to follow .NET naming conventions, and Android `set` and `get` methods are often replaced by properties. The reason for this is that APIs should be easier to use for .NET developers.

Mono (https://www.mono-project.com) is an open source implementation of the Microsoft .NET framework, which is based on the **European Computer Manufacturers Association (ECMA)** standards for C# and the **common language runtime (CLR)**. Mono was created to bring the .NET framework to platforms other than Windows. It is part of the .NET foundation (http://www.dotnetfoundation.org), an independent organization that supports open development and collaboration involving the .NET ecosystem.

With the combination of Xamarin platforms and Mono, we will be able to use both all platform-specific APIs and all platform-independent parts of .NET, including, for example, namespaces, systems, `System.Linq`, `System.IO`, `System.Net`, and `System.Threading.Tasks`.

There are several reasons to use Xamarin for mobile application development, as we will see in the following sections.

Code sharing

If there is one common programming language for multiple mobile platforms, and even server platforms, then we can share a lot of code between our target platforms, as illustrated in the following diagram. All code that isn't related to the target platform can be shared with other .NET platforms. Code that is typically shared in this way includes business logic, network calls, and data models:

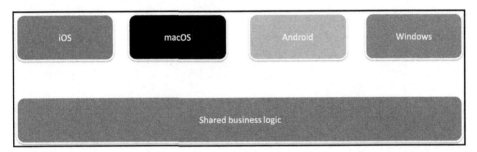

There is also a large community based around the .NET platforms and a wide range of third-party libraries and components that can be downloaded from NuGet (`https://nuget.org`) and used across the .NET platforms.

Code sharing across platforms will lead to shorter development times. It will also lead to applications of a higher quality because we only need to write the code for business logic once. There will be a lower risk of bugs, and we will also be able to guarantee that a calculation will return the same result, no matter what platform our users are using.

Using existing knowledge

For .NET developers who want to start building native mobile applications, it is easier to just learn the APIs for the new platforms than it is to learn programming languages and APIs for both old and new platforms.

Similarly, organizations that want to build native mobile applications could use their existing developers with their knowledge of .NET to develop applications. Because there are more .NET developers than Objective-C and Swift developers, it would be easier to find new developers for mobile application development projects.

Xamarin.iOS

Xamarin.iOS is used for building applications for iOS with .NET, and contains the bindings to the iOS APIs mentioned previously. Xamarin.iOS uses **ahead of time** (**AOT**) compiling to compile the C# code to **Advanced RISC Machines** (**ARM**) assembly language. The Mono runtime runs along with the Objective-C runtime. Code that uses .NET namespaces, such as System.Linq or System.Net, will be executed by the Mono runtime, while code that uses iOS-specific namespaces will be executed by the Objective-C runtime. Both the Mono runtime and the Objective-C runtime will run on top of the Unix-like kernel, **X is Not Unix** (**XNU**) (https://en.wikipedia.org/wiki/XNU), which is developed by Apple. The following diagram shows an overview of the iOS architecture:

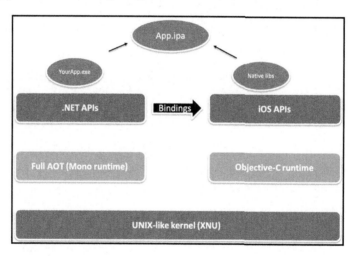

Xamarin.Android

Xamarin.Android is used to build applications for Android with .NET, and contains the bindings to the Android APIs. The Mono runtime and the Android runtime run side by side on top of a Linux kernel. Xamarin.Android applications could either be **just-in-time** (**JIT**)-compiled or AOT-compiled, but to AOT-compile them, you need to use Visual Studio Enterprise.

Communication between the Mono runtime and the Android runtime occurs via a **Java Native Interface (JNI)** bridge. There are two types of JNI bridges: **manage callable wrapper (MCW)** and **Android callable wrapper (ACW)**. An **MCW** is used when the code needs to run in the **Android runtime (ART)** and an **ACW** is used when **ART** needs to run code in the Mono runtime, as shown in the following diagram:

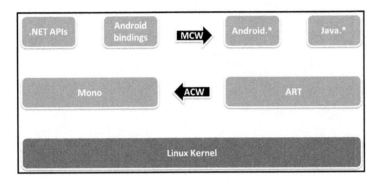

Xamarin.Mac

Xamarin.Mac is for building applications for macOS with .NET, and contains the bindings to the macOS APIs. Xamarin.Mac has the same architecture as Xamarin.iOS—the only difference is that Xamarin.Mac applications are JIT compiled, unlike Xamarin.iOS apps, which are AOT-compiled. This is shown in the following diagram:

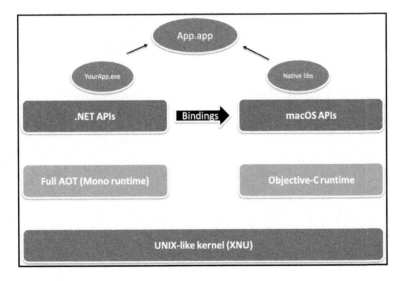

Xamarin.Forms

Xamarin.Forms is a UI framework that is built on top of Xamarin (for iOS and Android) and the **Universal Windows Platform** (**UWP**). Xamarin.Forms enables developers to create a UI for iOS, Android, and UWP with one shared code base, as illustrated in the following diagram. If we are building an application with Xamarin.Forms, we can use XAML, C#, or a combination of both to create the UI:

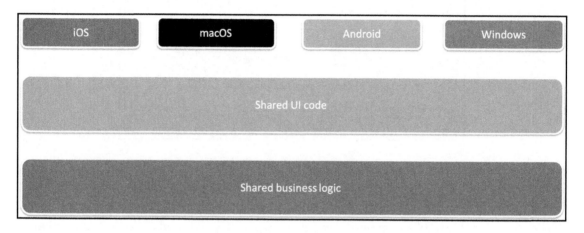

The architecture of Xamarin.Forms

Xamarin.Forms is more or less just an abstract layer on top of each platform. Xamarin.Forms has a shared layer, which is used by all platforms, as well as a platform-specific layer. The platform-specific layer contains renderers. A renderer is a class that maps a Xamarin.Forms control into a platform-specific native control. Each Xamarin.Forms control has a platform-specific renderer.

The following diagram illustrates how an entry control in Xamarin.Forms is rendered to a **UITextField** control from the **UIKit** namespace when the shared Xamarin.Forms code is used in an iOS app. The same code in Android renders an **EditText** control from the **Android.Widget** namespace:

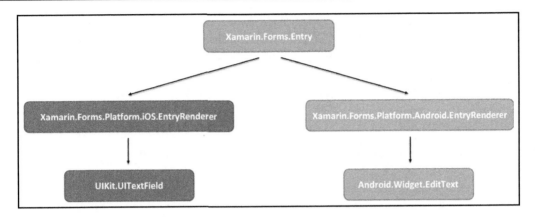

Defining a user interface using XAML

The most common way to declare your user interface in Xamarin.Forms is by defining it in a XAML document. It is also possible to create the GUI in C#, since XAML is really only a markup language for instantiating objects. You could, in theory, use XAML to create any type of object, as long as it has a parameterless constructor. A XAML document is an **Extensible Markup Language** (**XML**) document with a specific schema.

Defining a Label control

As a simple example, let's look at the following snippet of XAML:

```
<Label Text="Hello World!" />
```

When the XAML parser encounters this snippet, it will create an instance of a `Label` object and then set the properties of the object that correspond to the attributes in the XAML. This means that if we set a `Text` property in XAML, it will set the `Text` property on the instance of the `Label` object that is created. The XAML in the preceding example will have the same effect as the following:

```
var obj = new Label()
{
    Text = "Hello World!"
};
```

XAML exists to make it easier to view the object hierarchy that you need to create in order to make a GUI. An object model for a GUI is also hierarchical by design, so XAML has support for adding child objects. You can simply add them as child nodes, as follows:

```
<StackLayout>
    <Label Text="Hello World" />
    <Entry Text="Ducks are us" />
</StackLayout>
```

The `StackLayout` is a container control that will organize the children vertically or horizontally within that container. A vertical organization is the default value, and will be used unless you specify otherwise. There are also a number of other containers, such as the `Grid` and the `FlexLayout`. These will be used in many of the projects in the following chapters.

Creating a page in XAML

A single control is no good unless it has a container that hosts it. Let's see what an entire page would look like. A fully valid `ContentPage` defined in XAML is an XML document. This means that we must start with an XML declaration. After that, we must have one, and only one, root node, as shown in the following code:

```
<?xml version="1.0" encoding="UTF-8"?>
<ContentPage
    xmlns="http://xamarin.com/schemas/2014/forms"
    xmlns:x="http://schemas.microsoft.com/winfx/2009/xaml"
    x:Class="MyApp.MainPage">

    <StackLayout>
        <Label Text="Hello world!" />
    </StackLayout>
</ContentPage>
```

In the preceding example, we have defined a `ContentPage` that translates into a single view on each platform. In order to make it valid XAML, you must specify a default namespace (`xmlns="http://xamarin.com/schemas/2014/forms"`) and then add the x namespace (`xmlns:x="http://schemas.microsoft.com/winfx/2009/xaml"`).

The default namespace lets you create objects without prefixing them, like the `StackLayout` object. The x namespace lets you access properties such as the `x:Class`, which tells the XAML parser which class to instantiate to control the page when the `ContentPage` object is being created.

A `ContentPage` can have only one child. In this case, it's a `StackLayout` control. Unless you specify otherwise, the default layout orientation is vertical. A `StackLayout` can, therefore, have multiple children. Later on, we will touch on more advanced layout controls, such as the `Grid` and the `FlexLayout` control.

In this specific example, we are going to create a `Label` control as the first child of the `StackLayout`.

Creating a page in C#

For clarity, the following code shows how the same thing would look in C#:

```
public class MainPage : ContentPage
{
}
```

A `page` is a class that inherits from the `Xamarin.Forms.ContentPage`. This class is autogenerated for you if you create a XAML page, but if you go code-only, then you will need to define it yourself.

Let's create the same control hierarchy as the XAML page we defined earlier using the following code:

```
var page = new MainPage();

var stacklayout = new StackLayout();
stacklayout.Children.Add(
    new Label()
    {
        Text = "Welcome to Xamarin.Forms"
    });

page.Content = stacklayout;
```

The first statement creates a `page`. You could, in theory, create a new page directly of the `ContentPage` type, but this would prohibit you from writing any code behind it. For this reason, it's a good practice to subclass each page that you are planning to create.

The block following this first statement creates the `StackLayout` control that contains the `Label` control that is added to the `Children` collection.

Finally, we need to assign the `StackLayout` to the `Content` property of the page.

XAML or C#?

Generally, using XAML will give you a much better overview, since the page is a hierarchical structure of objects and XAML is a very nice way of defining that structure. In code, the structure gets flipped around since you must define the innermost object first, making it harder to read the structure of your page. This was shown in an earlier example in this chapter. Having said that, it is generally a matter of preference as to how you decide to define the GUI. This book will use XAML rather than C# in the projects to come.

Xamarin.Forms versus traditional Xamarin

While this book is about Xamarin.Forms, we will highlight the difference between using traditional Xamarin and Xamarin.Forms. Traditional Xamarin is used when developing applications that use iOS and Android SDK without any means of abstraction. For example, we can create an iOS app that defines its user interface in a storyboard or in the code directly. This code will not be reusable for other platforms, such as Android. Applications built using this approach can still share non-platform-specific code by simply referencing a .NET standard library. This relationship is shown in the following diagram:

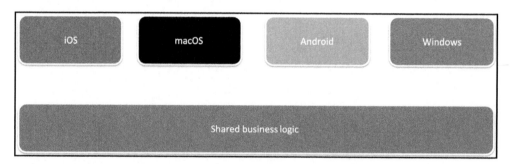

Xamarin.Forms, on the other hand, is an abstraction of the GUI, which allows us to define user interfaces in a platform-agnostic way. It still builds on top of Xamarin.iOS, Xamarin.Android, and all other supported platforms. The Xamarin.Forms application can be created as a .NET standard library or as a shared code project, where the source files are linked as copies and built within the same project as the platform you are currently building for. This relationship is shown in the following diagram:

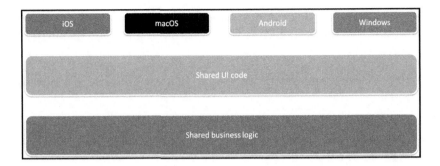

Having said that, Xamarin.Forms cannot exist without traditional Xamarin, since it's bootstrapped through an application for each platform. This gives you the ability to extend Xamarin.Forms on each platform using custom renderers and platform-specific code that can be exposed to your shared code base through interfaces. We'll look at these concepts in detail later in this chapter.

When to use Xamarin.Forms

We can use Xamarin.Forms in most cases and for most types of applications. If we need to use controls that not are available in Xamarin.Forms, we can always use the platform-specific APIs. There are, however, cases where Xamarin.Forms is not useful. The most common situation in which we might want to avoid using Xamarin.Forms is if we are building an app that we want to look very different across our target platforms.

Setting up a development machine

To develop an app for multiple platforms imposes higher demands on our development machine. One reason for this is that we often want to run one or multiple simulators or emulators on our development machine. Different platforms also have different requirements with regard to what is needed to begin development. Regardless of whether we are using Mac or Windows, Visual Studio will be our IDE. There are several versions of Visual Studio, including the free community edition. Go to `https://visualstudio.microsoft.com/` to compare the available versions of Visual Studio. The following list is a summary of what we need to begin development for each platform:

- **iOS**: To develop an app for iOS, we need a Mac. This could either be the machine that we are developing on or a machine on our network, if we are using one. The reason that we need to connect to a Mac is that we need Xcode for compiling and debugging an app. Xcode also provides the iOS simulator.

- **Android**: Android apps can be developed on either macOS or Windows. Everything you need, including SDKs and simulators, are installed with Visual Studio.

- **UWP**: UWP apps can only be developed in Visual Studio on a Windows machine.

Setting up a Mac

There are two main tools that are required to develop applications for iOS and Android with Xamarin on a Mac. These are Visual Studio for Mac (if we are only developing Android applications, this is the only tool we need) and Xcode. In the following sections, we will take a look at how to set up a Mac for app development.

Installing Xcode

Before we install Visual Studio, we need to download and install Xcode. Xcode is the official development IDE from Apple and contains all the tools they provide for iOS development, including SDKs for iOS, macOS, tvOS, and watchOS.

We can download Xcode from the Apple developer portal (`https://developer.apple.com`) or from Apple App Store. I recommend that you download it from App Store because this will always provide you with the latest stable version. The only reason to download Xcode from the developer portal is if we want to use a prerelease version of Xcode, to develop for a prerelease of iOS, for example.

After the first installation, and after each update of Xcode, it is important to open it. Xcode often needs to install additional components after an installation or an update. You also need to open Xcode to accept the license agreement with Apple.

Installing Visual Studio

To install Visual Studio, we first need to download it from `https://visualstudio.microsoft.com`.

When we start the Visual Studio installer via the file we downloaded, it will start to check what we already have installed on our machine. When the check has finished, we will be able to select which platforms and tools we would like to install. Note that Xamarin Inspector requires a Visual Studio Enterprise license.

Once we have selected the platforms that we want to install, Visual Studio will download and install everything that we need to get started with app development using Xamarin, as shown in the following screenshot:

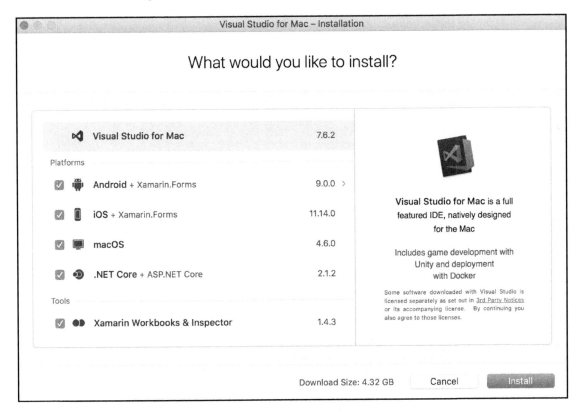

Configuring the Android emulator

Visual Studio will use the Android emulators provided by Google. If we would like the emulator to be fast, then we need to ensure that it is hardware-accelerated. To hardware-accelerate the Android emulator, we need to install the **Intel Hardware Accelerated Execution Manager (HAXM)**, which can be downloaded from `https://software.intel.com/en-us/articles/intel-hardware-accelerated-execution-manager-intel-haxm`.

The next step is to create an **Android Emulator**. First, we need to ensure that the Android emulator and the Android OS images are installed. To do this, go through the following steps:

1. Go to the **Tools** tab to install the **Android Emulator**:

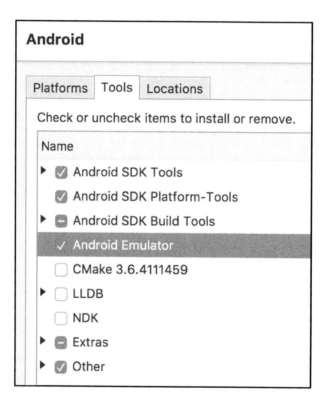

2. We also need to install one or multiple images to use with the emulator. We can install multiple images if, for example, we want to run our application on different versions of Android. We will select emulators with **Google Play** (as shown in the following screenshot) so that we can use Google Play services in our app, even when we are running it in an emulator. This is required if, for example, we want to use Google Maps in our app:

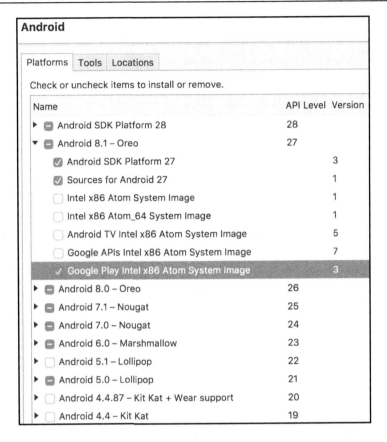

3. Then, to create and configure an emulator, go to the **Android Device Manager** from the **Tools** tab in Visual Studio. From the **Android Device Manager**, we can start an emulator if we have already created one, or we can create new emulators, as shown in the following screenshot:

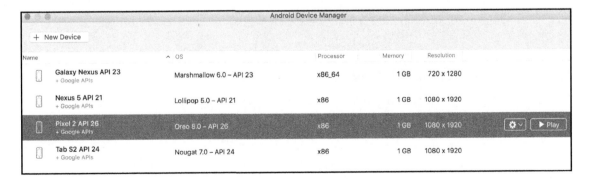

4. If we click the **New Device** button, we can create a new emulator with the specifications that we need. The easiest way to create a new emulator here is to select a base device that matches our needs. These base devices will be preconfigured, and that is often enough. However, it is also possible to edit the properties of the device so that we can get an emulator that matches our specific needs.

Because we will not run the emulator on a device with an ARM processor, we have to select either an **x86** processor or an **x64** processor, as shown in the following screenshot. If we try to use an ARM processor, the emulator will be very slow:

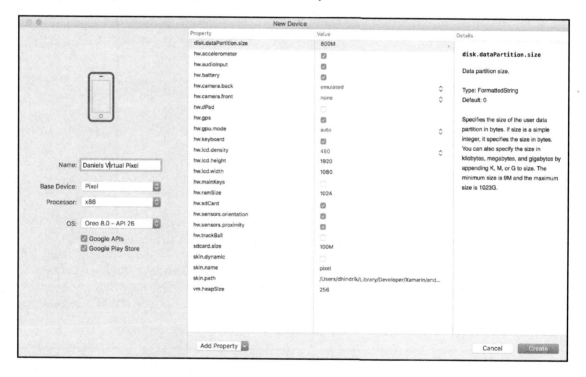

Setting up a Windows machine

We can either use a virtual or a physical Windows machine for development with Xamarin. We can, for example, run a virtual Windows machine on our Mac. The only tool we need for app development on our Windows machine is Visual Studio.

Installing Xamarin for Visual Studio

If we already have Visual Studio installed, we must first open **Visual Studio Installer**; otherwise, we need to go to `https://visualstudio.microsoft.com` to download the installation files.

Before the installation starts, we need to select which workloads we want to install.

If we want to develop apps for Windows, we need to select the **Universal Windows Platform development** workload, as shown in the following screenshot:

For Xamarin development, we need to install **Mobile development with .NET**. If you want to use Hyper-V for hardware acceleration, we can deselect the checkbox for Intel HAXM in the detailed description of the **Mobile development with .NET** workload on the left-hand side, as shown in the following screenshot. When we deselect Intel HAXM, the Android emulator will also be deselected, but we can install it later:

When we first start Visual Studio, we will be asked whether we want to sign in. It is not necessary for us to sign in unless we want to use Visual Studio Professional or Enterprise, in which case we have to sign in so that our license can be verified.

Pairing Visual Studio with a Mac

If we want to run, debug, and compile our iOS app, then we need to connect it to a Mac. We can set up the Mac manually, as described earlier in this chapter, or we can use **Automatic Mac Provisioning**. This will install Mono and Xamarin.iOS on the Mac that we are connecting to. It will not install the Visual Studio IDE, but this isn't necessary if you just want to use it as a build machine. We do, however, need to install Xcode manually.

To be able to connect to the Mac—either to a manually-installed Mac or using **Automatic Mac Provisioning**—the Mac needs to be accessible via our network and we need to enable **Remote Login** on the Mac. To do this, go to **Settings | Sharing** and select the checkbox for **Remote Login**. To the left of the window, we can select which users are allowed to connect with **Remote Login**, as shown in the following screenshot:

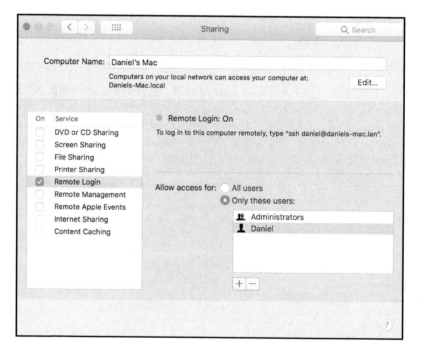

To connect to the Mac from Visual Studio, use the **Pair to Mac** button in the toolbar (as shown in the following screenshot), or, in the top menu, select **Tools** I **iOS** and finally **Pair to Mac**:

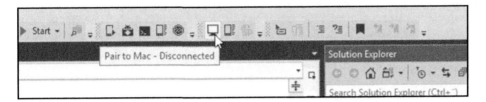

A dialog will appear showing all the Macs that can be found on the network. If the Mac doesn't appear in the list of available Macs, we can use the **Add Mac** button in the bottom left corner to enter an IP address, as shown in the following screenshot:

If everything that you require is installed on the Mac, then Visual Studio will connect and we can start building and debugging our iOS app. If Mono is missing on the Mac, a warning will appear. This warning will also give us the option to install it, as shown in the following screenshot:

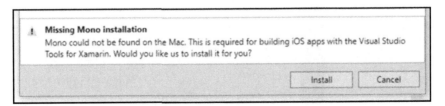

Configuring an Android emulator and hardware acceleration

If we want a fast Android emulator that works smoothly, we need to enable hardware acceleration. This can be done using either Intel HAXM or Hyper-V. The disadvantage of Intel HAXM is that it can't be used on machines with an **Advanced Micro Devices (AMD)** processor; you have to have a machine with an Intel processor. We can't use Intel HAXM in parallel with Hyper-V.

For these reasons, Hyper-V is the preferred way to hardware accelerate the Android emulator on a Windows machine. To use Hyper-V with the Android emulator, we need to have the April 2018 update (or later) for Windows and Visual Studio version 15.8 (or later) installed. To enable Hyper-V, you need to go through the following steps:

1. Open the **Start** menu and type **Turn Windows features on or off**. Click the option that appears to open it, as shown in the following screenshot:

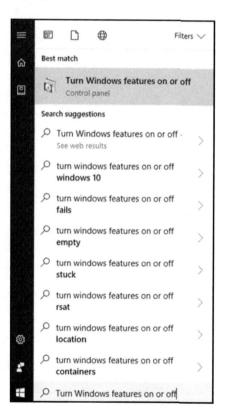

2. To enable Hyper-V, select the **Hyper-V** checkbox. Also, expand the Hyper-V option and check the **Hyper-V Platform** checkbox. We also need to select the **Windows Hypervisor Platform** checkbox, as shown in the following screenshot:

3. Restart the machine when Windows prompts you to.

Because we didn't install an Android emulator during the installation of Visual Studio, we need to install it now. Go to the **Tools** menu in Visual Studio, click on **Android**, and then **Android SDK Manager**.

Under **Tools** in **Android SDK Manager**, we can install the emulator by selecting **Android Emulator**, as shown in the following screenshot. Also, we should ensure that the latest version of **Android SDK Build Tools** is installed:

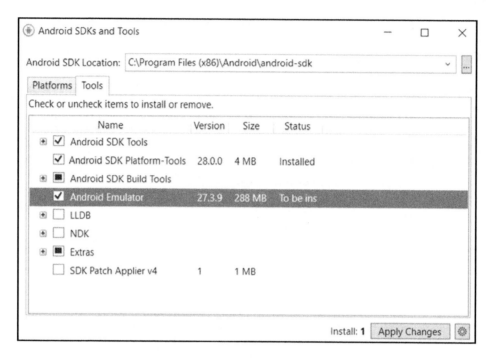

We recommend installing the **NDK** (**Native Development Kit**). The NDK makes it possible to import libraries that are written in C or C++. NDK is also required if we want to AOT compile an app.

The Android SDK allows for multiple emulator images to be installed simultaneously. We can install multiple images if, for example, we want to run our application on different versions of Android. Select emulators with **Google Play** (as shown in the following screenshot) so we can use Google Play services in our app even when we are running it in an emulator.

This is required if we want to use Google Maps in our app, for example:

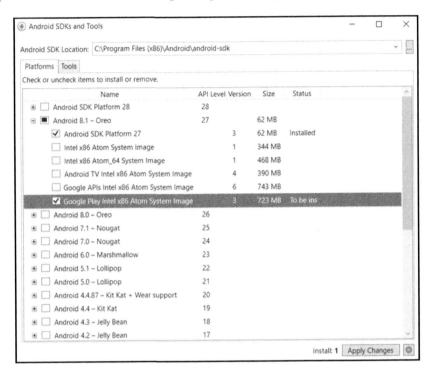

The next step is to create a virtual device to use the emulator image. To create and configure an emulator, go to the **Android Device Manager**, which we will open from the **Tools** tab in Visual Studio. From the **Device Manager**, we can either start an emulator—if we already have created one—or we can create new emulators, as shown in the following screenshot:

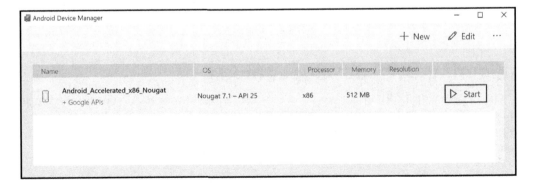

If we click the **New Device** button, we can create a new emulator with the specifications that we need. The easiest way to create a new emulator here is to select a base device that matches our needs. These base devices will be preconfigured, which is often enough. However, it is possible to edit the properties of the device so that we can get an emulator that matches our specific needs.

We have to select either an **x86** processor (as shown in the following screenshot) or an **x64** processor since we will not run the emulator on a device with an ARM processor. If we try to use an ARM processor, the emulator will be very slow:

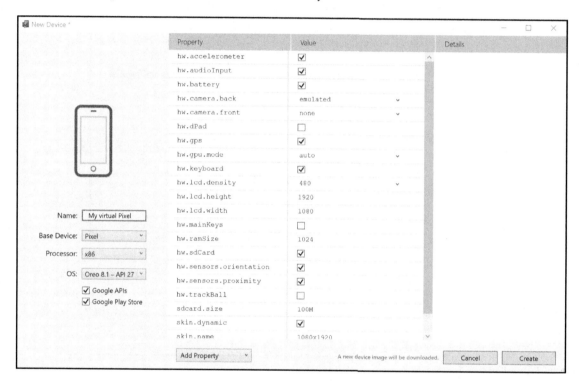

Configuring UWP developer mode

If we want to develop UWP apps, we need to activate developer mode on our development machine. To do this, go to **Settings** | **Update & Security** | **For developers**. Then, click on **Developer Mode**, as shown in the following screenshot. This makes it possible for us to sideload and debug apps via Visual Studio:

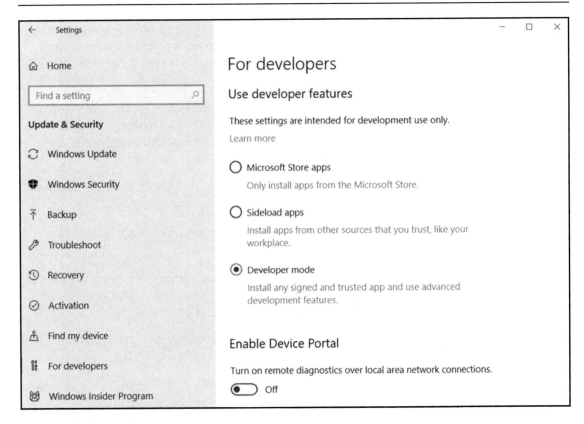

If we select **Sideload apps** instead of **Developer Mode**, we will only be able to install apps without going via Microsoft Store. If we have a machine to test, rather than debug our apps on, we can just select **Sideload apps**.

Summary

After reading this chapter, you should feel a little bit more comfortable about what Xamarin is and how Xamarin.Forms relates to Xamarin itself.

In this chapter, we established our definition of what a native application is, which includes the following elements:

- Native user interface
- Native performance
- Native API access

We talked about how Xamarin is based on Mono, which is an open source implementation of the .NET framework, and discussed how, at its core, Xamarin is a set of bindings to platform-specific APIs. We then looked in detail at how Xamarin.iOS and Xamarin.Android work under the hood.

After that, we started to touch upon the core topic of this book, which is Xamarin.Forms. We started off with an overview of how platform-agnostic controls are rendered into platform-specific controls and how to use XAML to define a hierarchy of controls to assemble a page.

We then spent some time looking at the difference between a Xamarin.Forms application and a traditional Xamarin application.

A traditional Xamarin app uses platform-specific APIs directly, without any abstraction other than what .NET adds as a platform.

Xamarin.Forms is an API that is built on top of the traditional Xamarin APIs, and allows us to define platform-agnostic GUIs in XAML or in code that is rendered to platform-specific controls. There's more to Xamarin.Forms than this, but this is what it does at its core.

In the last part of this chapter, we discussed how to set up a development machine on Windows or macOS.

Now it's time to put our newly acquired knowledge to use! We will start off by creating a To-Do app from the ground up in the next chapter. We will look at concepts such as **Model–View–ViewModel (MVVM)**, for a clean separation between business logic and the user interface, and SQLite.NET, for persisting data to a local database on your device. We will do this for three platforms at the same time—read on!

2
Building Our First Xamarin.Forms App

In this chapter, we will create a to-do list app and, in doing so, we'll explore all the bits and pieces of what makes an app. We will look at creating pages, adding content to those pages, navigating between them, and creating a stunning layout. Well, *stunning* might be a bit of a stretch, but we will be sure to design the app so that you can tweak it to your needs once it is complete!

The following topics will be covered in this chapter:

- Setting up the project
- Persisting data locally on a device
- Using the repository pattern
- What MVVM is and why it's a great fit for Xamarin.Forms
- Using Xamarin.Forms pages (as Views) and navigating between them
- Using Xamarin.Forms Control in XAML
- Using data binding
- Using styling in Xamarin.Forms

Technical requirements

To be able to complete this project, we need to have Visual Studio for Mac or PC installed, as well as the Xamarin components. See `Chapter 1`, *Introduction to Xamarin*, for more details on how to set up your environment.

An overview of the project

Everyone needs a way of keeping track of things. To kick-start our Xamarin.Forms development learning curve, we've decided that a to-do list app is the best way to get started and also to help you keep track of things. A simple, classic, win-win scenario.

We will start by creating the project and defining a repository in which to store the items of a to-do list. We will render these items in list form and allow the user to edit them using a detailed user interface. We will also look at how to store the to-do list items locally on the device through **SQLite-net** so they don't get lost when we exit the app.

The build time for this project is about two hours.

Beginning the project

It's time to start coding! Before moving on, however, make sure you have your development environment set up as described in `Chapter 1`, *Introduction to Xamarin*.

This chapter will be a classic **File** | **New Project** chapter, guiding you step-by-step through the process of creating your first to-do list app. There will be no downloads required whatsoever.

Setting up the project

A Xamarin app can essentially be created using one of two code-sharing strategies:

- As a shared project
- As a .NET Standard library

The first choice, a **shared project**, will create a project type that is essentially a linked copy of each file in it. The file exists in one common place and is linked in at build time. This means that we cannot determine the runtime when writing the code and we are only allowed to access the APIs that are available on each target platform. It does allow us to use conditional compilations, which can be useful in certain circumstances but can also be confusing for someone who reads the code later on. Going for the shared project option may also be a bad choice as it locks down our code to specific platforms.

We will use the second choice, a **.NET Standard library**. This is, of course, a matter of choice and both ways will still work. With a little imagination, you can still follow this chapter, even if you select a shared project.

Let's get started!

Creating the new project

The first step is to create a new Xamarin.Forms project. Open up Visual Studio 2017 and click on **File | New| Project**:

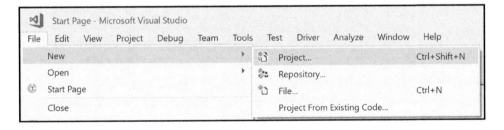

This will open the **New Project** dialog box. Expand the **Visual C#** node and click on **Cross-Platform**. Select the **Mobile App (Xamarin.Forms)** item in the list. Complete the form by naming your project and click **OK.** Make sure to name the project `DoToo` to avoid namespace issues:

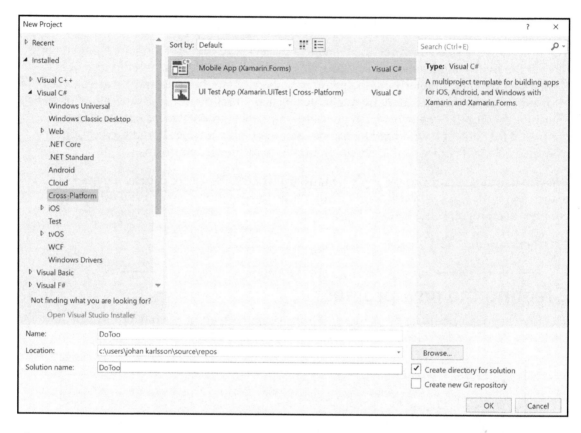

The next step is to select a project template and a **Code Sharing Strategy** to use. Select **Blank App** to create a bare Xamarin.Forms app and change the **Code Sharing Strategy** to **.NET Standard**. Finalize the setup by clicking **OK** and wait for Visual Studio to create the necessary projects:

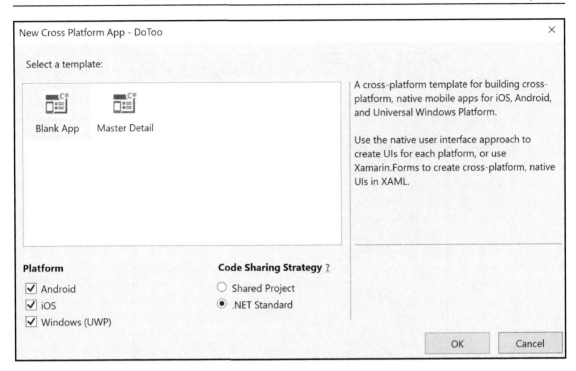

Congratulations, we've just created our first Xamarin.Forms app!

Examining the files

The template selected has now created four projects:

- **DoToo**: This is a .NET Standard library targeting .NET Standard 2.0. It can be imported by any runtime that supports this version of .NET Standard.
- **DoToo.Android**: This is an Android app for bootstrapping Xamarin.Forms on Android.
- **DoToo.iOS**: This is an iOS app for bootstrapping Xamarin.Forms on iOS.
- **DoToo.UWP**: This is a **Universal Windows Platform** (**UWP**) app for bootstrapping Xamarin.Forms on UWP.

The three platform-specific libraries reference the .NET Standard library. Most of our code will be written in the .NET Standard library and only a small portion of platform-specific code will be added to each target platform.

The project should now look like as follows:

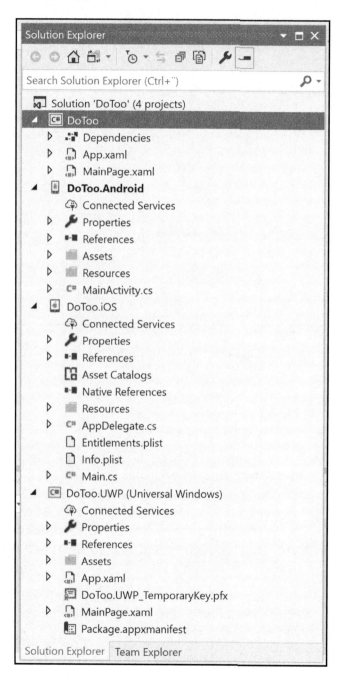

We will highlight a few important files in each project so that we can have a basic understanding of what they each are. We'll go through these project by project.

DoToo

This is the .NET Standard library that all the platform-specific projects reference and the location to which most of our code will be added. The following screenshot displays the structure of the .NET Standard library:

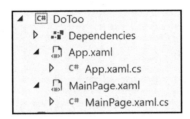

Under **Dependencies**, we will find references to external dependencies such as Xamarin.Forms. We will update the Xamarin.Forms package version in the *Updating Xamarin.Forms packages* section. We will add more dependencies as we progress throughout the chapter.

The App.xaml file is a XAML file that represents the app. This is a good place to put application-wide resources, which we will do later on. We can also see the App.xaml.cs file, which contains the startup code and some lifetime events to which we can add custom code, such as OnStart or OnSleep.

If we open up App.xaml.cs, we can see the starting point for our Xamarin.Forms application:

```
public partial class App : Application
{
    public App()
    {
        InitializeComponent();
        MainPage = new DoToo.MainPage();
    }

    protected override void OnStart()
    {
        // Handle when your app starts
    }

    // code omitted for brevity
}
```

The assignment of a page to the `MainPage` property is particularly important, as this is what determines which page will be displayed to the user first. In the template, this is the `DoToo.MainPage()` class.

The last two files are the `MainPage.xaml` file, which contains the first page of the application and the code-behind file, which is called `MainPage.xaml.cs`. These files will be removed in order to comply with the **Model–View–ViewModel (MVVM)** naming standards.

DoToo.Android

This is the Android app. It only has one file:

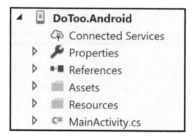

The important file here is `MainActivity.cs`. This contains the entry point for our application if we run the app on an Android device. The entry point method for an Android app is `OnCreate(...)`.

If you open the `MainActivity.cs` and examine the `OnCreate(...)` method, it should look something like this:

```
protected override void OnCreate(Bundle bundle)
{
    TabLayoutResource = Resource.Layout.Tabbar;
    ToolbarResource = Resource.Layout.Toolbar;
    base.OnCreate(bundle);
    global::Xamarin.Forms.Forms.Init(this, bundle);
    LoadApplication(new App());
}
```

The first two lines assign resources for the `Tabbar` and the `Toolbar`. We then call the base method, followed by the mandatory initialization of Xamarin.Forms. Finally, we have the call to load the Xamarin.Forms application that we have defined in the .NET Standard library.

We don't need to understand these files in detail, just remember that they are important for the initialization of our app.

DoToo.iOS

This is the iOS app. It contains a few more files than its Android counterpart:

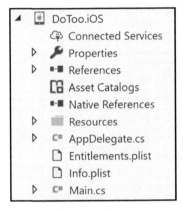

The `AppDelegate.cs` file is the entry point for an iOS app. This file contains a method called `FinishedLaunching(...)`, which is where we start writing code:

```
public override bool FinishedLaunching(UIApplication app, NSDictionary
options)
{
    global::Xamarin.Forms.Forms.Init();
    LoadApplication(new App());
    return base.FinishedLaunching(app, options);
}
```

The code starts off by initializing Xamarin.Forms and then loads the application from the .NET Standard library. After that, it returns the control to iOS. It must do this within 17 seconds, or the app will be terminated by the OS.

The `info.plist` file is an iOS-specific file that contains information about the app, such as the bundle ID and its provisioning profiles. It has a graphical editor, but can also be edited in any text editor, since it's a standard XML file.

The `Entitlements.plist` file is also an iOS-specific file that configures the entitlements that we want our app to take advantage of, such as **in-app purchases** or **push notifications**.

As with the Android app's startup code, we don't need to understand what is going on here in detail, other than that it's important for the initialization of our app.

DoToo.UWP

The last project to examine is the UWP app. The file structure of the project looks like the following screenshot:

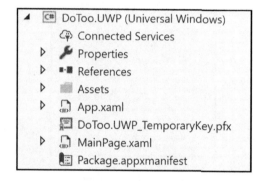

It has an `App.xaml` file, which is similar to the one in the .NET Standard library, but specific to the UWP app. It also has a related file called `App.xaml.cs`. This contains a method called `OnLaunched(...)`, which is the entry point for a UWP app. This file is quite large, so we won't be printing it out here, but do open it up and see if we can locate the Xamarin.Forms initialization code in it.

Updating the Xamarin.Forms packages

After creating the project, we should always update our Xamarin.Forms packages to the latest version. To do this, follow these steps:

1. Right-click on our **Solution** in the **Solution Explorer**.
2. Click on **Manage NuGet Packages for Solution...**:

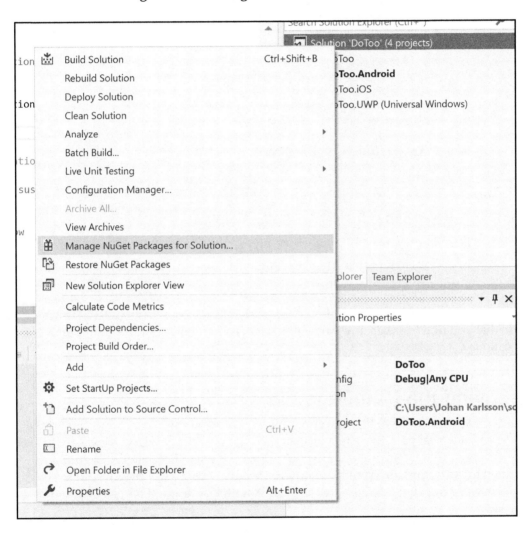

3. This brings up the **NuGet Package Manager** in Visual Studio:

To update Xamarin.Forms to the latest version, do this:

1. Click the **Updates** tab
2. Check **Xamarin.Forms** and click **Update**
3. Accept any license agreements

Keep an eye on the output pane and wait for all the packages to be updated. However, ensure that you don't update any Android packages manually, as this might break your application.

Removing the MainPage file

In Xamarin.Forms, we have the concept of pages. This is not the case, however, for the MVVM architectural pattern, which instead uses the concept of views. Views are the same thing as pages but they are not suffixed with -Page, so we will delete the MainPage generated by the template. We will go into more detail on MVVM shortly, but for the time being, we will remove the MainPage.cs class from the solution. This can be done as follows:

1. Right-click on the MainPage.xaml file in the DoToo project (the .NET Standard library)
2. Click **Delete** and confirm the delete action

Creating a repository and a TodoItem model

Any good architecture always involves abstraction. In this app, we need something to store and retrieve the items of our to-do list. These will later be stored in an SQLite database, but adding a reference to the database directly from the code that is responsible for the GUI is generally a bad idea.

What we need instead is something to abstract our database from the GUI. For this app, we've chosen to use a simple repository pattern. This repository is simply a class that sits in between the SQLite database and our upcoming `ViewModels`. This is the class that handles the interaction with the view, which in turn handles the GUI.

The repository will expose methods for getting items, adding items, and updating items, as well as events that allow other parts of the app to react to changes in the repository. It will be hidden behind an interface so that we can replace the entire implementation later on, without modifying anything but a line of code in the initialization of the app. This is made possible by **Autofac**.

Defining a to-do list item

We will start off by creating a `TodoItem` class, which will represent a single item in the list. This will be a simple **Plain Old CLR Object (POCO)** class, where **CLR** stands from **Common Language Runtime**. In other words, this will be a .NET class without any dependencies on third-party assemblies. To create the class, follow the steps:

1. In the .NET Standard library project, create a folder called `Models`.
2. Add a class called `TodoItem.cs` in that folder and enter the following code:

```
public class TodoItem
{
    public int Id { get; set; }
    public string Title { get; set; }
    public bool Completed { get; set; }
    public DateTime Due { get; set; }
}
```

The code is pretty self-explanatory; it's a simple **Plain Old CLR Object (POCO)** class that only contains properties and no logic. We have a `Title` that describes what we want to be done, a flag (`Completed`) that determines if the to-do list item is done, a `Due` date when we expect it to be done, and a unique `id` that we need later on for the database.

Creating a repository and its interface

Now that we have the `TodoItem` class, let's define an interface that describes a repository to store our to-do list items:

1. In the .NET Standard library project, create a folder called `Repositories`.
2. Create an interface called `ITodoItemRepository.cs` in the `Repositories` folder and write the following code:

```
using System;
using System.Collections.Generic;
using System.Threading.Tasks;
using DoToo.Models;

namespace DoToo.Repositories
{
    public interface ITodoItemRepository
    {
        event EventHandler<TodoItem> OnItemAdded;
        event EventHandler<TodoItem> OnItemUpdated;

        Task<List<TodoItem>> GetItems();
        Task AddItem(TodoItem item);
        Task UpdateItem(TodoItem item);
        Task AddOrUpdate(TodoItem item);
    }
}
```

 The eagle-eyed among you might notice that we are not defining a `Delete` method in this interface. This is definitely something that should be there in a real-world app. While the app that we are creating in this chapter will not support the deleting of items, we are quite sure that you could add this yourself if you want to!

This interface defines everything we need for our app. It is there to create logical insulation between your implementation of a repository and the user of that repository. If any other part of your application wants an instance of `TodoItemRepository`, we can pass it any object that implements `ITodoItemRepository`, regardless of how it's implemented.

Having that said, let's implement `ITodoItemRepository`:

1. Create a class called `TodoItemRepository.cs`.
2. Enter the following code:

```csharp
using DoToo.Models;
using System.Collections.Generic;
using System.IO;
using System.Threading.Tasks;

namespace DoToo.Repositories
{
    public class TodoItemRepository : ITodoItemRepository
    {
        public event EventHandler<TodoItem> OnItemAdded;
        public event EventHandler<TodoItem> OnItemUpdated;

        public async Task<List<TodoItem>> GetItems()
        {
        }

        public async Task AddItem(TodoItem item)
        {
        }

        public async Task UpdateItem(TodoItem item)
        {
        }

        public async Task AddOrUpdate(TodoItem item)
        {
            if (item.Id == 0)
            {
                await AddItem(item);
            }
            else
            {
                await UpdateItem(item);
            }
        }
    }
}
```

This code is the bare-bones implementation of the interface, except for the `AddOrUpdate(...)` method. This handles a small piece of logic that states that if the ID of an item is 0, it's a new item. Any item with an ID larger than 0 is stored in the database. This is because the database assigns a value larger than zero when we create rows in a table.

There are also two events defined in the preceding code. These will be used for notifying any subscriber that items have been updated or added.

Connecting SQLite to persist data

We now have an interface and a skeleton to implement that interface. The last thing we need to do to finish this section is to connect SQLite inside the implementation of the repository.

Adding the SQLite NuGet package

To access SQLite in this project, we need to add a NuGet package called **sqlite-net-pcl** to the .NET Standard library project. To do this, right-click on the **Dependencies** item under the **DoToo** project node of the **Solution** and click **Manage NuGet Packages**:

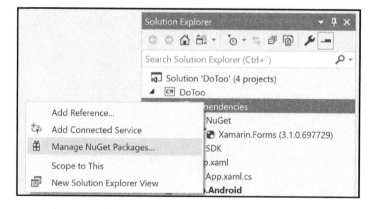

You might notice that the NuGet package is suffixed with -pcl. This is an example of what happens when naming conventions go wrong. This package actually supports .NET Standard 1.0, even though the name says **Portable Class Library (PCL)**, which was the predecessor to .NET Standard.

This brings up the **NuGet Package Manager**:

1. Click **Browse** and enter **sqlite-net-pcl** in the search box
2. Select the package by **Frank A. Krueger** and click **Install**

Wait for the installation to complete. We'll then add some code to the `TodoItem` class and the repository.

Updating the TodoItem class

Since SQLite is a relational database, it needs to know some basic information about how to create the tables that will store our objects. This is done using attributes, which are defined in the SQLite namespace:

1. Open up the `Models/TodoItem`.
2. Add a `using SQLite` statement at the start of the file right below the existing `using` statements, as shown in the following code:

```
using System;
using SQLite;
```

3. Add the `PrimaryKey` and `AutoIncrement` attributes right before the ID property, as demonstrated in the following code:

```
[PrimaryKey, AutoIncrement]
public int Id { get; set; }
```

The `PrimaryKey` attribute instructs SQLite that the `Id` property is the primary key of the table. The `AutoIncrement` attribute will make sure that the value of `Id` will be increased by one for each new `TodoItem` class that is added to the table.

Creating a connection to the SQLite database

We will now add all the code needed to communicate with the database. The first thing we need to do is to define a connection field that will hold the connection to the database:

1. Open up the `Repositories/TodoItemRepository` file.
2. Add a `using SQLite` statement at the start of the file right below the existing `using` statements, as shown in the following code:

```
using DoToo.Models;
using System.Collections.Generic;
using System.IO;
using System.Threading.Tasks;
using SQLite
```

3. Add the following field right below the class declaration:

```
private SQLiteAsyncConnection connection;
```

The connection needs to be initialized. Once it is initialized, it can be reused throughout the lifespan of the repository. Since the method is asynchronous, it cannot be called from the constructor without introducing a locking strategy. To keep things simple, we will simply call it from each of the methods that are defined by the interface:

1. Add the following code to the `TodoItemRepository` class.
2. Add a `using System.IO` statement at the start of the file so that we can use `Path.Combine(...)`:

```
private async Task CreateConnection()
{
    if (connection != null)
    {
        return;
    }
    var documentPath = Environment.GetFolderPath(
```

```
                          Environment.SpecialFolder.MyDocuments);
        var databasePath = Path.Combine(documentPath, "TodoItems.db");

        connection = new SQLiteAsyncConnection(databasePath);
        await connection.CreateTableAsync<TodoItem>();

        if (await connection.Table<TodoItem>().CountAsync() == 0)
        {
            await connection.InsertAsync(new TodoItem() { Title =
            "Welcome to DoToo" });
        }
    }
```

The method begins by checking whether we already have a connection. If we do, we can simply return. If we don't have a connection set up, we define a path on the disk to indicate where we want the database file to be located. In this case, we will choose the `MyDocuments` folder. Xamarin will find the closest match to this on each platform that we target.

We then create the connection and store the reference to that connection in the `connection` field. We need to make sure that SQLite has created a table that mirrors the schema of the `TodoItem` table. To make the development of the app easier, we add a default to-do list item if the `TodoItem` table is empty.

Implementing the Get, Add, and Update methods

The only thing left to do in the repository is to implement the methods for getting, adding, and updating items:

1. Locate the `GetItems()` method in the `TodoItemRepository` class.
2. Update the `GetItems()` method with the following code:

```
public async Task<List<TodoItem>> GetItems()
{
    await CreateConnection();
    return await connection.Table<TodoItem>().ToListAsync();
}
```

To ensure that the connection to the database is valid, we call the `CreateConnection()` method we created in the previous section. When this method returns, we can make sure that it is initialized and that the `TodoItem` table has been created.

We then use the connection to access the `TodoItem` table and return a `List<TodoItem>` that contains all the to-do list items in the database.

SQLite supports querying data using **Language Integrated Query (LINQ)**. You could play around with this after the project is complete to get a better understanding of how to work with databases inside your app.

The code for adding items is even simpler:

1. Locate the `AddItem()` method in the `TodoItemRepository` class.
2. Update the `AddItem()` method with the following code:

```
public async Task AddItem(TodoItem item)
{
    await CreateConnection();
    await connection.InsertAsync(item);
    OnItemAdded?.Invoke(this, item);
}
```

The call to `CreateConnection()` makes sure that we have a connection in the same way as we did for the `GetItems()` method. After this, we perform the actual insertion into the database using the `InsertAsync(...)` method on the connection object. After an item has been inserted into the table, we invoke the `OnItemAdded` event to notify any subscribers.

The code to update an item is basically the same as the `AddItem()` method, but also includes calls to `UpdateAsync` and `OnItemUpdated`. Let's finish up by updating the `UpdateItem()` method with the following code:

1. Locate the `UpdateItem()` method in the `TodoItemRepository` class.
2. Update the `UpdateItem()` method with the following code:

```
public async Task UpdateItem(TodoItem item)
{
    await CreateConnection();
    await connection.UpdateAsync(item);
    OnItemUpdated?.Invoke(this, item);
}
```

In the next section, we'll get started with MVVM. Grab a cup of coffee and let's get started.

Using MVVM – creating Views and ViewModels

MVVM is all about the separation of concerns. Each part has a specific meaning:

- **Model**: This relates to anything that represents data and that can be referenced by the ViewModel
- **View**: This is the visual component. In Xamarin.Forms, this is represented by a page
- **ViewModel**: This is a class that acts as the glue between the Model and the View

In our app, we could say that the Model is the repository and the to-do list items it returns. The ViewModel has a reference to this repository and exposes properties that the View can bind to. The ground rule is that any logic should reside in the ViewModel and no logic should be in the View. The View should know how to present data, such as converting a Boolean value to *Yes* or *No*.

MVVM can be implemented in many ways and there are quite a few frameworks that we could use. In this chapter, we have chosen to keep things simple and implement MVVM in a vanilla way, without any framework at all.

Defining a ViewModel base class

A ViewModel is the mediator between the View and the Model. We can benefit greatly by creating a common base class for all our ViewModels to inherit from. To do this, follow these steps:

1. Create a folder called ViewModels in the DoToo .NET Standard project.
2. Create a class called ViewModel in the ViewModels folder.
3. Resolve references to System.ComponentModel and Xamarin.Forms and add the following code:

```
public abstract class ViewModel : INotifyPropertyChanged
{
    public event PropertyChangedEventHandler PropertyChanged;

    public void RaisePropertyChanged(params string[] propertyNames)
    {
        foreach (var propertyName in propertyNames)
        {
            PropertyChanged?.Invoke(this, new
            PropertyChangedEventArgs(propertyName));
        }
    }
}
```

```
        public INavigation Navigation { get; set; }
    }
```

The `ViewModel` class is a base class for all `ViewModels`. This is not meant to be instantiated on its own, so we mark it as abstract. It implements `INotifyPropertyChanged`, which is an interface defined in `System.ComponentModel` in the .NET base class libraries. This interface only defines one thing: the `PropertyChanged` event. Our `ViewModel` must raise this event whenever we want the GUI to be aware of any changes to a property. This can be done manually, by adding code to a setter in a property, or by using an **intermediate language (IL)** weaver such as `PropertyChanged.Fody`. We will talk about this in detail in the next section.

We are also taking a little shortcut here by adding an `INavigation` property in the `ViewModel`. This will help us with navigation later on. This is also something that can (and should) be abstracted, since we don't want the `ViewModel` to be dependent on Xamarin.Forms, in order to be able to reuse the `ViewModels` on any platform.

Introducing PropertyChanged.Fody

The traditional way of implementing a `ViewModel` is to inherit from a base class (such as the `ViewModel` that we defined previously) and then add code that might look as follows:

```
public class MyTestViewModel : ViewModel
{
    private string name;
    public string Name
    {
        get { return name; }
        set { name = value; RaisePropertyChanged(nameof(Name)); }
    }
}
```

Each property that we want to add to a `ViewModel` yields six lines of code. Not too bad, you might think. However, considering that a `ViewModel` could potentially contain 10 to 20 properties, this rapidly turns into a lot of code. We can do better than this.

In just a few simple steps, we can use a tool called `PropertyChanged.Fody` to automatically inject almost all the code during the build process:

1. In the .NET Standard library, install the `PropertyChanged.Fody` NuGet package.
2. Create a file called `FodyWeavers.xml` and add the following XML to it:

```xml
<?xml version="1.0" encoding="utf-8" ?>
<Weavers>
    <PropertyChanged />
</Weavers>
```

`PropertyChanged.Fody` will scan the assembly for any class that implements the `INotifyPropertyChanged` interface and adds the code needed to raise the `PropertyChanged` event. It will also take care of dependencies between properties, meaning that if you have a property that returns values based on two other properties, it will be raised if either of those two values changes.

The result is that the test class we had previously is reduced to a single line of code per property. This makes the code base more readable because everything happens behind the scenes:

```csharp
public class MyTestViewModel : ViewModel
{
    public string Name { get; set; }
}
```

 It is worth noting that there are a lot of different plugins that can be used to make Fody automate tasks, such as logging or method decoration. Check out `https://github.com/Fody/Fody` for more info.

Creating the MainViewModel

Up to this point, we have mainly been preparing to write the code that will make up the app itself. The `MainViewModel` is the `ViewModel` for the first view that will be displayed to the user. It will be responsible for providing data and logic to a list of to-do list items. We will create the bare-bones `ViewModels` and add code to them as we move through the chapter:

1. Create a class called `MainViewModel` inside the `ViewModels` folder.
2. Add the following template code and resolve the references:

```
public class MainViewModel : ViewModel
{
    private readonly TodoItemRepository repository;

    public MainViewModel(TodoItemRepository repository)
    {
        this.repository = repository;
        Task.Run(async () => await LoadData());
    }

    private async Task LoadData()
    {
    }
}
```

The structure in this class is something that we will reuse for all the `ViewModels` to come.

Let's summarize the important features we want the `ViewModel` to have:

- We inherit from the `ViewModel` to gain access to shared logic, such as the `INotifyPropertyChanged` interface and common navigation code.
- All dependencies to other classes, such as repositories and services, are passed through the constructor of the `ViewModel`. This will be handled by the **dependency injection** pattern and, more specifically for our case, by Autofac, which is the implementation of dependency injection we are using.
- We use an asynchronous call to `LoadData()` as an entry point to initialize the `ViewModel`. Different MVVM libraries might do this in different ways, but the basic functionally is the same.

Creating the TodoItemViewModel

The `TodoItemViewModel` is the `ViewModel` that represents each item in the to-do list on the `MainView`. It will not have an entire view of its own (although it could have), but instead will be rendered by a template in the `ListView`. We will get back to this when we create the controls for the `MainView`.

The important thing here is that this `ViewModel` will represent a single item, regardless of where we choose to render it.

Let's create the `TodoItemViewModel`:

1. Create a class called `TodoItemViewModel` inside the `ViewModels` folder.
2. Add the following template code and resolve the references:

```
public class TodoItemViewModel : ViewModel
{
    public TodoItemViewModel(TodoItem item) => Item = item;

    public event EventHandler ItemStatusChanged;
    public TodoItem Item { get; private set; }
    public string StatusText => Item.Completed ? "Reactivate" :
    "Completed";
}
```

As with any other `ViewModel`, we inherit the `TodoItemViewModel` from `ViewModel`. We conform to the pattern of injecting all dependencies in the constructor. In this case, we pass an instance of the `TodoItem` class in the constructor that the `ViewModel` will use to expose to the view.

The `ItemStatusChanged` event handler will be used later when we want to signal to the view that the state of the `TodoItem` has changed. The `Item` property allows us to access the item that we passed in.

The `StatusText` property is used for making the status of the to-do item human readable in the view.

Creating the ItemViewModel

The `ItemViewModel` represents the to-do list item in a view that can be used to create new items and to edit existing items:

1. In the `ViewModels` folder, create a class called `ItemViewModel`.
2. Add the code as following:

```
using DoToo.Models;
using DoToo.Repositories;
using System;
using System.Windows.Input;
using Xamarin.Forms;

namespace DoToo.ViewModels
{
    public class ItemViewModel : ViewModel
    {
        private TodoItemRepository repository;

        public ItemViewModel(TodoItemRepository repository)
        {
            this.repository = repository;
        }
    }
}
```

The pattern is the same as for the previous two `ViewModels`:

- We use dependency injection to pass the `TodoItemRepository` into the `ViewModel`
- We use inheritance from the `ViewModel` base class to add the common features defined by the base class

Creating the MainView

Now that we are done with the `ViewModels`, let's create the skeleton code and the XAML needed for the views. The first view that we are going to create is the `MainView`, which is the view that will be loaded first:

1. Create a folder named `Views` in the .NET Standard library.
2. Right-click the `Views` folder, select **Add**, and then click **New Item...**.
3. Select **Xamarin.Forms** under the **Visual C# Items** node on the left.

4. Select **Content Page** and name it `MainView`.

5. Click **Add** to create the page:

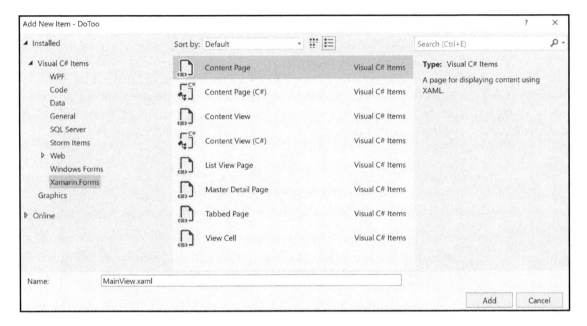

Let's add some content to the newly created view:

1. Open `MainView.xaml`.

2. Remove all the template code below the `ContentPage` root node and add the XAML code marked in bold in the following code:

```
<?xml version="1.0" encoding="utf-8"?>
<ContentPage xmlns="http://xamarin.com/schemas/2014/forms"
             xmlns:x="http://schemas.microsoft.com/winfx/2009/xaml"
             xmlns:local="clr-namespace:DoToo"
             x:Class="DoToo.Views.MainView"
             Title="Do Too!">

    <ContentPage.ToolbarItems>
        <ToolbarItem Text="Add" />
    </ContentPage.ToolbarItems>

    <Grid>
        <Grid.RowDefinitions>
            <RowDefinition Height="auto" />
            <RowDefinition Height="*" />
        </Grid.RowDefinitions>
```

```
        <Button Text="Toggle filter" />

        <ListView Grid.Row="1">
        </ListView>
      </Grid>
  </ContentPage>
```

To be able to access custom converters, we need to add a reference to a local namespace. The line `xmlns:local="clr-namespace:DoToo"` defines this namespace for us. We will not be using it directly in this case, but it's a good idea to have a local namespace defined. If we create custom controls, we can then access these by writing something like `<local:MyControl />`.

The `Title` property on the `ContentPage` gives the page a title. Depending on the platform we are running on, the title is displayed differently. If we are using a standard navigation bar, it will be displayed at the top in both iOS and Android, for example. A page should always have a title.

The `ContentPage.Toolbar` node defines a toolbar item for adding new to-do items. It will also be rendered differently based on the platform, but it will always follow the platform-specific UI guidelines.

A page in Xamarin.Forms (and also an XML document in general) can only have one root node. The root node in a Xamarin.Forms page will populate the `Content` property of the page itself. Since we want our `MainView` to contain a list of items and a button at the top to toggle a filter (to switch between all items and only active items), we need to add a `Layout` control to position them on the page. The `Grid` is a control that allows you to partition the available space based on rows and columns.

For our `MainView`, we want to add two rows. The first row is a space calculated by the height of the button (`Height="auto"`) and the second row takes up all of the remaining available space for the `Listview` (`Height="*"`). Elements, like the `ListView`, are positioned in the grid using the `Grid.Row` and `Grid.Column` attributes. Both of these properties default to `0` if they are not specified, just like the `Button`.

If you are interested in how the `Grid` works, you should search for more information about Xamarin.Forms `Grid` on the internet or study the official documentation at `https://docs.microsoft.com/en-us/xamarin/xamarin-forms/user-interface/layouts/grid`.

We also need to wire up the `ViewModel` to the view. This can be done by passing the `ViewModel` in the constructor of the view:

1. Open up the code-behind file of the `MainView` by expanding the `MainView.xaml` file in the **Solution Explorer**.
2. Add a *using* `DoToo.ViewModels` statement at the top of the following file the existing `using` statements.
3. Modify the constructor of the class to look like the following code by adding the code marked in bold:

```
public MainView(MainViewModel viewModel)
{
    InitializeComponent();
    viewModel.Navigation = Navigation;
    BindingContext = viewModel;
}
```

We follow the same pattern as we did with the `ViewModels` by passing any dependencies through the constructor. A view is always dependent on a `ViewModel`. To simplify the project, we also assign the `Navigation` property of the page directly to the `Navigation` property defined in the `ViewModel` base class. In a larger project, we might want to abstract this property as well, to make sure that we separate the `ViewModels` completely from Xamarin.Forms. For the sake of this app, however, it is OK to reference it directly.

Lastly, we assign the `ViewModel` to the `BindingContext` of the page. This tells the Xamarin.Forms binding engine to use our `ViewModel` for the bindings that we will create later on.

Creating the ItemView

Next up is the second view. We will use this for adding and editing to-do list items:

1. Create a new **Content Page** (the same way as we created the `MainView`) and name it `ItemView`.
2. Edit the XAML and make it look like the following code:

```
<?xml version="1.0" encoding="UTF-8"?>
<ContentPage xmlns="http://xamarin.com/schemas/2014/forms"

xmlns:x="http://schemas.microsoft.com/winfx/2009/xaml"
             x:Class="DoToo.Views.ItemView"
             Title="New todo item">
```

```
<ContentPage.ToolbarItems>
    <ToolbarItem Text="Save" />
</ContentPage.ToolbarItems>

<StackLayout Padding="14">
    <Label Text="Title" />
    <Entry />
    <Label Text="Due" />
    <DatePicker />
    <StackLayout Orientation="Horizontal">
        <Switch />
        <Label Text="Completed" />
    </StackLayout>
</StackLayout>
</ContentPage>
```

As with the `MainView`, we need a title. We will give it a default title of `"New todo item"` for now, but we will change this to `"Edit todo item"` when we reuse this view for editing later on. The user must be able to save a new or edited item, so we have added a toolbar save button. The content of the page uses a `StackLayout` to structure the controls. A `StackLayout` adds an element vertically (the default option) or horizontally based on the space it calculates that the element takes up. This is a CPU-intensive process, so we should only use it on small portions of our layout. In the `StackLayout`, we add a `Label` that will be a line of text over the `Entry` control that comes underneath it. The `Entry` control is a text input control that will contain the name of the to-do list item. We then have a section for a `DatePicker`, where the user can select a due date for the to-do list item. The final control is a `Switch` control, which renders a toggle button to control when an item is completed, and a heading next to that. Since we want these to be displayed next to each other horizontally, we use a horizontal `StackLayout` to do this.

The last step for the views is to wire up the `ItemViewModel` to the `ItemView`:

1. Open up the code-behind file of the `ItemView` by expanding the `ItemView.xaml` file in the **Solution Explorer.**
2. Modify the constructor of the class to look like the following code. Add the code that is marked in bold.

3. Add a using `DoToo.ViewModels` statement at the top of the following file the existing `using` statements:

```
public ItemView (ItemViewModel viewmodel)
{
    InitializeComponent ();
    viewmodel.Navigation = Navigation;
    BindingContext = viewmodel;
}
```

This code is identical to the code that we added for `MainView`, except for the type of the `ViewModel`.

Wiring up a dependency injection through Autofac

Earlier, we discussed the dependency injection pattern, which states that all dependencies, such as the repositories and view models, must be passed through the constructor of the class. This has several benefits:

- It increases the readability of the code, since we can quickly determine all external dependencies
- It makes dependency injection possible
- It makes unit testing possible by mocking classes
- We can control the lifetime of an object by specifying whether it should be a singleton or a new instance for each resolution

Dependency injection is a pattern that lets us determine at runtime which instance of an object should be passed to a constructor when an object is created. We do this by defining a container where we register all the types of a class. We let the framework that we are using resolve any dependencies between them. Let's say that we ask the container for a `MainView`. The container takes care of resolving the `MainViewModel` and any dependencies that the class has.

To set this up, we need to reference a library called Autofac. There are other options out there, so feel free to switch to one that better fits your needs. We also need an entry point to resolve the types into instances. To do this, we will define a bare-bones `Resolver` class. To wrap it all up, we need a bootstrapper that we will call to initialize the dependency injection configuration.

Adding a reference to Autofac

We need a reference to Autofac to get started. We will use NuGet to install the packages needed:

1. Open up the NuGet-manager by right-clicking on the **Solution** node and clicking on **Manage NuGet packages for solution...**.
2. Click on **Browse** and type `autofac` in the search box.
3. Tick all checkboxes under **Project**, scroll down, and click **Install**:

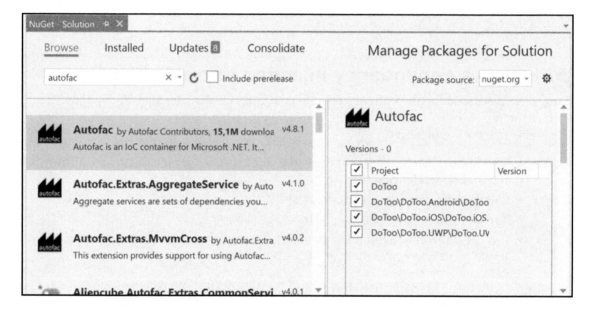

Creating the resolver

The resolver will be responsible for creating our objects for us based on the type that we request. Let's create the resolver:

1. In the root of the .NET Standard library project, create a new file called `Resolver.cs`.
2. Add the following code to the file:

```
using Autofac;

namespace DoToo
{
    public static class Resolver
```

```
    {
        private static IContainer container;

        public static void Initialize(IContainer container)
        {
            Resolver.container = container;
        }

        public static T Resolve<T>()
        {
            return container.Resolve<T>();
        }
    }
}
```

The `container` property of the `IContainer` type is defined in `Autofac` and represents a container that holds the configuration on how to resolve types. The `Initialize` method takes an instance of an object that implements the `IContainer` interface and assigns it to the `container` property. The `Resolve` method uses the `container` to resolve a type to an instance of an object. While it might seem strange to use this at first, it will become much easier with experience.

Creating the bootstrapper

The bootstrapper's responsibility is to initialize Autofac. It will be called at the startup of the application. We can create it as follows:

1. In the root of the .NET Standard library project, create a new file called `Bootstrapper.cs`.
2. Enter the following code:

```
using Autofac;
using System.Linq;
using Xamarin.Forms;
using DoToo.Views;
using DoToo.Repositories;
using DoToo.ViewModels;

namespace DoToo
{
    public abstract class Bootstrapper
    {
        protected ContainerBuilder ContainerBuilder { get; private
        set; }

        public Bootstrapper()
```

```
        {
            Initialize();
            FinishInitialization();
        }

        protected virtual void Initialize()
        {
            var currentAssembly = Assembly.GetExecutingAssembly();
            ContainerBuilder = new ContainerBuilder();

            foreach (var type in currentAssembly.DefinedTypes
                    .Where(e =>
                            e.IsSubclassOf(typeof(Page)) ||
                            e.IsSubclassOf(typeof(ViewModel)))))
            {
                ContainerBuilder.RegisterType(type.AsType());
            }


ContainerBuilder.RegisterType<TodoItemRepository>().SingleInstance(
);
        }

        private void FinishInitialization()
        {
            var container = ContainerBuilder.Build();
            Resolver.Initialize(container);
        }
    }
}
```

The Bootstrapper will be inherited by each platform since this is where the execution of the app begins. This will also give us the option to add platform-specific configurations. To ensure that we inherit from the class, we define it as abstract.

The ContainerBuilder is a class defined in Autofac that takes care of creating the container for us after we are finished with the configuration. The building of the container happens in the FinishInitialization method defined at the end and is called by the constructor right after we call the virtual Initialize method. We can override the Initialize method to add custom registrations on each platform.

The `Initialize` method scans the assembly for any types that inherit from the `Page` or `ViewModel` and adds them to the `container`. It also adds the `TodoItemRepository` as a singleton to the `container`. This means that each time we ask for a `TodoItemRepository`, we will get the same instance. The default behavior for Autofac (this may vary between libraries) is that we get a new instance for each resolution.

Adding a bootstrapper on iOS

The `Bootstrapper` for iOS is a simple wrapper for the common bootstrapper defined in the .NET Standard library, but with the addition of an `Init` method that will be called at startup:

1. In the root of the iOS project, create a new class called `Bootstrapper.cs`.
2. Add the following code to it:

```
public class Bootstrapper : DoToo.Bootstrapper
{
    public static void Init()
    {
        var instance = new Bootstrapper();
    }
}
```

The `Init` method may look strange since we don't retain a reference to the instance we create. Keep in mind, however, that we do keep a reference to a `Resolver` instance inside the `Resolver` class, which is itself a singleton.

The final step for iOS is to call this `Init` method in the right place:

1. Open up `AppDelegate.cs`.
2. Locate the `FinishedLaunching` method and add the code in bold:

```
public override bool FinishedLaunching(UIApplication app,
NSDictionary options)
{
    global::Xamarin.Forms.Forms.Init();
    Bootstrapper.Init();
    LoadApplication(new App());

    return base.FinishedLaunching(app, options);
}
```

Adding a bootstrapper in Android

Just like for iOS, the `Bootstrapper` for Android is a simple wrapper for the common bootstrapper defined in the .NET Standard library, but with the addition of an `Init` method that will be called at startup:

1. In the root of the Android project, create a new class called `Bootstrapper.cs`.
2. Add the following code to it:

```
public class Bootstrapper : DoToo.Bootstrapper
{
    public static void Init()
    {
        var instance = new Bootstrapper();
    }
}
```

We then need to call this `Init` method. A good place to do this is right before the `LoadApplication` call in `OnCreate`:

1. Open up `MainActivity.cs`.
2. Locate the `OnCreate` method and add the code in bold:

```
protected override void OnCreate(Bundle bundle)
{
    TabLayoutResource = Resource.Layout.Tabbar;
    ToolbarResource = Resource.Layout.Toolbar;

    base.OnCreate(bundle);

    global::Xamarin.Forms.Forms.Init(this, bundle);
    Bootstrapper.Init();
    LoadApplication(new App());
}
```

Adding a bootstrapper in UWP

The bootstrapper for UWP is identical to the other platforms:

1. In the root of the UWP project, create a new class called `Bootstrapper.cs`.
2. Add the following code to it:

```
public class Bootstrapper : DoToo.Bootstrapper
{
    public static void Init()
    {
```

```
            var instance = new Bootstrapper();
    }
}
```

And as with the other platforms, we need to call the `Init` method in a good place:

1. In the UWP project, open up the `App.xaml.cs` file.
2. Locate the call to the `Xamarin.Forms.Forms.Init()` method and add the code in bold:

```
Xamarin.Forms.Forms.Init(e);
Bootstrapper.Init();
```

Making the app run

We can start the app for the first time as follows:

1. Open up `App.xaml.cs` by expanding the `App.xaml` node in the .NET Standard library.
2. Locate the constructor.
3. Add a `using` statement for `DoToo.Views` and add the following code line in bold:

```
public App ()
{
    InitializeComponent();
    MainPage = new NavigationPage(Resolver.Resolve<MainView>());
}
```

The line added resolves the `MainView` (and all dependencies, including `MainViewModel` and the `TodoItemRepository`) and wraps it into a `NavigationPage`. The `NavigationPage` is a page defined in Xamarin.Forms that adds a navigation bar and enables the user to navigate to other views.

That's it! At this point, your project should start. Depending on the platform you are using, it might look like the following screenshot:

Adding data bindings

Data binding is the heart and soul of MVVM. This is the way that the `Views` and the `ViewModel` communicate with each other. In Xamarin.Forms, we need two things to make data binding happen:

1. We need an object to implement `INotifyPropertyChanged`.
2. We need to set the `BindingContext` of the page to that object. We already do this on both the `ItemView` and the `MainView`.

A really useful feature of data binding is that it allows us to use two-way communication. For example, when data binding text to an `Entry` control, the property on the data-bound object will be updated directly. Consider the following XAML:

```
<Entry Text="{Binding Title} />
```

To make this work, we need a property named `Title` on the object that is a string. We have to look at the documentation, define an object, and let **Intellisense** provide us with a hint to find out what type our property should be.

Controls that perform some kind of action, like a `Button`, usually expose a property called `Command`. This property is of the `ICommand` type and we can either return a `Xamarin.Forms.Command` or an implementation of our own. The `Command` property is explained in the next section, where we will use it to navigate to the `ItemView`.

Navigating from the MainView to the ItemView to add a new item

We have an **Add** toolbar button in the `MainView`. When the user taps this button, we want to navigate to the `ItemView`. The MVVM way to do this is to define a command and then bind that command to the button. Let's add the code:

1. Open `ViewModels/MainViewModel.cs`.
2. Add using statements for `System.Windows.Input`, `DoToo.Views`, and `Xamarin.Forms`.
3. Add the following property to the class:

```
public ICommand AddItem => new Command(async () =>
{
    var itemView = Resolver.Resolve<ItemView>();
    await Navigation.PushAsync(itemView);
});
```

All commands should be exposed as a generic `ICommand`. This abstracts the actual command implementation, which is a good general practice to follow. The command must be a property; in our case, we are creating a new `Command` object that we assign to this property. The property is read-only, which is usually fine for a `Command`. The action of the command (the code that we want to run when the command is executed) is passed to the constructor of the `Command` object.

The action of the command creates a new `ItemView` through the `Resolver` and Autofac builds the necessary dependencies. Once the new `ItemView` has been created, we simply tell the `Navigation` service to push it onto the stack for us.

After that, we just have to wire up the `AddItem` command from the `ViewModel` to the add button in the view:

1. Open `Views/MainView.xaml`.
2. Add the `Command` attribute to the `ToolbarItem`:

```
<ContentPage.ToolbarItems>
    <ToolbarItem Text="Add" Command="{Binding AddItem}" />
</ContentPage.ToolbarItems>
```

Run the app and tap the **Add** button to navigate to the new item view. Notice that the back button appears automatically.

Adding new items to the list

We have now finished adding the navigation to a new item. Let's now add the code needed to create a new item and save it to the database:

1. Open up `ViewModels/ItemViewModel.cs`.
2. Add the following code in bold.
3. Resolve the reference to `System.Windows.Input`:

```
public class ItemViewModel : ViewModel
{
    private TodoItemRepository repository;

    public TodoItem Item { get; set; }

    public ItemViewModel(TodoItemRepository repository)
    {
        this.repository = repository;
        Item = new TodoItem() { Due = DateTime.Now.AddDays(1) };
    }
    public ICommand Save => new Command(async () =>
    {
        await repository.AddOrUpdate(Item);
        await Navigation.PopAsync();
    });
}
```

The `Item` property holds a reference to the current item that we want to add or edit. A new item is created in the constructor and when we want to edit an item, we can simply assign our own item to this property. The new item is not added to the database unless we execute the `Save` command defined at the end. After the item is added or updated, we remove the view from the navigation stack and return to the `MainView` again.

 Since the navigation keeps pages in a stack, the framework declares methods that reflect operations that you can perform on a stack. The operation of removing the topmost item in a stack is known as **popping the stack**, so instead of `RemoveAsync()`, we have `PopAsync()`. To add a page to the navigation stack, we push it, so that method is called `PushAsync()`.

Now that we have extended the `ItemViewModel` with the necessary commands and properties, it's time to data-bind them in the XAML:

1. Open `ViewModels/ItemView.xaml`.
2. Add the code marked in bold:

```xml
<?xml version="1.0" encoding="UTF-8"?>
<ContentPage xmlns="http://xamarin.com/schemas/2014/forms"
             xmlns:x="http://schemas.microsoft.com/winfx/2009/xaml"
             x:Class="DoToo.Views.ItemView">
    <ContentPage.ToolbarItems>
        <ToolbarItem Text="Save" Command="{Binding Save}" />
    </ContentPage.ToolbarItems>
    <StackLayout Padding="14">
        <Label Text="Title" />
        <Entry Text="{Binding Item.Title}" />
        <Label Text="Due" />
        <DatePicker Date="{Binding Item.Due}" />
        <StackLayout Orientation="Horizontal">
            <Switch IsToggled="{Binding Item.Completed}" />
            <Label Text="Completed" />
        </StackLayout>
    </StackLayout>
</ContentPage>
```

The binding to the `ToolbarItems` command attribute triggers the `Save` command exposed by the `ItemViewModel` when a user taps the `Save` link. It's worth nothing again that any attribute called `Command` indicates that an action will take place and that we must bind it to an instance of an object implementing the `ICommand` interface.

The `Entry` control that represents the title is data-bound to the `Item.Title` property of the `ItemViewModel`, and the `Datepicker` and `Switch` control bind in a similar way to their respective properties.

We could have exposed `Title`, `Due`, and `Complete` as properties directly on the `ItemViewModel`, but chose to reuse the already existing `TodoItem` as a reference. This is fine, as long as the properties of the `TodoItem` object implement the `INotifyPropertyChange` interface.

Binding the ListView in the MainView

A to-do list is not much use without a list of items. Let's extend the `MainViewModel` with a list of items:

1. Open `ViewModels/MainViewModel.cs`.
2. Add `using` statements for `System.Collections.ObjectModel` and `System.Linq`.
3. Add a property for the to-do list items:

   ```
   public ObservableCollection<TodoItemViewModel> Items { get; set; }
   ```

An `ObservableCollection` is like an ordinary collection, but it has a useful superpower. It can notify listeners about changes in the list, such as when `items` are added or deleted. The `Listview` will listen to changes in the list and update itself automatically based on these.

We now need some data:

1. Open `ViewModels/MainViewModel.cs`.
2. Replace (or complete) the `LoadData` method and create the `CreateTodoItemViewModel` and `ItemStatusChanged` methods.
3. Resolve the reference to `DoToo.Models` by adding a `using` statement:

   ```
   private async Task LoadData()
   {
       var items = await repository.GetItems();
       var itemViewModels = items.Select(i =>
       CreateTodoItemViewModel(i));
       Items = new ObservableCollection<TodoItemViewModel>
       (itemViewModels);
   }
   ```

```
private TodoItemViewModel CreateTodoItemViewModel(TodoItem item)
{
    var itemViewModel = new TodoItemViewModel(item);
    itemViewModel.ItemStatusChanged += ItemStatusChanged;
    return itemViewModel;
}

private void ItemStatusChanged(object sender, EventArgs e)
{
}
```

The `LoadData` method calls the repository to fetch all items. We then wrap each to-do list item in the `TodoItemViewModel`. This will contain more information that is specific to the view and that we don't want to add to the `TodoItem` class. It is a good practice to wrap plain objects in a `ViewModel`; this makes it simpler to add actions or extra properties to it. The `ItemStatusChanged` is a stub that will be called when we change the status of the to-do list item from *active* to *completed* and vice versa.

We also need to hook up some events from the repository to know when data changes:

1. Open `ViewModels/MainViewModel.cs`.
2. Add the following code in bold:

```
public MainViewModel(TodoItemRepository repository)
{
    repository.OnItemAdded += (sender, item) =>
        Items.Add(CreateTodoItemViewModel(item));
    repository.OnItemUpdated += (sender, item) =>
        Task.Run(async () => await LoadData());

    this.repository = repository;
    Task.Run(async () => await LoadData());
}
```

When an item is added to the repository, no matter who added it, the `MainView` will add it to the items list. Since the items collection is an observable collection, the list will update. If an item gets updated, we simply reload the list.

Let's data-bind our items to the `ListView`:

1. Open up `MainView.xaml` and locate the `ListView` element.
2. Modify it to reflect the following code:

```
<ListView Grid.Row="1"
          RowHeight="70"
          ItemsSource="{Binding Items}">
```

```xml
<ListView.ItemTemplate>
    <DataTemplate>
        <ViewCell>
            <Grid Padding="15,10">
                <Grid.ColumnDefinitions>
                    <ColumnDefinition Width="10" />
                    <ColumnDefinition Width="*" />
                </Grid.ColumnDefinitions>

                <BoxView Grid.RowSpan="2" />
                <Label Grid.Column="1"
                        Text="{Binding Item.Title}"
                        FontSize="Large" />
                <Label Grid.Column="1"
                        Grid.Row="1"
                        Text="{Binding Item.Due}"
                        FontSize="Micro" />
                <Label Grid.Column="1"
                        Grid.Row="1"
                        HorizontalTextAlignment="End"
                        Text="Completed"
                        IsVisible="{Binding Item.Completed}"
                        FontSize="Micro" />
            </Grid>
        </ViewCell>
    </DataTemplate>
</ListView.ItemTemplate>
</ListView>
```

The `ItemsSource` binding tells the `ListView` where to find the collection to iterate over and is local to the `ViewModel`. Any bindings inside the `ViewCell` node, however, are local to each item that we iterate in the list. In this case, we are binding to the `TodoItemViewModel`, which contains a property named `Item`. This, in turn, has properties such as `Title`, `Due`, and `Completed`. We can navigate down the hierarchy of objects without any problem when defining a binding.

The `DataTemplate` defined what each row will look like. We use a grid to partition the space just like we did earlier.

Creating a ValueConverter for the item status

Sometimes, we want to bind to objects that are a representation of the original value. This could be a piece of text that is based on a Boolean value. Instead of *true* and *false*, for example, we might want to write *Yes* and *No*, or return a color. This is where `ValueConverter` comes in handy. It can be used to convert a value to and from another value. We are going to write a `ValueConverter` that converts the status of a to-do list item to a color:

1. In the root of the .NET Standard library project, create a folder called `Converters`.

2. Create a class called `StatusColorConverter.cs` and add the following code:

```
using System;
using System.Globalization;
using Xamarin.Forms;

namespace DoToo.Converters
{
    public class StatusColorConverter : IValueConverter
    {
        public object Convert(object value, Type targetType,
                              object parameter, CultureInfo
                              culture)
        {
            return (bool)value ?
(Color)Application.Current.Resources["CompletedColor"]:

            (Color)Application.Current.Resources["ActiveColor"];
        }

        public object ConvertBack(object value, Type
targetType,
                                  object parameter, CultureInfo
                                  culture)
        {
            return null;
        }
    }
}
```

A `ValueConverter` is a class that implements `IValueConverter`. This, in turn, only has two methods defined. The `Convert` method is called when the view reads data from the `ViewModel`, and the `ConvertBack` method is used when the `ViewModel` gets data from the view. The `ConvertBack` method is only used for controls that return data from plain text, such as the `Entry` control.

If we look at the implementation of the `Convert` method, we notice that any value passed into the method is of the object type. This is because we don't know what type the user has bound to the property to which we are adding this `ValueConverter`. We may also notice that we fetch colors from a resource file. We could have defined the colors in the code, but this is not recommended, so instead, we went the extra mile and added them as a global resource in the `App.xaml` file. Resources are a good thing to take another look at once we've finished with the chapter:

1. Open `App.xaml` in the .NET Standard library project.
2. Add the following `ResourceDictionary`:

```
<Application ...>
    <Application.Resources>
        <ResourceDictionary>
            <Color x:Key="CompletedColor">#1C8859</Color>
            <Color x:Key="ActiveColor">#D3D3D3</Color>
        </ResourceDictionary>
    </Application.Resources>
</Application>
```

A `ResourceDictionary` can define a wide range of different objects. We settle for the two colors that we want to access from the `ValueConverter`. Notice that these are accessible by the key given to them and they can also be accessed from any other XAML file using a static resource binding. The `ValueConverter` itself will be referenced as a static resource, but from a local scope.

Using the ValueConverter

We want to use our brand new `StatusColorConverter` in the `MainView`. Unfortunately, we have to jump through some hoops to make this happen. We need to do three things:

- Define a namespace in XAML
- Define a local resource that represents an instance of the converter
- Declare in the binding that we want to use that converter

Let's start with the namespace:

1. Open `Views/MainView.xaml`.
2. Add the following namespace to the page:

```
<ContentPage xmlns="http://xamarin.com/schemas/2014/forms"
             xmlns:x="http://schemas.microsoft.com/winfx/2009/xaml"
             xmlns:converters="clr-namespace:DoToo.Converters"
             x:Class="DoToo.Views.MainView"
             Title="Do Too!>
```

Add a `Resource` node to the `MainView.xaml` file:

1. Open Views/MainView.Xaml.
2. Add the following `ResourceDictionary`, shown in bold under the root element of the XAML file:

```
<ContentPage ...>
    <ContentPage.Resources>
        <ResourceDictionary>
            <converters:StatusColorConverter
            x:Key="statusColorConverter" />
        </ResourceDictionary>
    </ContentPage.Resources>
    <ContentPage.ToolBarItems>
        <ToolbarItem Text="Add" Command="{Binding AddItem}" />
    </ContentPage.ToolBarItems>
    <Grid ...>
    </Grid>
</ContentPage>
```

This has the same form as the global resource dictionary, but since this one is defined in the `MainView`, it will only be accessible from there. We could have defined this in the global resource dictionary, but it's usually best to define objects that you only consume in one place as close to that place as possible.

The last step is to add the converter:

1. Locate the `BoxView` node in the XAML.
2. Add the `BackgroundColor` XAML, which is marked in bold:

```
<BoxView Grid.RowSpan="2"
    BackgroundColor="{Binding Item.Completed,
                     Converter={StaticResource
                     statusColorConverter}}" />
```

What we have done here is bound a Boolean value to a property that takes a `Color` object. Right before the data binding takes place, however, the `ValueConverter` converts the Boolean value to a color. This is just one of the many cases where a `ValueConverter` comes in handy. Keep this in mind when you are defining the GUI.

Navigating to an item using a command

We want to be able to see the details for a selected to-do list item. When we tap a row, we should navigate to the item in that row.

To do this, we need to add the following code:

1. Open `ViewModels/MainViewModel.cs`.
2. Add the `SelectedItem` property and the `NavigateToItem` method to the class:

```
public TodoItemViewModel SelectedItem
{
    get { return null; }
    set
    {
        Device.BeginInvokeOnMainThread(async () => await
        NavigateToItem(value));
        RaisePropertyChanged(nameof(SelectedItem));
    }
}

private async Task NavigateToItem(TodoItemViewModel item)
{
    if (item == null)
    {
        return;
    }

    var itemView = Resolver.Resolve<ItemView>();
    var vm = itemView.BindingContext as ItemViewModel;
    vm.Item = item.Item;

    await Navigation.PushAsync(itemView);
}
```

The `SelectedItem` property is a property that we will data-bind to the `ListView`. When we select a row in the `ListView`, this property will be set to the `TodoItemViewModel` that represents that row. Since we can't really use Fody here to carry out its `PropertyChanged` magic, because of the need to do a method call in the setter, we need to go old-school and manually add a getter and a setter.

The setter then calls `NavigateToItem`, which creates a new `ItemView` using the `Resolver`. We extract the `ViewModel` from the newly created `ItemView` and assign the current `TodoItem` that the `TodoItemViewModel` contains. Confused? Remember that the `TodoItemViewModel` actually wraps a `TodoItem` and it is that item that we want to pass to the `ItemView`.

We are not done yet. We now need to data-bind the new `SelectedItem` property to the right place in the view:

1. Open `Views/MainView.xaml`.
2. Locate the `ListView` and add the attributes in bold:

```
<ListView x:Name="ItemsListView"
          Grid.Row="1"
          RowHeight="70"
          ItemsSource="{Binding Items}"
          SelectedItem="{Binding SelectedItem}">
```

The `SelectedItem` attribute binds the, `SelectedItem` property `ListView` to the `ViewModel` property. When the selection of an item in the `ListView` changes, the `ViewModels` `SelectedItem` property will be called and we will navigate to the new and exciting views.

The `x:Name` attribute is for naming the `ListView`, because we do need to make a small and ugly hack to make this work. The `ListView` will actually stay selected after the navigation is done. When we navigate back, it cannot be selected again until we select another row. To mitigate this, we need to hook up to the `ItemSelected` event of `ListView` and reset the selected item directly on the `ListView`. This is not recommended, because we shouldn't really have any logic in our `Views`, but sometimes we have no other choice:

1. Open `Views/MainView.xaml.cs`.
2. Add the following code in bold:

```
public MainView(MainViewModel viewmodel)
{
    InitializeComponent();
    viewmodel.Navigation = Navigation;
```

```
        BindingContext = viewmodel;

        ItemsListView.ItemSelected += (s, e) =>
        ItemsListView.SelectedItem = null;
}
```

We should now be able to navigate to an item in the list.

Marking an item as complete using a command

We need to add a functionality that allows us to toggle the items between *complete* and *active*. It is possible to navigate to the detailed view of the to-do list item, but this is too much work for a user. Instead, we'll add a `ContextAction` to the `ListView`. In iOS, for example, this will be accessed by swiping left on a row:

1. Open `ViewModel/TodoItemViewModel.cs`.
2. Add a `using` statement for `System.Windows.Input` and `Xamarin.Forms`.
3. Add a command to toggle the status of the item and a piece of text that describes the status:

```
public ICommand ToggleCompleted => new Command((arg) =>
{
    Item.Completed = !Item.Completed;
    ItemStatusChanged?.Invoke(this, new EventArgs());
});
```

Here, we have added a command for toggling the state of an item. When executed, it inverses the current state and raises the `ItemStatusChanged` event so that subscribers are notified. To change the text of the context action button depending on the status, we added a `StatusText` property. This is not a recommended practice, because we are adding code that only exists because of a specific UI case into the `ViewModel`. Ideally, this would be handled by the view, perhaps by using a `ValueConverter`. To save us having to implement these steps, however, we have left it as a string property:

1. Open `Views/MainView.xaml`.
2. Locate the `ListView.ItemTemplate` node and add the following `ViewCell.ContextActions` node:

```
<ListView.ItemTemplate>
    <DataTemplate>
        <ViewCell>
            <ViewCell.ContextActions>
                <MenuItem Text="{Binding StatusText}"
```

```
                Command="{Binding ToggleCompleted}" />
            </ViewCell.ContextActions>
        <Grid Padding="15,10">
        ...
        </Grid>
    </DataTemplate>
</ListView.ItemTemplate>
```

Creating the filter toggle function using a command

We want to be able to toggle between viewing only active items and all items. We will create a simple mechanism to do this.

Hook up the changes in the MainViewModel as follows:

1. Open ViewModels/MainViewModel.cs and locate the ItemStatusChangeMethod.

2. Add the implementation to the ItemStatusChanged method and a property called ShowAll to control the filtering:

```
private void ItemStatusChanged(object sender, EventArgs e)
{
    if (sender is TodoItemViewModel item)
    {
        if (!ShowAll && item.Item.Completed)
        {
            Items.Remove(item);
        }

        Task.Run(async () => await
        repository.UpdateItem(item.Item));
    }
}

public bool ShowAll { get; set; }
```

The ItemStatusChanged event handler is triggered when we use the context action from the last section. Since the sender is always an object, we try to cast it to a TodoItemViewModel. If this is successful, we check whether we can remove it from the list if ShowAll is not true. This is a small optimization; we could have called LoadData and reloaded the entire list, but since the Items list is an ObservableCollection, it communicates to the ListView that one item has been removed from the list. We also call the repository to update the item to persist the change of status.

The `ShowAll` property is what controls which state our filter is in. We need to adjust the `LoadData` method to reflect this:

1. Locate the Load method in the `MainViewModel`.
2. Add the lines of code marked in bold:

```
private async Task LoadData()
{
    var items = await repository.GetItems();

    if (!ShowAll)
    {
        items = items.Where(x => x.Completed == false).ToList();
    }

    var itemViewModels = items.Select(i =>
    CreateTodoItemViewModel(i));
    Items = new ObservableCollection<TodoItemViewModel>
    (itemViewModels);
}
```

If `ShowAll` is false, we limit the content of the list to the items that have not been completed. We could do this either by having two methods, `GetAllItems()` and `GetActiveItems()`, or by using a filter argument that could be passed to `GetItems()`. Take a minute to think about how we would have implemented this.

Let's add the code that toggles the filter:

1. Open `ViewModels/MainViewModel.cs`.
2. Add the `FilterText` and `ToggleFilter` properties:

```
public string FilterText => ShowAll ? "All" : "Active";

public ICommand ToggleFilter => new Command(async () =>
{
    ShowAll = !ShowAll;
    await LoadData();
});
```

The `FilterText` property is a read-only property used to display the status as a string in human-readable form. We could have used a `ValueConverter` for this, but to save some time, we simply expose it as a property. The logic for the `ToggleFilter` command is a simple inversion of the state and then a call to `LoadData`. This, in turn, causes a reload of the list.

Before we can filter the items, we need to hook up the filter button:

1. Open `Views/MainView.xaml`.
2. Locate the `Button` that controls the filter (the only button in the file).
3. Adjust the code to reflect the following code:

```
<Button Text="{Binding FilterText, StringFormat='Filter: {0}'}"
        Command="{Binding ToggleFilter}" />
```

The app is now complete with regard to this feature! But it isn't very attractive; we'll deal with this in the following section.

Laying out contents

This last section is about making the app look a bit nicer. We are just going to scratch the surface of the possibilities here, but this should give you some ideas about how styling works.

Setting an application-wide background color

Styles are a great way to apply styling to elements. They can be applied either to all elements of a type or to the elements referenced by a key, if you add an x:Key attribute:

1. Open `App.xaml` in the .NET Standard project.
2. Add the following XAML, which is in bold, to the file:

```
<ResourceDictionary>
    <Style TargetType="NavigationPage">
        <Setter Property="BarBackgroundColor" Value="#A25EBB" />
        <Setter Property="BarTextColor" Value="#FFFFFF" />
    </Style>
    <Style x:Key="FilterButton" TargetType="Button">
        <Setter Property="Margin" Value="15" />
        <Setter Property="BorderWidth" Value="1" />
        <Setter Property="BorderRadius" Value="6" />
        <Setter Property="BorderColor" Value="Silver" />
        <Setter Property="TextColor" Value="Black" />
    </Style>
    <Color x:Key="CompletedColor">#1C8859</Color>
    <Color x:Key="ActiveColor">#D3D3D3</Color>
</ResourceDictionary>
```

The first style we are going to apply is a new background color and text color in the navigation bar. The second style will be applied to the filter button. We can define a style by setting the `TargetType` that instructs Xamarin.Forms which type of object this style can be applied to. We can then add one or more properties that we want to set. The result is the same as if we had added these properties directly to the element in the XAML code.

Styles that lack the `x:Key` attribute will be applied to all instances of the type defined in `TargetType`. The styles that have a key must be explicitly assigned in the XAML of the user interface. We will see examples of this when we define the filter button in the next section.

Laying out the MainView and ListView items

In this section, we'll be improving the appearance of the `MainView` and the `ListView`. Open up `Views/MainView.xaml` and apply the changes in bold in the XAML code for each section following.

The filter button

The filter button allows us to toggle the state of the list to show only active to-do items and all to-do items. Let's style it to make it stand out a bit in the layout:

1. Find the filter button.
2. Make the following changes:

```
<Button Style="{StaticResource FilterButton}"
        Text="{Binding FilterText, StringFormat='Filter: {0}'}"
        BackgroundColor="{Binding ShowAll,
Converter={StaticResource
        statusColorConverter}}"
        TextColor="Black"
        Command="{Binding ToggleFilter}">
  <Button.Triggers>
    <DataTrigger TargetType="Button" Binding="{Binding ShowAll}"
        Value="True">
      <Setter Property="TextColor" Value="White" />
    </DataTrigger>
  </Button.Triggers>
</Button>
```

The style is applied using a `StaticResource`. Anything defined in a resource dictionary, either in the `App.xaml` file or in the local XAML file, is accessible through it. We then set the `BackgroundColor`, based on the `ShowAll` property of the `MainViewModel`, and the `TextColor` to `Black`.

The `Button.Triggers` node is a useful feature. We can define a number of types of triggers that fire when a certain criteria is met. In this case, we use a data trigger that checks whether the value of `ShowAll` changes to true. If it does, we set the `TextColor` to white. The coolest part is that when `ShowAll` becomes false again, it switches back to whichever color it was before.

Touching up the ListView

The `ListView` could use a couple of minor changes. The first change is formatting the due-date string to a more human, readable format, and the second is to change the color of the completed label to a nice green tint:

1. Open up `Views/MainView.xaml`.
2. Locate the labels that bind `Item.Due` and `Item.Completed` in the `ListView`:

```
<Label Grid.Column="1"
       Grid.Row="1"
       Text="{Binding Item.Due, StringFormat='{0:MMMM d, yyyy}'}"
       FontSize="Micro" />
<Label Grid.Column="1"
       Grid.Row="1"
       HorizontalTextAlignment="End"
       Text="Completed"
       IsVisible="{Binding Item.Completed}"
       FontSize="Micro"
       TextColor="{StaticResource CompletedColor}" />
```

We added a string formatting in the binding to format the date using a specific format. In this case, the `0:MMMM d, yyyy` format that will display the date as a string in the format of May 5, 2019.

We also added a text color to the `Completed` label that is only visible if an item is completed. We do this by referencing our dictionary in `App.xaml`.

Summary

We should now have a good grasp of all the steps involved in creating a Xamarin.Forms application from scratch. We have learned about the project structure and the important files in a newly created project. We talked about dependency injection, using Autofac, and learned the basics of MVVM by creating all the Views and ViewModels needed. We also covered data storage in SQLite, to be able to persist data on the device in a fast and secure way. Using the knowledge gained from this chapter, you should now be able to create the backbone of any app you like.

The next chapter will focus on creating a richer user experience by creating a match-making application that displays images that you can pan around the screen. We will take a closer look at XAML and how to create custom controls.

3
A Matchmaking App with a Rich UX Using Animations

In this chapter, we will create the base functionality for a matchmaking app. We won't be rating people, however, because of privacy issues. Instead, we will download images from a random source on the internet. This project is for anyone who wants an introduction to how to write reusable controls. We will also look at using animations to make our application feel nicer to use. This app will not be an MVVM application, since we want to isolate the creation and usage of a control from the slight overhead of MVVM.

The following topics will be covered in this chapter:

- Creating a custom control
- How to style the app to look like a photo with descriptive text beneath it
- Animations using Xamarin.Forms
- Subscribing to custom events
- Reusing the custom control over and over again
- Handling pan gestures

Technical requirements

To be able to complete this project, you will need to have Visual Studio for Mac or Windows installed, as well as the necessary Xamarin components. See `Chapter 1`, *Introduction to Xamarin*, for more details on how to set up your environment.

Project overview

Many of us have been there, faced with the conundrum to swipe left or right. All of a sudden, you may find yourself wondering: how does this work? How does the swipe magic happen? Well, in this project, we're going to learn all about it. We will start by defining a `MainPage` file, in which the images of our application will reside. After that, we will create the image control and gradually add the GUI and functionality to it until we have nailed the perfect swiping experience.

The build time for this project is about 90 minutes.

Creating the matchmaking app

In this project, we will learn more about creating reusable controls that can be added to a XAML page. To keep things simple, we will not be using MVVM, but bare-metal Xamarin.Forms without any data binding. What we aim to create is an app that allows the user to swipe images, either to the right or the left, just like most popular matchmaking applications do.

Well, let's get started by creating the project!

Creating the project

Just as with the to-do list app in `Chapter 2`, *Building our First Xamarin.Forms App*, this chapter will start with a clean **File | New Project** approach. We are going to opt for a .NET Standard approach rather than a shared code approach in this chapter; please refer back to `Chapter 2`, *Building our First Xamarin.Forms App* to gain more insight into the differences between them if you're not sure why we're doing this.

Let's get started!

Creating the new project

Open up Visual Studio and click on **File** | **New** | **Project**:

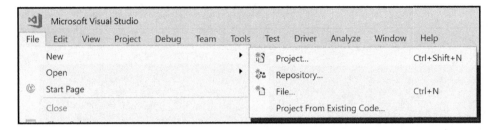

This will open up the **New Project** dialog. Expand the **Visual C#** node and click on **Cross-Platform**. Select the **Mobile App (Xamarin.Forms)** item from the list. Complete the form by naming your project. We will be calling our application `Swiper` in this case. Move on to the next dialog by clicking **OK**:

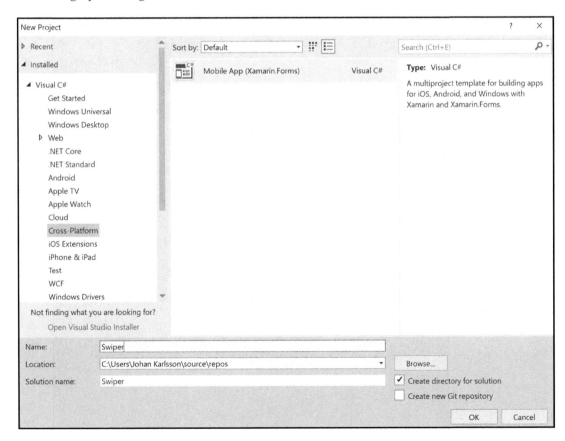

The next step is to select a project template and a **Code Sharing Strategy**. Select **Blank** to create a bare minimum Xamarin.Forms app and make sure that the **Code Sharing Strategy** is set to **.NET Standard**. Finish the setup wizard by clicking **OK** and let Visual Studio scaffold the project for you. This might take a couple of minutes:

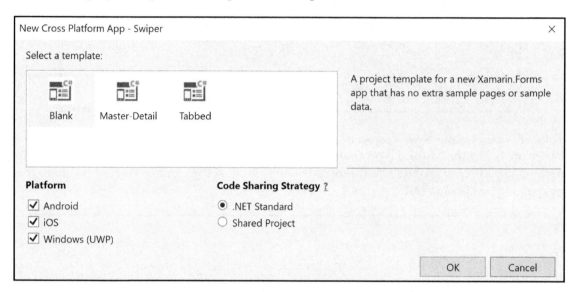

Just like that, the app is created. Let's move on to updating Xamarin.Forms to the latest version.

Updating the Xamarin.Forms NuGet packages

Currently, the Xamarin.Forms version that your project will be created with is most likely a bit old. To rectify this, we need to update the **NuGet Packages**. Please note that you should only update the Xamarin.Forms packages and not the Android packages; doing the latter might cause your packages to get out of sync with each other, resulting in the app not building at all. To update the NuGet packages, perform the following steps:

1. Right-click on our **Solution** in the **Solution Explorer.**
2. Click **Manage NuGet Packages for Solution...**:

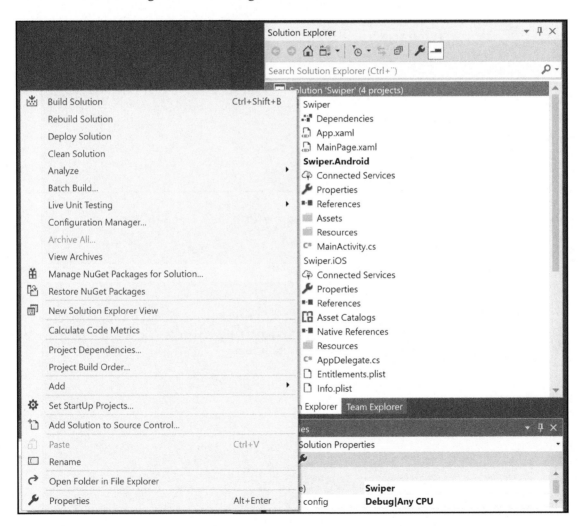

This will open the **NuGet** Package Manager in Visual Studio:

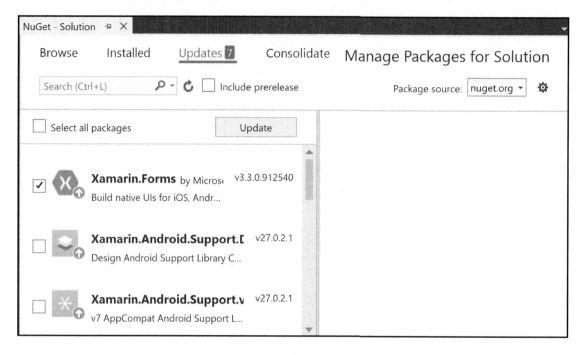

To update Xamarin.Forms to the latest version, perform the following steps:

1. Click the **Updates** tab.
2. Check **Xamarin.Forms** and click **Update.**
3. Accept any license agreements.

The update takes at most a few minutes. Check the output pane to find information about the update. At this point, we can run the app to make sure it works. We should see the text **Welcome to Xamarin.Forms!** in the middle of the screen:

Designing the MainPage file

A brand new blank Xamarin.Forms app named `Swiper` is created with a single page called `MainPage.xaml`. This is located in the .NET Standard Project that is referenced by all platform-specific projects. We will need to replace the XAML template with a new layout that will contain our `Swiper` control.

Let's edit the already existing `MainView.xaml` file by replacing the default content with what we need:

1. Open the `MainView.xaml` file.
2. Replace the content of the page with the following XAML code marked in bold:

```
<?xml version="1.0" encoding="utf-8"?>
<ContentPage xmlns="http://xamarin.com/schemas/2014/forms"
             xmlns:x="http://schemas.microsoft.com/winfx/2009/xaml"
             xmlns:local="clr-namespace:Swiper"
             x:Class="Swiper.MainPage">
```

```
<Grid Padding="0,40" x:Name="MainGrid">
    <Grid.RowDefinitions>
        <RowDefinition Height="400" />
        <RowDefinition Height="*" />
    </Grid.RowDefinitions>
    <Grid Grid.Row="1" Padding="30">
        <!-- Placeholder for later -->
    </Grid>
</Grid>
</ContentPage>
```

The XAML within the `ContentPage` node defines two grids in the application. A grid is simply a container for other controls. It positions those controls based on rows and columns. The outer grid, in this case, defines two rows that will cover the entire available area of the screen. The first row is `400` units high and the second row, with `height="*"`, uses the rest of the available space.

The inner grid, which is defined within the first grid, is assigned to the second row with the attribute `Grid.Row="1"`. The row and column indexes are zero-based, so `"1"` actually refers to the second row. We will add some content to this grid later on in the chapter, but we'll leave it empty for now.

Both grids define their padding. You could enter a single number, meaning that all sides will have the same padding, or as in this case, enter two numbers. We have entered `0,40`, which means that the left and right sides should have zero units of padding and the top and bottom should have `40` units of padding. There is also a third option with four digits, which sets the padding of the *left* side, the *top*, the *right* side, and the *bottom*, in that specific order.

The last thing to notice is that we give the outer grid a name, `x:Name="MainGrid"`. This will make it directly accessible from the code-behind defined in the `MainPage.xaml.cs` file. Since we are not using MVVM in this example, we will need a way to access the grid without data binding.

Creating the Swiper control

The main part of this project involves creating the `Swiper` control. A control is a self-contained UI with a code-behind to go with it. It can be added to any XAML page as an element or in code in the code-behind file. We will be adding the control from code in this project.

Creating the control

Creating the `Swiper` control is a straightforward process. We just need to make sure that we select the correct item template, which is the **Content View**:

1. In the .NET Standard library project, create a folder called `Controls`.
2. Right-click on the `Controls` folder, select **Add**, and then click **New item....**
3. Select **Visual C# Items** and then **Xamarin.Forms** in the left pane of the **Add New Item** dialog box.
4. Select the **Content View (C#)** item. Make sure you don't select the C# version; this only creates a `C#` file and not an `XAML` file.
5. Name the control `SwiperControl.xaml`.
6. Click **Add:**

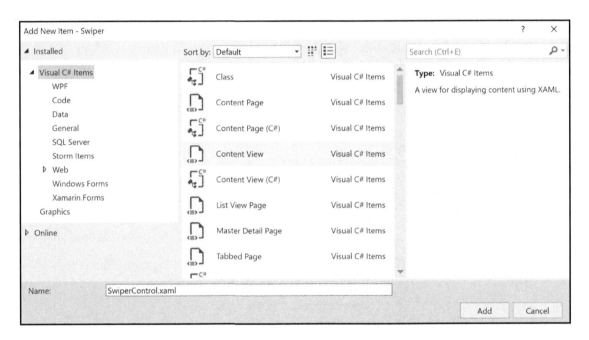

This adds an XAML file for the UI and a C# code-behind file. It should look like the following screenshot:

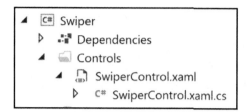

Defining the main grid

Let's set the basic structure of the Swiper control:

1. Open the SwiperControl.xaml file.

2. Replace the content with the code marked in bold:

```xml
<?xml version="1.0" encoding="UTF-8"?>
<ContentView xmlns="http://xamarin.com/schemas/2014/forms"
             xmlns:x="http://schemas.microsoft.com/winfx/2009/xaml"
             x:Class="Swiper.Controls.SwiperControl">
    <ContentView.Content>
        <Grid>
            <Grid.ColumnDefinitions>
                <ColumnDefinition Width="100" />
                <ColumnDefinition Width="*" />
                <ColumnDefinition Width="100" />
            </Grid.ColumnDefinitions>

            <!-- ContentView for photo here -->

            <!-- StackLayout for like here -->

            <!-- StackLayout for deny here -->
        </Grid>
    </ContentView.Content>
</ContentView>
```

This defines a grid with three columns. The leftmost and the rightmost columns will take up 100 units of space and the center will occupy the rest of the available space. The spaces on the sides will be areas in which we will add labels to highlight the choice that the user has made. We've also added three comments that act as placeholders for the XAML to come.

Adding a content view for the photo

We will now extend the `SwiperControl.xaml` file by adding a definition of what we want the photo to look like. Our final result will look like the following photo. Since we are going to pull images off the internet, we'll display a loading text to make sure that the user gets feedback on what's going on. To make it look like an instantly printed photo, we add some handwritten text under the photo:

A horrible picture of grandpa

The preceding photo is what we would like the photo to look like. To make it a reality, we need to add some XAML to the `SwiperControl`:

1. Open up `SwiperControl.xaml`.
2. Add the XAML in bold to the following comment: `<!-- ContentView for photo here -->`. Make sure that you do not replace the entire `ContentView` for the page; just add this under the comment as follows. The rest of the page should be untouched:

    ```
    <!-- ContentView for photo here -->
    <ContentView x:Name="photo" Padding="40" Grid.ColumnSpan="3" >
        <Grid x:Name="photoGrid" BackgroundColor="Black" Padding="1" >
            <Grid.RowDefinitions>
                <RowDefinition Height="*" />
                <RowDefinition Height="40" />
            </Grid.RowDefinitions>

            <BoxView BackgroundColor="White" Grid.RowSpan="2" />
    ```

```
<Image x:Name="image" Margin="10"
        BackgroundColor="#AAAAAA"
        Aspect="AspectFill" />

<Label x:Name="loadingLabel"
        Text="Loading..."
        TextColor="White"
        FontSize="Large"
        FontAttributes="Bold"
        HorizontalOptions="Center"
        VerticalOptions="Center" />

<Label x:Name="descriptionLabel"
        Margin="10,0"
        Text="A picture of grandpa"
        Grid.Row="1"
        FontFamily="Bradley Hand" />
    </Grid>
</ContentView>
```

A ContentView control defines a new area where we can add other controls. One very important feature of a ContentView is that it only takes one child control. Most of the time, we would add one of the layout controls that are available. In this case, we'll use a Grid control to lay out the control, as shown in the preceding code.

The grid defines two rows:

- A row for the photo itself, which takes up all the available space when the other rows have been allocated space
- A row for the comment, which will be exactly 40 units in height

The Grid itself is set to use a black background and a padding of 1. This, in combination with a BoxView, which has a white background, creates the frame that we see around the control. The BoxView is also set to span both rows of the grid (Grid.RowSpan="2"), taking up the entire area of the grid, minus the padding.

The Image control comes next. It has a background color set to a nice gray tone (#AAAAAA) and a margin of 40, which will separate it a bit from the frame around it. It also has a hardcoded name (x:Name="image"), which will allow us to interact with it from the code-behind. The last attribute, called Aspect, determines what we should do if the image control isn't of the same ratio as the source image. In this case, we want to fill the entire image area, but not show any blank areas. This effectively crops the image either in height or in width.

We finish off by adding two labels, which also have hardcoded names for later reference.

Creating the DescriptionGenerator

At the bottom of the image, we see a description. Since we don't have any general descriptions of the images from our upcoming image source, we need to create a generator that makes up descriptions. Here's how we would do it:

1. Create a folder called Utils in the .NET Standard project.
2. Create a new class called DescriptionGenerator in that folder.
3. Add a using statement for System.Linq (using System.Linq;).
4. Add the following code to the class:

```
public class DescriptionGenerator
{
    private string[] _adjectives = { "nice", "horrible", "great",
    "terribly old", "brand new" };
    private string[] _other = { "picture of grandpa", "car", "photo
    of a forest", "duck" };
    private static Random random = new Random();

    public string Generate()
    {
        var a = _adjectives[random.Next(_adjectives.Count())];
        var b = _other[random.Next(_other.Count())];
        return $"A {a} {b}";
    }
}
```

This class only has one purpose. It takes one random word from the _adjectives array and combines it with a random word from the _other array. By calling the Generate() method, we get a fresh new combination. Feel free to enter your own words in the arrays. Note that the Random instance is a static field. This is because if we create new instances of the Random class that are too close to each other in time, they get seeded with the same value and return the same sequence of random numbers.

Creating a picture class

To abstract all the information about the image we want to display, we'll create a class that encapsulates this information. There isn't much information in our `Picture` class, but it is good coding practice to do this:

1. Create a new class called `Picture` in the `Utils` folder.
2. Add the following code to the class:

```
public class Picture
{
 public Uri Uri { get; set; }
  public string Description { get; set; }

 public Picture()
 {
 Uri = new Uri($"https://picsum.photos/400/400/?random&ts=
 {DateTime.Now.Ticks}");

 var generator = new DescriptionGenerator();
 Description = generator.Generate();
 }
}
```

The `Picture` class has two public properties:

-   The `Uri` of an image, which points to its location on the internet
-   The description of that image

In the constructor, we create a new **Uniform Resource Identifier** (**URI**), which points to a public source of test photos that we can use. The width and height are specified in the query string part of the URI. We also append a random timestamp to avoid the images being cached by Xamarin.Forms. This generates a unique URI each time we request an image.

We then use the `DescriptionGenerator` class that we created to generate a random description for the image.

Binding the picture to the control

Let's begin to wire up the `Swiper` control so that it starts displaying images. We need to set the source of an image and then control the visibility of the loading label based on the status of the image. Since we are using an image fetched from the internet, it might take a couple of seconds to download. This has to be communicated to the user to avoid confusion about what is going on.

Setting the source

We begin by setting the source of the image. The `image` control (referred to as `image` in the code) has a `source` property. This property is of the abstract type, `ImageSource`. There are a few different types of image sources that you can use. The one we are interested in is the `UriImageSource`, which takes a URI, downloads the image, and allows the image control to display it.

Let's extend the `Swiper` control to set the source and description:

1. Open the `Controls/Swiper.Xaml.cs` file (the code-behind for the `Swiper` control).
2. Add a using statement for `Swiper.Utils` (`using Swiper.Utils;`).
3. Add the code marked in bold to the constructor:

```
public SwiperControl()
{
    InitializeComponent();
    var picture = new Picture();
    descriptionLabel.Text = picture.Description;
    image.Source = new UriImageSource() { Uri = picture.Uri };
}
```

We create a new instance of a `Picture` class and assign the description to the `descriptionLabel` in the GUI by setting the text property of that control. We then set the source of the image to a new instance of a `UriImageSource` class and assign the URI from the picture instance. This will start the download of the image from the internet and display it as soon as it is downloaded.

Controlling the loading label

While the image is downloading, we want to show a loading text centered over the image. This is already in the XAML file that we created earlier, so what we really need to do is hide it once the image is downloaded. We will do this by controlling the `IsVisibleProperty` of the `loadingLabel` by setting a binding to the `IsLoading` property of the image. Any time the `IsLoading` property is changed on the image, the binding changes the `IsVisible` property on the label. This is a nice fire-and-forget approach.

Let's add the code needed to control the loading label:

1. Open the `Swiper.xaml.cs` code-behind file.
2. Add the code marked in bold to the constructor:

```
public SwiperControl()
{
    InitializeComponent();
    var picture = new Picture();
    descriptionLabel.Text = picture.Description;
    image.Source = new  UriImageSource() { Uri = picture.Uri };

    loadingLabel.SetBinding(IsVisibleProperty, "IsLoading");
    loadingLabel.BindingContext = image;
}
```

In the preceding code, the `loadingLabel` sets a binding to the `IsVisibleProperty`, which actually belongs to the `VisualElement` class that all controls inherit from. It tells the `loadingLabel` to listen to changes in the `IsLoading` property of whichever object is assigned to the binding context. In this case, this is the `image` control.

Handling pan gestures

A core feature of this app is the pan gesture. A pan gesture is when a user presses on the control and moves it around the screen. We will also add a random rotation to the `Swiper` control to make it look like there are photos in a stack when we add multiple images.

We start by adding some fields to the `SwiperControl`:

1. Open the `SwiperControl.xaml.cs` file.
2. Add the following fields in the code to the class:

```
private readonly double _initialRotation;
private static readonly Random _random = new Random();
```

The first field, _initialRotation, stores the initial rotation of the image. We will set this in the constructor. The second field is a `static` field containing a `Random` object. As you might remember, it's better to create one static random object to make sure multiple random objects don't get created with the same seed. The seed is based on time, so if we create objects too close in time to each other, they get the same random sequence generated, so it wouldn't actually be that random at all.

The next thing we have to do is create an event handler for the `PanUpdated` event that we will bind to at the end of this section:

1. Open the `SwiperControl.xaml.cs` code-behind file.
2. Add the `OnPanUpdated` method to the class:

```
private void OnPanUpdated(object sender, PanUpdatedEventArgs e)
{
    switch (e.StatusType)
    {
        case GestureStatus.Started:
            PanStarted();
            break;

        case GestureStatus.Running:
            PanRunning(e);
            break;

        case GestureStatus.Completed:
            PanCompleted();
            break;
    }
}
```

The code is really straightforward. We handle an event that takes a `PanUpdatedEventArgs` object as the second argument. This is a standard method of handling events. We then have a `switch` clause that checks which status the event refers to.

A pan gesture can have three states:

- `GestureStatus.Started`: The event is raised once with this state when the panning begins
- `GestureStatus.Running`: The event is then raised multiple times, once for each time you move your finger
- `GestureStatus.Completed`: The event is raised one last time when you let go

For each of these states, we call specific methods that handle the different states. We'll continue with adding those methods now:

1. Open the `SwiperControl.xaml.cs` code-behind file.
2. Add these three methods to the class:

```
private void PanStarted()
{
    photo.ScaleTo(1.1, 100);
}

private void PanRunning(PanUpdatedEventArgs e)
{
    photo.TranslationX = e.TotalX;
    photo.TranslationY = e.TotalY;
    photo.Rotation = _initialRotation + (photo.TranslationX / 25);
}

private void PanCompleted()
{
    photo.TranslateTo(0, 0, 250, Easing.SpringOut);
    photo.RotateTo(_initialRotation, 250, Easing.SpringOut);
    photo.ScaleTo(1, 250);
}
```

Let's start by looking at `PanStarted()`. When the user starts dragging the image, we want to add the effect of it raising up a little bit over the surface. This is done by scaling the image by 10%. Xamarin.Forms has a set of excellent functions to do this. In this case, we call the `ScaleTo()` method on the image control (named `Photo`) and tell it to scale to `1.1`, which corresponds to 10% of its original size. We also tell it to do this in a duration of `100` ms. This call is also awaitable, which means we can wait for the control to finish animating before executing the next call. In this case, we are going to use a fire-and-forget approach.

Next, we have `PanRunning()`, which is called multiple times during the pan operation. This takes an argument, which is the `PanUpdatedEventArgs` from the event handler that `PanRunning()` is called from. We could also just pass in an X and a Y value as arguments to reduce the coupling of the code. This is something that you can experiment with. The method extracts the X and Y components from the `TotalX`/`TotalY` properties of the event and assigns them to the `TranslationX`/`TranslationY` properties of the image control. We also adjust the rotation slightly, based on how far the image has been moved.

The last thing to do is to restore everything to its initial state when the image is released. This can be done in `PanCompleted()`. First, we translate (or move) the image back to its original local coordinates (`0,0`) in `250` ms. We also add an easing function to make it overshoot the target a bit and then animate back. We can play around with the different predefined easing functions; these are really useful for creating nice animations. We do the same to move the image back to its initial rotation. Finally, we scale it back to its original size in `250` ms.

It's now time to add the code in the constructor that will wire up the pan gesture and set some initial rotation values:

1. Open the `SwiperControl.xaml.cs` code-behind file.
2. Add the code in bold to the constructor. Note that there is more code in the constructor, so don't copy and paste the whole method, just add the bold text:

```
public SwiperControl()
{
    InitializeComponent();

    var panGesture = new PanGestureRecognizer();
    panGesture.PanUpdated += OnPanUpdated;
    this.GestureRecognizers.Add(panGesture);

    _initialRotation = _random.Next(-10, 10);
    photo.RotateTo(_initialRotation, 100, Easing.SinOut);

    <!-- other code omitted for brevity -->
}
```

All Xamarin.Forms controls have a property called `GestureRecognizers`. There are different types of gesture recognizers, such as `TapGestureRecognizer` or `SwipeGestureRecognizer`. In our case, we are interested in the `PanGestureRecognizer`. We create a new `PanGestureRecognizer` and subscribe to the `PanUpdated` event by hooking it up to the `OnPanUpdated()` method we created earlier. We then add it to the `Swiper` controls, `GestureRecognizers` collection.

We then set an initial rotation of the image and make sure we store it so that we can modify the rotation and then rotate it back to the original state.

Testing the control

We now have all the code written to take the control for a test run:

1. Open `MainPage.xaml.cs`.
2. Add a `using` statement for the `Swiper.Controls` (using `Swiper.Controls;`).
3. Add the code marked in bold to the constructor:

```
public MainPage()
{
    InitializeComponent();
    MainGrid.Children.Add(new SwiperControl());
}
```

If all goes well with the build, we should end up with an image like the following one:

We can also drag the image around (pan it). Notice the slight lift effect when you begin dragging and the rotation of the image based on the amount of translation, which is the total movement. If you let go of the image, it animates back in place.

Creating decision zones

A matchmaking app is nothing without those special drop-zones on each side of the screen. We want to do a few things here:

- When a user drags an image to either side, text should appear that says *LIKE* or *DENY* (the decision zones)
- When the users drop an image on a decision zone, the app should remove the image from the page

We will create the zones by adding some XAML to the `SwiperControl.xaml` file and then move on to adding the necessary code to make this happen. It is worth noting here that the zones are not actually hotspots for dropping the image, but rather for displaying labels on top of the control surface. The actual drop-zones are calculated and determined based on how far you drag the image.

Extending the grid

The `Swiper` control has three columns defined. We want to add some kind of visual feedback to the user if the image is dragged to either side of the page. We will do this by adding a `StackLayout` with a `Label` on each side.

Adding the StackLayout for liking photos

The first thing to do is to add the `StackLayout` for liking photos on the right-hand side of the control:

1. Open `Controls/SwiperControl.xaml`.
2. Add the following code under the comment `<!-- StackLayout for like here -->`:

```
<StackLayout x:Name="likeStackLayout" Grid.Column="2"
            Opacity="0" Padding="0, 100">
    <Label Text="LIKE"
           TextColor="Lime"
           FontSize="30"
           Rotation="30"
           FontAttributes="Bold" />
</StackLayout>
```

The `StackLayout` is the container of what we want to display. It has a name and is assigned to be rendered in the third column (it says `Grid.Column="2"` in the code due to the zero indexing). The `Opacity` is set to `0`, making it completely invisible, and the `Padding` is adjusted to make it move down a bit from the top.

Inside the `StackLayout`, we'll add a `Label`.

Adding the StackLayout for denying photos

The next step is to add the `StackLayout` for denying photos on the left-hand side of the control:

1. Open `Controls/SwiperControl.xaml`.
2. Add the following code under the comment `<!-- StackLayout for deny here -->`:

```
<StackLayout x:Name="denyStackLayout" Opacity="0"
             Padding="0, 100" HorizontalOptions="End">
    <Label Text="DENY"
           TextColor="Red"
           FontSize="30"
           Rotation="-20"
           FontAttributes="Bold" />
</StackLayout>
```

The setup for the left-hand side `StackLayout` is the same, except that it should be in the first column, which is the default, so there is no need to add a `Grid.Column` attribute. We have also specified `HorizontalOptions="End"`, which means that the content should be right-justified.

Determining the screen size

To be able to calculate a percentage of how far the user has dragged the image, we need to know the size of the control. This is not determined until the control is laid out by Xamarin.Forms.

We will override the `OnSizeAllocated()` method and add a field in the class called `_screenWidth` to keep track of the current width of the window by following these few steps:

1. Open `SwiperControl.xaml.cs`.
2. Add the following code to the file. Put the field at the beginning of the class and the `OnSizeAllocated()` method below the constructor:

```
private double _screenWidth = -1;

protected override void OnSizeAllocated(double width, double height)
{
    base.OnSizeAllocated(width, height);

    if (Application.Current.MainPage == null)
    {
        return;
    }

    _screenWidth = Application.Current.MainPage.Width;
}
```

The `_screenWidth` field is used to store the width as soon as we have resolved it. We do this by overriding the `OnSizeAllocated()` method that is called by Xamarin.Forms when the size of the control is allocated. This is called multiple times. The first time it's called is actually before the width and height have been set and before the `MainPage` of the current app is set. At this time, the width and height are set to -1 and the `Application.Current.MainPage` is null. We look for this state by null checking `Application.Current.MainPage` and returning if it is null. We could also have checked for -1 values on the width. Either method would work. If it does have a value, however, we want to store it in our `_screenWidth` field for later use.

Xamarin.Forms will call the `OnSizeAllocated()` method any time the frame of the app changes. This is most relevant for UWP apps since they are in a window that a user can easily change. Android and iOS apps are less likely to get a call to this method a second time, since the app will take up the entire screen's real estate.

Adding a clamp function

To be able to calculate the state, we need to clamp a value later on. At the time of writing, this function is already in Xamarin.Forms, but it's marked as an internal function, meaning that we shouldn't really be using it. According to the rumors, it will soon be made public in later versions of Xamarin.Forms, but for now, we need to redefine it ourselves:

1. Open `SwiperControl.xaml.cs`.
2. Add the following `static` method to the class:

```
private static double Clamp(double value, double min, double max)
{
    return (value < min) ? min : (value > max) ? max : value;
}
```

The method takes a value to clamp, a minimum boundary, and a maximum boundary. It returns either the value itself, or the edge value, if it's greater or larger than the set boundaries.

Adding code to calculate the state

To calculate the state of the image, we need to define what our zones are and then create a function that takes the current amount of movement and updates the opacity of the GUI decision zones based on how far we panned the image.

Defining a method for calculating the state

Let's add the `CalculatePanState()` method to calculate how far we have panned the image, and if it should start to affect the GUI, by following these few steps:

1. Open `Controls/SwiperControl.xaml.cs`.
2. Add the properties at the top and the `CalculatePanState()` method anywhere in the class, as shown in the following code:

```
private const double DeadZone = 0.4d;
private const double DecisionThreshold = 0.4d;

private void CalculatePanState(double panX)
{
    var halfScreenWidth = _screenWidth / 2;
    var deadZoneEnd = DeadZone * halfScreenWidth;

    if (Math.Abs(panX) < deadZoneEnd)
    {
```

```
            return;
    }

    var passedDeadzone = panX < 0 ? panX + deadZoneEnd : panX -
    deadZoneEnd;
    var decisionZoneEnd = DecisionThreshold * halfScreenWidth;
    var opacity = passedDeadzone / decisionZoneEnd;

    opacity = Clamp(opacity, -1, 1);

    likeStackLayout.Opacity = opacity;
    denyStackLayout.Opacity = -opacity;
}
```

We define two values as constants:

- The `DeadZone`, which defines that 40% (0.4) of the available space on either side of the center point is a dead zone when panning an image. If we release the image in this zone, it simply returns to the center of the screen without any action being taken.
- The next constant is the `DecisionThreshold`, which defines another 40% (0.4) of the available space. This is used for interpolating the opacity of the `StackLayout` on either side of the layout.

We then use these values to check the state of the panning action whenever the panning changes. If the absolute panning value of X (panX) is less than the dead zone, we return without any action being taken. If not, we calculate how far over the dead zone we have passed and how far into the decision zone we are. We calculate the opacity values based on this interpolation and clamp the value between -1 and 1.

Finally, we set the opacity to this value for both `likeStackLayout` and `denyStackLayout`.

Wiring up the pan state check

While the image is being panned, we want to update the state:

1. Open `Controls/SwiperControl.xaml.cs`.
2. Add the code in bold to the `PanRunning()` method:

```
private void PanRunning(PanUpdatedEventArgs e)
{
    photo.TranslationX = e.TotalX;
    photo.TranslationY = e.TotalY;
```

```
photo.Rotation = _initialRotation + (photo.TranslationX / 25);

CalculatePanState(e.TotalX);
}
```

This addition to the `PanRunning()` method passes the total amount of movement on the *x* axis to the `CalculatePanState()` method to determine if we need to adjust the opacity of either the `StackLayout` on the right or the left of the control.

Adding exit logic

So far, all is good, except for the fact that if we drag an image to the edge and let go, the text stays. We need to determine when the user stops dragging the image, and, if so, whether or not the image is in a decision zone.

Checking if the image should exit

We want a simple function that determines if an image has panned far enough for it to count as an exit of that image:

1. Open `Controls/SwiperControl.xaml.cs`.
2. Add the `CheckForExitCritera()` method to the class, as shown in the following code:

```
private bool CheckForExitCriteria()
{
    var halfScreenWidth = _screenWidth / 2;
    var decisionBreakpoint = DeadZone * halfScreenWidth;
    return (Math.Abs(photo.TranslationX) > decisionBreakpoint);
}
```

This function calculates whether we have passed over the dead zone and into the decision zone. We need to use the `Math.Abs()` method to get the total absolute value to compare it against. We could have used a < and > operator as well, but we are using this approach as it is more readable. This is a matter of code style and taste—feel free to do it your own way.

Removing the image

If we determine that an image has panned far enough for it to exit, we want to animate it off the screen and then remove the image from the page:

1. Open `Controls/SwiperControl.xaml.cs`.
2. Add the `Exit()` method to the class, as shown in the following code:

```
private void Exit()
{
    Device.BeginInvokeOnMainThread(async () =>
    {
        var direction = photo.TranslationX < 0 ? -1 : 1;

        await photo.TranslateTo(photo.TranslationX +
        (_screenWidth * direction),
        photo.TranslationY, 200, Easing.CubicIn);
        var parent = Parent as Layout<View>;
        parent?.Children.Remove(this);
    });
}
```

The `Exit()` method does the following:

1. We begin by making sure that this call is done on the UI thread, which is also known as the `MainThread`. This is because only the UI thread can do animations.
2. We also need to run this thread asynchronously, so that we can kill two birds with one stone. Since this method is all about animating the image to either side of the screen, we need to determine in which direction to animate it.
3. We do this by determining if the total translation of the image is positive or negative.
4. We then use this value to await a translation through the `photo.TranslateTo()` call.
5. We await this call since we don't want the code execution to continue until it's done. Once it has finished, we remove the control from the parent's collection of children, causing it to disappear from existence forever.

Updating PanCompleted

The decision on whether the image should disappear or simply return to its original state is triggered in the `PanCompleted()` method. Here, we wire up the two methods that we created in the previous two sections:

1. Open `Controls/SwiperControl.xaml.cs`.
2. Add the code in bold to the `PanCompleted()` method:

```
private void PanCompleted()
{
    if (CheckForExitCriteria())
    {
        Exit();
    }

    likeStackLayout.Opacity = 0;
    denyStackLayout.Opacity = 0;

    photo.TranslateTo(0, 0, 250, Easing.SpringOut);
    photo.RotateTo(_initialRotation, 250, Easing.SpringOut);
    photo.ScaleTo(1, 250);
}
```

The last step in this section is to use the `CheckForExitCriteria()` method, and the `Exit()` method if those criteria are met. If the exit criteria are not met, we need to reset the state and the opacity of the `StackLayout` to make everything go back to normal.

Adding events to the control

The last thing we have left to do in the control itself is to add some events that indicate whether the image has been *Liked* or *Denied*. We are going to use a clean interface, allowing for a simple use of the control while hiding all the implementation details.

Declaring two events

To make the control easier to interact with from the application itself, we'll need to add events for `Like` and `Deny`:

1. Open `Controls/SwiperControl.xaml.cs`.
2. Add two event declarations at the beginning of the class, as shown in the following code:

```
public event EventHandler OnLike;
public event EventHandler OnDeny;
```

These are two standard event declarations with out-of-the-box event handlers.

Raising the events

We need to add code in the `Exit()` method to raise the events we created earlier:

1. Open `Controls/SwiperControl.xaml.cs`.
2. Add the code in bold to the `Exit()` method:

```
private void Exit()
{
    Device.BeginInvokeOnMainThread(async () =>
    {
        var direction = photo.TranslationX < 0 ? -1 : 1;

        if (direction > 0)
        {
            OnLike?.Invoke(this, new EventArgs());
        }

        if (direction < 0)
        {
            OnDeny?.Invoke(this, new EventArgs());
        }

        await photo.TranslateTo(photo.TranslationX + (_screenWidth
        * direction),
        photo.TranslationY, 200, Easing.CubicIn);
        var parent = Parent as Layout<View>;
        parent?.Children.Remove(this);
    });
}
```

Here, we inject the code to check whether we are liking or disliking an image. We then raise the correct event based on this information.

Wiring up the Swiper control

We have now reached the final part of the chapter. In this section, we are going to wire up the images and make our app a closed-loop app that can be used forever. We will add 10 images that we will download from the internet when the app starts up. Each time an image is removed, we'll simply add another one.

Adding images

Let's start by creating some code that will be adding the images to the MainView. We will first add the initial images, and then create logic for adding a new image to the bottom of the stack each time an image is liked or disliked.

Adding initial photos

To make the photos look like they are stacked, we need at least 10 of them:

1. Open `MainPage.xaml.cs`.
2. Add the `AddInitalPhotos()` method and the `InsertPhotoMethod()` to the class:

```
private void AddInitialPhotos()
{
    for (int i = 0; i < 10; i++)
    {
        InsertPhoto();
    }
}

private void InsertPhoto()
{
    var photo = new SwiperControl();
    this.MainGrid.Children.Insert(0, photo);
}
```

First, we create a method called `AddInitialPhotos()` that will be called upon startup. This method simply calls the `InsertPhoto()` method 10 times and adds a new `SwiperControl` to the `MainGrid` each time. It inserts the control at the first position in the stack, effectively putting it at the bottom of the pile, since the collection of controls is rendered from the beginning to the end.

Making the call from the constructor

We need to call this method in order for the magic to happen:

1. Open `MainPage.xaml.cs`.
2. Add the code in bold to the constructor and make sure it looks like the following:

```
public MainPage()
{
    InitializeComponent();
    AddInitialPhotos();
}
```

There isn't much to say here. After the `MainPage` is initialized, we call the method to add 10 random photos that we will download from the internet.

Adding count labels

We want to add some values to the app as well. We can do this by adding two labels below the collection of `Swiper` controls. Each time a user rates an image, we will increment one of two counters and display the result.

So, let's add the XAML needed to display the labels:

1. Open `MainPage.xaml`.
2. Replace the comment `<!-- Placeholder for later -->` with the code marked in bold:

```
<Grid Grid.Row="1" Padding="30">
    <Grid.RowDefinitions>
        <RowDefinition Height="auto" />
        <RowDefinition Height="auto" />
        <RowDefinition Height="auto" />
        <RowDefinition Height="auto" />
    </Grid.RowDefinitions>
    <Label Text="LIKES" />
    <Label x:Name="likeLabel"
           Grid.Row="1"
```

```
                    Text="0"
                    FontSize="Large"
                    FontAttributes="Bold" />
            <Label Grid.Row="2"
                    Text="DENIED" />
            <Label x:Name="denyLabel"
                    Grid.Row="3"
                    Text="0"
                    FontSize="Large"
                    FontAttributes="Bold" />
    </Grid>
```

This code adds a new `Grid` with four auto-height rows. This means that we calculate the height of the content of each row and use this for the layout. It is basically the same thing as a `StackLayout`, but we wanted to demonstrate a better way of doing this.

We add a `Label` in each row and name two of them as `likeLabel` and `denyLabel`. The two named labels will hold how many images have been liked and how many have been denied.

Subscribing to events

The last step is to wire up the `OnLike` and `OnDeny` events and display the total count to the user.

Adding methods to update the GUI and respond to events

We need some code to update the GUI and to keep track of the count:

1. Open `MainPage.xaml.cs`.
2. Add the following code to the class, as shown here:

```
private int _likeCount;
private int _denyCount;

private void UpdateGui()
{
    likeLabel.Text = _likeCount.ToString();
    denyLabel.Text = _denyCount.ToString();
}

private void Handle_OnLike(object sender, EventArgs e)
{
    _likeCount++;
    InsertPhoto();
```

```
        UpdateGui();
    }

    private void Handle_OnDeny(object sender, EventArgs e)
    {
        _denyCount++;
        InsertPhoto();
        UpdateGui();
    }
```

The two fields at the top keep track of the number of likes and denies. Since they are value-type variables, they default to zero.

To make the changes of these labels propagate to the UI, we've created a method called `UpdateGui()`. This takes the value of the two aforementioned fields and assigns it to the `Text` properties of both labels.

The two methods that follow are the event handlers that will be handling the `OnLike` and `OnDeny` events. They increase the appropriate field, add a new photo, and then update the GUI to reflect the change.

Wiring up events

Each time a new `SwiperControl` is created, we need to wire up the events:

1. Open `MainPage.xaml.cs`.
2. Add the code in bold to the `InsertPhoto()` method:

```
    private void InsertPhoto()
    {
        var photo = new SwiperControl();
        photo.OnDeny += Handle_OnDeny;
        photo.OnLike += Handle_OnLike;

        this.MainGrid.Children.Insert(0, photo);
    }
```

The added code wires up the event handlers that we defined earlier. The events really make it easy to interact with our new control. Try it for yourself and have a play around with the app that you have created.

Summary

Good job! In this chapter, we have learned how to create a reusable, good-looking control that can be used in any Xamarin.Forms app. To enhance the **User Experience (UX)** of the app, we used some animations that give the user more visual feedback. We also got creative with the use of XAML to define a GUI of the control that looks like a photo with a hand-written description.

After that, we used events to expose the behavior of the control back to the `MainPage` to limit the contact surface between your app and the control. Most importantly of all, we touched on the subject of `GestureRecognizers`, which can make our life much easier when dealing with common gestures.

In the next chapter, we will take a look at how to use track the location of a user in the background on an iOS and Android device. To visualize what we are tracking, we will use the map component in Xamarin.Forms.

4
Building a Location Tracking App Using GPS and Maps

In this chapter, we will create a location tracking app that saves the location of the user and display it as a heat map. We will look at how to run tasks in the background on iOS and Android devices and how to use custom renderers to extend the functionality of Xamarin.Forms maps.

The following topics will be covered in this chapter:

- Tracking the location of a user in the background on an iOS device
- Tracking the location of a user in the background on an Android device
- How to show maps in a Xamarin.Forms app
- How to extend the functionality of Xamarin.Forms maps with custom renderers

Technical requirements

To be able to complete the project, you need to have Visual Studio for Mac or PC installed, as well as the Xamarin components. See `Chapter 1`, *Introduction to Xamarin*, for more details on how to set up your environment.

Project overview

Many apps could be made richer by adding a map and location services. In this project, we will build a location tracking app that we will call **MeTracker**. The app will track the position of the user and save it to an SQLite database so we can visualize the result in the form of a heat map. To build this app, we will learn how to set up processes in the background, on both iOS and Android, because we cannot share code between iOS and Android. For the map, we will use the `Xamarin.Forms.Maps` component and extend its functionality in order to build a heat map. To do this, we will use a custom renderer for iOS and a custom renderer for Android so that we can use the platform APIs.

Getting started

We can use either Visual Studio 2017 on a PC or Visual Studio for Mac to do this project. To build an iOS app using Visual Studio for PC, you have to have a Mac connected. If you don't have access to a Mac at all, you can just do the Android part of this project.

Building the MeTracker app

It's time to start building the app. Create a **Mobile App (Xamarin.Forms)**. We will find that template under the **Cross-Platform** ta in the New Project dialog. We will name the project MeTracker.

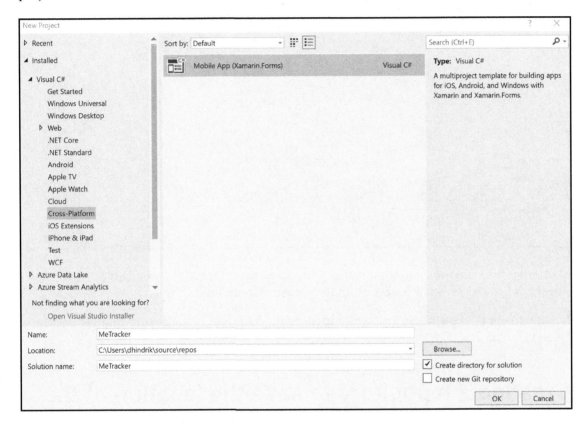

Use .NET Standard as the code sharing strategy and select iOS and Android as the platforms.

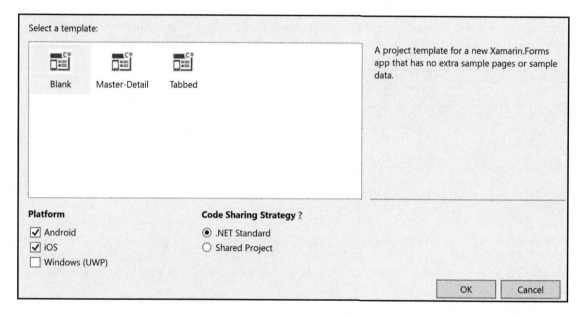

Make sure that you are compiling using Android version Oreo (API level 26) or higher. We can set this in the project **Properties** under the **Application** tab.

Update the NuGet packages that was added by the template to make sure that we use the latest versions.

Creating a repository to save the location of the users

The first thing we will do is create a repository that we can use to save the location of the users.

Creating a model for the location data

Before we create the repository, we will create a model class that will represent a user location by going through the following steps:

1. Create a new folder that we can use for this and other models, called `Models`.

2. Create a class with the name `Location` in the `Models` folder and add properties for the `Id`, the `Latitude`, and the `Longitude`.

3. Create two constructors, one empty and one that takes the `latitude` and `longitude` as arguments, using the following code:

```
using System;

namespace MeTracker.Models
{
    public class Location
    {
        public Location() {}

        public Location(double latitude, double longitude)
        {
            Latitude = latitude;
            Longitude = longitude;
        }

        public int Id { get; set; }
        public double Latitude { get; set; }
        public double Longitude { get; set; }
    }
}
```

Creating the repository

Now that we have created a model, we can move on to creating the repository. First, we will create an interface for the repository by going through the following steps:

1. In the `MeTracker` project, create a new folder, called `Repositories`.

2. In our new folder, we will create an interface that we will call `ILocationRepository`.

3. Write the following code in the new file that we created for the `interface`:

```
using MeTracker.Models;
using System;
using System.Threading.Tasks;
```

```
namespace MeTracker.Repositories
{
    public interface ILocationRepository
    {
        Task Save(Location location);
    }
}
```

4. Add a `using` directive for `MeTracker.Models` and `System.Threading.Tasks` to resolve the references for `Location` and `Task`.

Once we have an `interface`, we need to create an implementation of it by going through the following steps:

1. In the `MeTracker` project, create a new class with the name `LocationRepository`.

2. Implement the `ILocationRepository` interface and add the `async` keyword to the `Save` method using the following code:

```
using System;
using System.Threading.Tasks;
using MeTracker.Models;

namespace MeTracker.Repositories
{
    public class LocationRepository : ILocationRepository
    {
        public async Task Save(Location location)
        {
        }
    }
}
```

To store the data, we will use an SQLite database and the **object relational mapper (ORM)**, SQLite-net, so that we can write code against a domain model instead of using SQL for operations against the database. This is an open source library created by Frank A. Krueger. Let's set this up by going through the following steps:

1. Install the NuGet package, `sqlite-net-pcl`, for the `MeTracker` project.

2. Go to the `Location` model class and add a `PrimaryKeyAttribute` and an `AutoIncrementAttribute` to the `Id` property. When we add the attributes, the `Id` property will be a primary key in the database, and a value for it will automatically be created.

3. Write the following code in the `LocationRepository` class to create a connection to the SQLite database. The `if` statement is to check whether we have already created a connection. If this is the case, we will not create a new one; we will instead use the connection that we already created:

```
private SQLiteAsyncConnection connection;
private async Task CreateConnection()
{
    if (connection != null)
    {
        return;
    }

    var databasePath =
    Path.Combine(Environment.GetFolderPath
    (Environment.SpecialFolder .MyDocuments), "Locations.db");

    connection = new SQLiteAsyncConnection(databasePath);
    await connection.CreateTableAsync<Location>();
}
```

Now, it's time to implement the `Save` method, which will take a location object as a parameter and store it in the database.

We will now use the `CreateConnection` method in the `Save` method so we can be sure that a connection is created when we try to save data to the database. When we know that we have an active connection, we can just use the `InsertAsync` method and pass the `location` parameter of the `Save` method as an argument.

Edit the `Save` method in the `LocationRepository` class to look like the following code:

```
public async Task Save(Location location)
{
    await CreateConnection();
    await connection.InsertAsync(location);
}
```

Xamarin.Essentials

Xamarin.Essentials is a library that was created by Microsoft and Xamarin to make it possible for developers to use platform-specific APIs from shared code. Xamarin.Essentials targets Xamarin.iOS, Xamarin.Android, and UWP. In this project, we will use Xamarin.Essentials for various tasks, including getting a location and executing code on the main thread.

Installing the NuGet package

At the time of writing, Xamarin.Essentials is in preview. To find the NuGet packages in preview, we will have to check the **Include Prerelease** checkbox.

Configuring Xamarin.Essentials on Android

We need to initialize Xamarin.Essentials on Android by calling an initialization method. We do this by going through the following steps:

1. In the Android project, open the `MainActivity.cs` file.
2. Add the code in bold under the `global::Xamarin.Forms.Forms.Init` method:

```
protected override void OnCreate(Bundle savedInstanceState)
{
    TabLayoutResource = Resource.Layout.Tabbar;
    ToolbarResource = Resource.Layout.Toolbar;

    base.OnCreate(savedInstanceState);

    global::Xamarin.Forms.Forms.Init(this, savedInstanceState);
    Xamarin.Essentials.Platform.Init(this, savedInstanceState);
    LoadApplication(new App());
}
```

That's it. We are all good to go.

Creating a service for location tracking

To track a user's location, we need to write the code according to the platform. Xamarin.Essentials has methods for getting the location of a user in shared code, but it cannot be used in the background. To be able to use the code that we will write for each platform, we need to create an interface. For the `ILocationRepository` interface, there will be just one implementation that will be used on both platforms, whereas for the location tracking service, we will have one implementation for the iOS platform and one for the Android platform.

Go through the following steps to create the `ILocationRepository` interface:

1. In the `MeTracker` project, create a new folder and name it `Services`.
2. Create a new interface in the `Services` folder with the name `ILocationTrackingService`.
3. In the interface, add a method called `StartTracking` as shown in the following code:

```
public interface ILocationTrackingService
{
        void StartTracking();
}
```

For the moment, we will just create an empty implementation of the interface in both the iOS and the Android projects by going through the following steps. We will come back to each implementation later in this chapter:

1. Create a folder named `Services` in both the iOS and Android projects.
2. Create an empty implementation as shown in the following code, in a class called `LocationTrackingService` in the new `Service` folder in both the iOS and Android projects:

```
public class LocationTrackingService : ILocationTrackingService
{
        public void StartTracking()
        {
        }
}
```

Setting up the app logic

We have now created the interfaces we need to track the location of the user and save it locally on the device. It's time to write code to start the tracking of a user. We still don't have any code that actually tracks the location of the user, but it will be easier to write this if we have already written the code that starts the tracking.

Creating a view with a map

To start with, we will create a view with a simple map that is centered on the position of the user. Let's set this up by going through the following steps:

1. In the `MeTracker` project, create a new folder called `Views`.
2. In the `Views` folder, create a XAML-based `ContentPage` and name it `MainView`.

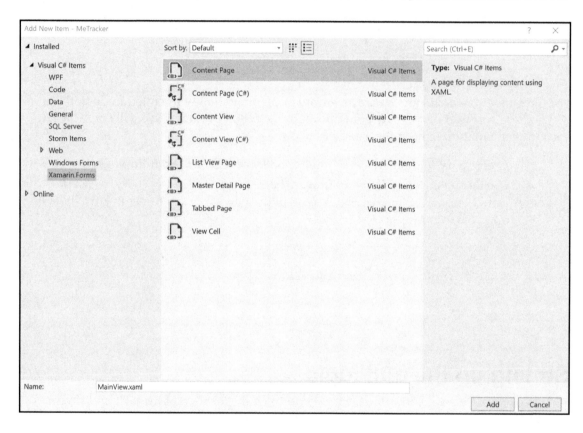

The Xamarin.Forms package has no map controls, but there is an official package from Microsoft and Xamarin that can be used to show maps in a Xamarin.Forms app. This package is called `Xamarin.Forms.Maps`, and we can install it from NuGet by following the steps below:

1. Install `Xamarin.Forms.Maps` in the `MeTracker`, `MeTracker.Android`, and `MeTracker.iOS` projects.
2. Add the namespace for `Xamarin.Forms.Maps` to the `MainView` using the following code:

```
<ContentPage xmlns="http://xamarin.com/schemas/2014/forms"

xmlns:x="http://schemas.microsoft.com/winfx/2009/xaml"
             xmlns:map="clr-
             namespace:Xamarin.Forms.Maps;assembly
             =Xamarin.Forms.Maps"
             x:Class="MeTracker.Views.MainView">
```

We can now use the map in our view. Because we want the `Map` to cover the whole page, we can add it to the root of the `ContentPage`. Let's set this up by going through the following steps:

1. Add the `map` to the `ContentPage`.
2. Give the map a name so we can access it from the code-behind. Name it `Map`, as shown in the following code:

```
<ContentPage xmlns="http://xamarin.com/schemas/2014/forms"
xmlns:x="http://schemas.microsoft.com/winfx/2009/xaml"
             xmlns:map="clr-
namespace:Xamarin.Forms.Maps;assembly=Xamarin.Forms.Maps"
             x:Class="MeTracker.Views.MainView">
             <map:Map x:Name="Map" />
</ContentPage>
```

To use the `map` control, we need to run code on each platform to initialize it by going through the following steps:

1. In the iOS project, go to `AppDelegate.cs`.
2. In the `FinishedLaunching` method, after the `Init` of `Xamarin.Forms`, add `global::Xamarin.FormsMaps.Init()` to initialize the `map` control for the iOS app using the following code:

```
public override bool FinishedLaunching(UIApplication app,
NSDictionary options)
{
```

```
        global::Xamarin.Forms.Forms.Init();
        global::Xamarin.FormsMaps.Init();

        LoadApplication(new App());

        return base.FinishedLaunching(app, options);
    }
```

Continue with to initialize it for Android:

1. In the Android project, go to `MainActivity.cs`.
2. In the `OnCreate` method, after the `Init` of `Xamarin.Forms`, add `global::Xamarin.FormsMaps.Init(this, savedInstanceState)` to initialize the `map` control for iOS.
3. Initialize Xamarin.Essentials by using `Xamarin.Essentials.Platform.Init(this, savedInstanceState)` as shown in the following code:

```
    protected override void OnCreate(Bundle savedInstanceState)
    {
        TabLayoutResource = Resource.Layout.Tabbar;
        ToolbarResource = Resource.Layout.Toolbar;

        base.OnCreate(savedInstanceState);
        global::Xamarin.Forms.Forms.Init(this, savedInstanceState);
        global::Xamarin.FormsMaps.Init(this, savedInstanceState);

        Xamarin.Essentials.Platform.Init(this, savedInstanceState);

        LoadApplication(new App());
    }
```

For Android, we also need to decide what happens when a user has answered a request for permission dialog and send the result to Xamarin.Essentials. We will do that by adding the following code to `MainActivity.cs`:

```
    public override void OnRequestPermissionsResult(int requestCode,
                string[] permissions,
                [GeneratedEnum] Android.Content.PM.Permission[]
                grantResults)
    {   Xamarin.Essentials.Platform.OnRequestPermissionsResult(requestCode,
                permissions, grantResults);
                base.OnRequestPermissionsResult(requestCode,
                permissions, grantResults);
    }
```

For Android, we will need an **API key** for Google Maps in order to get the maps to work. The Microsoft documentation about how to obtain an API key can be found at `https://docs.microsoft.com/en-us/xamarin/android/platform/maps-and-location/maps/obtaining-a-google-maps-api-key`. Here's how we go about obtaining the API key:

1. Open `AndroidMainfest.xml`, which is located in the `Properties` folder in the Android project.
2. Insert a metadata element as a child of the application element, as shown in the following code:

```
<application android:label="MeTracker.Android">
    <meta-data android:name="com.google.android.maps.v2.API_KEY"
    android:value="{YourKeyHere}" />
</application>
```

We also want the map to be centered on the position of the user. We will do this in the constructor of the `MainView.xaml.cs`. Because we want to run the fetching of the user's location asynchronously and it needs to be executed on the main thread, we will wrap it in `MainThread.BeginInvokeOnMainThread`. To get the current location of the user, we will use Xamarin.Essentials. When we have the location, we can use the `MoveToRegion` method of the `Map`. We can set this up by going through the following steps:

1. In the `MeTracker` project, open `MainView.xaml.cs`.
2. Add the code in bold in the following code fragment to the constructor of the `MainView.xaml.cs` class:

```
public MainView ()
{
    InitializeComponent ();
    MainThread.BeginInvokeOnMainThread(async() =>
    {
        var location = await Geolocation.GetLocationAsync();
        Map.MoveToRegion (MapSpan.FromCenterAndRadius (
        new Position(location.Latitude, location.Longitude),
        Distance.FromKilometers(5)));
    });
}
```

Creating a ViewModel

Before we create an actual view model, we will create an abstract base view model that all view models can inherit from. The idea behind this base view model is that we can write common code in it. In this case, we will implement the `INotifyPropertyChanged` interface by going through the following steps:

1. Create a folder with the name `ViewModels` in the `MeTracker` project.
2. Write the following code and resolve all references:

```
public abstract class ViewModel : INotifyPropertyChanged
{
    public event PropertyChangedEventHandler PropertyChanged;

    public void RaisePropertyChanged(params string[] propertyNames)
    {
        foreach(var propertyName in propertyNames)
        {
            PropertyChanged?.Invoke(this, new
            PropertyChangedEventArgs(propertyName));
        }
    }
}
```

The next step is to create the actual view model that will use `ViewModel` as a base class. Let's set this up by going through the following steps:

1. In the `MeTracker` project, create a new class called `MainViewModel` in the `ViewModels` folder.
2. Make the `MainViewModel` inherit the `ViewModel`.
3. Add a read-only field of the `ILocationTrackingService` type and name it `locationTrackingService`.
4. Add a read-only field of the `ILocationRepository` type and name it `locationRepository`.
5. Create a constructor with the `ILocationTrackingService` and the `ILocationRepository` as parameters.
6. Set the values of the fields that we created in *step 3* and *step 4* with the values from the parameters, as shown in the following code:

```
public class MainViewModel : ViewModel
{
        private readonly ILocationRepository
locationRepository;
        private readonly ILocationTrackingService
```

```
locationTrackingService;

public MainViewModel(ILocationTrackingService
locationTrackingService,
ILocationRepository locationRepository)
{
    this.locationTrackingService =
    locationTrackingTrackingService;
    this.locationRepository = locationRepository;
}
}
```

In order to make the iOS app start tracking the location of a user, we need to run the code that starts the tracking on the main thread by going through the following steps:

1. In the constructor of the newly created `MainViewModel`, add an invocation to the main thread using `MainThread.BeginInvokeOnMainThread` from Xamarin.Essentials. Xamarin.Forms has a helper method for invoking code on the main thread, but if we use the one from Xamarin.Essentials, we can have a view model without any dependencies on Xamarin.Forms. If we do not have any dependencies to Xamarin.Forms in the ViewModels we can reuse them in apps where we not using Xamarin.Forms if we will add other platforms in the future.

2. Call `locationService.StartTracking` in the action that we pass to the `BeginInvokeOnMainThread` method, shown in the following code marked in bold:

```
public MainViewModel(ILocationTrackingService
                    locationTrackingService,
                    ILocationRepository locationRepository)
{
    this.locationTrackingService = locationTrackingTrackingService;
    this.locationRepository = locationRepository;
    MainThread.BeginInvokeOnMainThread(async() =>
    {
    locationTrackingService.StartTracking();
    });
}
```

Finally, we need to inject a `MainViewModel` into the constructor of the `MainView` and assign the `MainViewModel` instance to the binding context of the view by going through the following steps. This will allow the data binding to be processed, and the properties of `MainViewModel` will be bound to the controls in the user interface:

1. In the `MeTracker` project, go to the constructor of the `Views/MainView.xaml.cs` file.
2. Add `MainViewModel` as a parameter of the constructor and call it `viewModel`.
3. Set `BindingContext` to the instance of the `MainViewModel`, as shown in the following code:

```
public MainView(MainViewModel viewModel)
{
    InitializeComponent();

    BindingContext = viewModel;

    MainThread.BeginInvokeOnMainThread(async () =>
    {
        var location = await
        Geolocation.GetLastKnownLocationAsync();
        Map.MoveToRegion(MapSpan.FromCenterAndRadius(
        new Position(location.Latitude, location.Longitude),
        Distance.FromKilometers(5)));
    });
}
```

Creating a resolver

We will be using dependency injection in this project, for which we will use a library called Autofac. Autofac is an open source **inversion of control (IoC)** container. We will create a `Resolver` class in order to easily resolve types that we will add to the container later in this chapter. To do so, we will go through the following steps:

1. Install Autofac from NuGet in the `MeTracker`, `MeTracker.Android`, and `MeTracker.iOS` projects.
2. In the `MeTracker` project, create a new class called `Resolver` in the root of the project.
3. Create a `private static IContainer` field called `container`.

4. Create a `static` method called `Initialized` that has an `IContainer` argument and set the value of the `container` field as shown in the following code:

```
using Autofac;
using System;
using System.Collections.Generic;
using System.Text;

namespace MeTracker
{
    public class Resolver
    {
        private static IContainer container;

        public static void Initialize(IContainer container)
        {
            Resolver.container = container;
        }
    }
}
```

The `Initialize` method will be called after the configuration of Autofac is complete, which we will do when we create the bootstrapper. This method simply takes the `container` that it gets as an argument and stores it in the `static` container field.

Now, we need a method to access it from. Create one more `static` method, called `Resolve`. This method will be generic, and when we use it, we will specify its type as the type that will be resolved. Use the `container` field to resolve the type as shown in the following code:

```
public static T Resolve<T>()
{
    return container.Resolve<T>();
}
```

The `Resolve<T>` method takes a type as an argument and looks in the container to see whether there is any information on how to construct this type. If there is, then we return it.

So, now that we have the `Resolver` that we will use to resolve instances of types of objects, we need to configure it. That's the job of the bootstrapper.

Creating the bootstrapper

To configure the dependency injection and initialize the `Resolver`, we will create a bootstrapper. We will have one shared bootstrapper, as well as other bootstrappers for each platform to meet their specific configurations. The reason that we need them to be platform-specific is that we will have different implementations of the `ILocationTrackingService` on iOS and Android. To create a bootstrapper, we go through the following steps:

1. Create a new class in the `MeTracker` project and name it `Bootstrapper`.
2. Write the following code in the new class:

```
using Autofac;
using MeTracker.Repositories;
using MeTracker.ViewModels;
using System;
using System.Collections.Generic;
using System.Linq;
using System.Reflection;
using System.Text;
using Xamarin.Forms;

namespace MeTracker
{
    public class Bootstrapper
    {
        protected ContainerBuilder ContainerBuilder { get; private
        set; }

        public Bootstrapper()
        {
            Initialize();
            FinishInitialization();
        }

        protected virtual void Initialize()
        {
            ContainerBuilder = new ContainerBuilder();

            var currentAssembly = Assembly.GetExecutingAssembly();

            foreach (var type in currentAssembly.DefinedTypes.
                    Where(e => e.IsSubclassOf(typeof(Page))))
            {
                ContainerBuilder.RegisterType(type.AsType());
            }
```

```
        foreach (var type in currentAssembly.DefinedTypes.
                Where(e => e.IsSubclassOf(typeof(ViewModel)))))
        {
            ContainerBuilder.RegisterType(type.AsType());
        }

        ContainerBuilder.RegisterType<LocationRepository>
        ().As<ILocationRepository>();
    }

    private void FinishInitialization()
    {
        var container = ContainerBuilder.Build();
        Resolver.Initialize(container);
    }
  }
}
```

Creating the iOS bootstrapper

In the iOS bootstrapper, we will have configurations that are specific to the iOS app. To create an iOS app, we go through the following steps:

1. In the iOS project, create a new class and name it Bootstrapper.
2. Make the new class inherit from MeTracker.Bootstrapper.
3. Write the following code:

```
using Autofac;
using MeTracker.iOS.Services;
using MeTracker.Services;

namespace MeTracker.iOS
{
    public class Bootstrapper : MeTracker.Bootstrapper
    {
        public static void Execute()
        {
            var instance = new Bootstrapper();
        }

        protected override void Initialize()
        {
            base.Initialize();


ContainerBuilder.RegisterType<LocationTrackingService>()
```

```
              .As<ILocationTrackingService>().SingleInstance();
        }
    }
}
```

4. Go to `AppDelegate.cs` in the iOS project.

5. Before the call to `LoadApplication`, in the `FinishedLaunching` method, call the `Init` method of the platform-specific bootstrapper, as shown in the following code:

```
public override bool FinishedLaunching(UIApplication app,
NSDictionary options)
{
    global::Xamarin.Forms.Forms.Init();
    global::Xamarin.FormsMaps.Init();
    Bootstrapper.Init();

    LoadApplication(new App());

    return base.FinishedLaunching(app, options);
}
```

Creating the Android bootstrapper

In the Android bootstrapper, we will have configurations that are specific to the Android app. To create the bootstrapper in Android, we go through the following steps:

1. In the Android project, create a new class and name it `Bootstrapper`.

2. Make the new class inherit from `MeTracker.Bootstrapper`.

3. Write the following code:

```
using Autofac;
using MeTracker.Droid.Services;
using MeTracker.Services;

namespace MeTracker.Droid
{
    public class Bootstrapper : MeTracker.Bootstrapper
    {
        public static void Init()
        {
            var instance = new Bootstrapper();
        }

        protected override void Initialize()
        {
```

```
                    base.Initialize();


ContainerBuilder.RegisterType<LocationTrackingService()
            .As<ILocationTrackingService>().SingleInstance();
        }
    }
}
```

4. Go to the `MainActivity.cs` file in the Android project.
5. Before the call to `LoadApplication`, in the `OnCreate` method, call the `Init` method of the platform-specific bootstrapper, as shown in the following code:

```
protected override void OnCreate(Bundle savedInstanceState)
{
    TabLayoutResource = Resource.Layout.Tabbar;
    ToolbarResource = Resource.Layout.Toolbar;

    base.OnCreate(savedInstanceState);
    Xamarin.Essentials.Platform.Init(this, savedInstanceState);

    global::Xamarin.Forms.Forms.Init(this, savedInstanceState);
    global::Xamarin.FormsMaps.Init(this, savedInstanceState);

    Bootstrapper.Init();

    LoadApplication(new App());
}
```

Setting the MainPage

The last step before we can start the app for the first time is to set the `MainPage` property in the `App.xaml.cs` file by going through the following steps. But first, we can delete the `MainPage.xaml` file and the `MainPage.xaml.cs` file that we created when we started the project because we are not using them here:

1. Delete the `MainPage.xaml` and the `MainPage.xaml.cs` in the `MeTracker` project, since we will be setting our `MainView` as the first view that the user sees.
2. Use the `Resolver` to create an instance of the `MainView`.

3. Set the `MainPage` in the constructor to the instance of the `MainView`, as shown in the following code:

```
public App()
{
    InitializeComponent();
    MainPage = Resolver.Resolve<MainView>();
}
```

The resolver uses Autofac to figure out all the dependencies we need in order to create a `MainView` instance. It looks at the constructor of the `MainView` and decides that it requires a `MainViewModel`. If the `MainViewModel` has further dependencies, then the process iterates through all those dependencies and builds all the instances we need.

We will now be able to run the app. It will be showing us a map centered at the current location of the user. We will now add code to track the location over time using background location tracking.

Background location tracking on iOS

The code for location tracking is something that we need to write for each platform. For iOS, we will use the `CLLocationManager` from the `CoreLocation` namespace.

Enabling location updates in the background

When we want to perform tasks in the background in an iOS app, we need to declare what we want to do in the `info.plist` file. The following steps show how we go about it:

1. In the `MeTracker.iOS` project, open `info.plist`.
2. Go to the **Capabilities** tab.
3. Select **Enable Background Modes** and **Location updates**, as shown in the following screenshot:

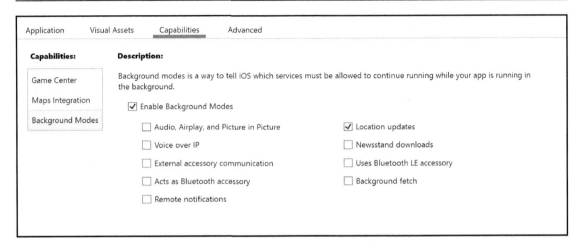

We can also enable background modes directly in the `info.plist` file, if we open it with an XML editor. In this case, we will add the following XML:

```
<key>UIBackgroundModes</key>
<array>
    <string>location</string>
</array>
```

Getting permissions to use the location of the user

Before we can request permissions for using the location of the user, we need to add a description of what we will use the location for. Since the introduction of iOS 11, we are no longer allowed to just ask for permission to track the location of the user all the time; the user has to be able to give us permission to only track their location while they are using the app. We will add the description to the `info.plist` file by going through the following steps:

1. Open `info.plist` with the XML (text) editor that can be found in the `MeTracker.iOS` project.
2. Add the key, `NSLocationWhenInUseUsageDescription`, with a description.
3. Add the key, `NSLocationAlwaysAndWhenInUsageDescription`, with a description, as shown in the following code:

```
<key>NSLocationWhenInUseUsageDescription</key>
<string>We will use your location to track you</string>
<key>NSLocationAlwaysAndWhenInUsageDescription</key>
<string>We will use your location to track you</string>
```

Subscribing to location updates

Now that we have prepared the `info.plist` file for location tracking, it is time to write the actual code that will track the location of the user. If we don't set the `CLLocationManager` to not pause location updates, location updates can be paused automatically by iOS when the location data is unlikely to change. In this app, we don't want that to happen because we want to save the location multiple times so that we can establish whether a user visits a particular location frequently. Let's set this up by going through the following steps:

1. In the `MeTracker.iOS` project, open the `LocationTrackingService`.
2. Add a private field for the `CLLocationManager`.
3. Create an instance of the `CLLocationMananger` in the `StartTracking` method.
4. Set `PausesLocationUpdatesAutomatically` to `false`.
5. Set `AllowBackgroundLocationUpdates` to `true` (as shown in the following code) so that the location updates will continue even when the app is running in the background:

```
public void StartTracking()
{
    locationManager = new CLLocationManager
    {
        PausesLocationUpdatesAutomatically = false,
        AllowsBackgroundLocationUpdates = true
    };

    // Add code here
}
```

The next step is to ask the user for permission to track their location. We will request permission to track their location all the time, but the user has the option of only giving us permission to track their location when they are using the app. Because the user also has the option of denying us permission to track their location, we need to check before we start to. Let's set this up by going through the following steps:

1. Add an event listener for when the authorization is changed by hooking up the `AuthorizationChanged` event on the `locationManager`.
2. In the event listener, create an `if` statement to check whether the user allows us to track their location.
3. Call the `RequestAlwaysAuthorization` method of the instance that we recently created in the `CLLocationManager`.

4. The code should be placed under the `// Add code here` comment, as shown in bold in the following code:

```
public void StartTracking()
{
    locationManager = new CLLocationManager
    {
        PausesLocationUpdatesAutomatically = false,
        AllowsBackgroundLocationUpdates = true
    };

    // Add code here
    locationManager.AuthorizationChanged += (s, args) =>
    {
        if (args.Status == CLAuthorizationStatus.Authorized)
        {
            // Next section of code goes here
        }
    };

    locationManager.RequestAlwaysAuthorization();
}
```

Before we start to track the location of the user, we will set the accuracy of the data that we want to receive from the `CLLocationManager`. We will also add an event handler to handle the location updates. Let's set this up by going through the following steps:

1. Set the `DesiredAccuracy` to `CLLocation.AccurracyBestForNavigation`. One of the constraints when running the app in the background is that the `DesiredAccuracy` needs to be set to either `AccurracyBest` or `AccurracyBestForNavigation`.

2. Add an event handler for `LocationsUpdated` and, after that, call the `StartUpdatingLocation` method.

3. The code should be placed at the `// Next section goes here` comment, and it should look like the code in bold in the following fragment:

```
locationManager.AuthorizationChanged += (s, args) =>
{
    if (args.Status == CLAuthorizationStatus.Authorized)
    {
        // Next section of code goes here
        locationManager.DesiredAccuracy =
        CLLocation.AccurracyBestForNavigation;
        locationManager.LocationsUpdated +=
        async (object sender, CLLocationsUpdatedEventArgs e) =>
            {
```

```
                        // Final block of code goes here
            };

        locationManager.StartUpdatingLocation();
    }
};
```

The higher the accuracy we set, the higher the battery consumption. If we only want to track where the user has been and not how popular a place is, we could also set `AllowDeferredLocationUpdatesUntil`. This way, we can specify that the user has to move a specific distance before the location is updated. We can also specify how often we want locations to be updated using the `timeout` argument. The most power-efficient solution to track how long a user has been at a place is to use the `StartMonitoringVisits` method of `CLLocationManager`.

Now, it's time to handle the `LocationsUpdated` event. Let's go through the following steps:

1. Add a private field with the name `locationRepository` that is of the `ILocationRepository` type.
2. Add a constructor that has `ILocationRepository` as a parameter. Set the value of the parameter to the `locationRepository` field.
3. Read the latest location of the `Locations` property on `CLLocationsUpdatedEventArgs`.
4. Create an instance of the `MeTracker.Models.Location` and pass the latitude and longitude of the latest location to it.
5. Save the location using the `Save` method of the `ILocationRepository`.
6. The code should be placed at the `// Final block of code goes here` comment, and it should look like the code in bold in the following fragment:

```
locationManager.LocationsUpdated +=
    async (object sender, CLLocationsUpdatedEventArgs e) =>
    {
        var lastLocation = e.Locations.Last();
        var newLocation = new
        Models.Location(lastLocation.Coordinate.Latitude,
        lastLocation.Coordinate.Longitude);

        await locationRepository.Save(newLocation);
    };
```

We have completed the tracking part of the app for iOS. We will now implement background tracking for Android. After this, we will visualize the data.

Background location tracking with Android

The Android way to carry out background updates is very different from how we implemented this with iOS. With Android, we need to create a `JobService` and schedule it.

Adding the required permissions to use the location of the user

To track the location of the user in the background with Android, we need to request five permissions, as shown in the following table:

ACCESS_COARSE_LOCATION	To get an approximate location for the user
ACCESS_FINE_LOCATION	To get a precise location for the user
ACCESS_NETWORK_STATE	Because the location services in Android use information from a network to determine the location of the user
ACCESS_WIFI_STATE	Because the location services in Android use information from a Wi-Fi network to determine the location of the user
RECEIVE_BOOT_COMPLETED	So that the background job can start again after the device is rebooted

Permissions can be set either from the **Android Manifest** tab in the properties of the `MeTracker.Android` project or via the `AndroidManifest.xml` file in the `Properties` folder. When changes are made from the **Android Manifest** tab, the changes will be written to the `AndroidMainfest.xml` file as well, so it doesn't matter which method you prefer.

The following is a screenshot of setting the permissions in the **Android Manifest** tab in the properties of the `MeTracker.Android` project:

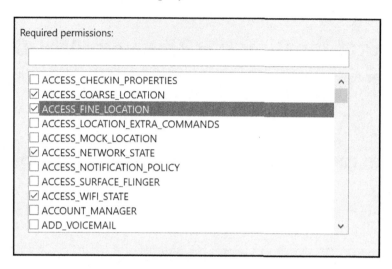

The `uses-permission` elements should be added to the `manifest` element in the `AndroidManifest.xml` file, as shown in the following code:

```
<uses-permission android:name="android.permission.ACCESS_FINE_LOCATION" />
<uses-permission android:name="android.permission.ACCESS_COARSE_LOCATION"
/>
<uses-permission android:name="android.permission.RECEIVE_BOOT_COMPLETED"
/>
<uses-permission android:name="android.permission.ACCESS_NETWORK_STATE" />
<uses-permission android:name="android.permission.ACCESS_WIFI_STATE" />
```

Creating a background job

To track the location of users in the background, we need to create a background job by going through the following steps:

1. In the Android project, create a new class with the name `LocationJobService` in the `Services` folder.
2. Make the class `public` and add `Android.App.Job.JobService` as a base class.
3. Implement the abstract methods `OnStartJob` and `OnStopJob`, as shown in the following code:

```
public class LocationJobService : JobService
{
```

```
public override bool OnStopJob(JobParameters @params)
{
    return true;
}

public override bool OnStartJob(JobParameters @params)
{
    return true;
}
}
```

All services in an Android app need to be added to the `AndroidManifest.xml` file. We don't have to do this manually; however, we can instead add an attribute to the class, which will then be generated in the `AndroidManifest.xml` file. We will use the `Name` and `Permission` properties to set the required information, as shown in the following code:

```
[Service(Name = "MeTracker.Droid.Services.LocationJobService",
         Permission = "android.permission.BIND_JOB_SERVICE")]
public class LocationJobService : JobService
```

Scheduling a background job

When we have created a job, we can schedule it. We will do this from the `LocationTrackingService` in the `MeTracker.Android` project. To configure the job, we will use the `JobInfo.Builder` class.

We will use the `SetPersisted` method to ensure that the job starts again after a reboot. This is why we added the `RECEIVE_BOOT_COMPLETED` permission earlier.

To schedule a job, at least one constraint is needed. In this case, we will use `SetOverrideDeadline`. This will specify that the job needs to run before the specified time (in milliseconds) has elapsed.

The `SetRequiresDeviceIdle` code phrase can be used to make sure that a job only runs when the device is not being used by a user. We could pass `true` to the method if we want to make sure that we don't slow down the device when the user is using it.

The `SetRequiresBatteryNotLow` code phrase can be used to specify that a job should not run when the battery level is low. We recommend that this should always be set to `true` if you don't have a good reason to run it when the battery is low. This is because we don't want our applications to drain the user's battery.

So, let's implement the `LocationTrackingService` that is found in the Android project in the `Services` folder by going through the following steps:

1. Create a `JobInfo.Builder` based on an ID that we specify (we will use 1 here) and on the component name (which we create from the application context and the Java class) in the `StartTracking` method. The component name is used to specify which code will run during the job.

2. Use the `SetOverrideDeadline` method and pass `1000` to it to make the job run before one second has elapsed from when the job was created.

3. Use the `SetPersisted` method and pass `true` to make the job persist even after the device is rebooted.

4. Use the `SetRequiresDeviceIdle` method and pass `false` so that the job will run even when a user is using the device.

5. Use the `SetRequiresBatteryLow` method and pass `true` to make sure that we don't drain the user's battery. This method was added in Android API level 26.

6. The code for the `LocationTrackingService` should now look as follows:

```
using Android.App;
using Android.App.Job;
using Android.Content;
using MeTracker.Services;

namespace MeTracker.Droid.Services
{
    public class LocationTrackingService : ILocationTrackingService
    {
        var javaClass =
        Java.Lang.Class.FromType(typeof(LocationJobService));
        var componentName = new ComponentName(Application.Context,
        javaClass);
        var jobBuilder = new JobInfo.Builder(1, componentName);

        jobBuilder.SetOverrideDeadline(1000);
        jobBuilder.SetPersisted(true);
        jobBuilder.SetRequiresDeviceIdle(false);
        jobBuilder.SetRequiresBatteryNotLow(true);

        var jobInfo = jobBuilder.Build();
    }
}
```

The `JobScheduler` service is a system service. To get an instance of a system service, we will use the application context by going through the following steps:

1. Use the `GetSystemService` method on the `Application.Context` to get the `JobScheduler`.
2. Cast the result to the `JobScheduler`.
3. Use the `Schedule` method on the `JobScheduler` class and pass the `JobInfo` object to schedule the job, as shown in the following code:

```
var jobScheduler =
    (JobScheduler)Application.Context.GetSystemService
    (Context.JobSchedulerService);
    jobScheduler.Schedule(jobInfo);
```

Subscribing to location updates

Once we have scheduled the job, we can write the code to specify what the job should do, which is track the location of a user. To do this, we will use the `LocationManager`, which is a `SystemService`. With the `LocationManager`, we can either request a single location update or we can subscribe to location updates. In this case, we want to subscribe to location updates.

We will start by creating an instance of the `ILocationRepository` interface that we will use to save the locations to the SQlite database. Let's set this up by going through the following steps:

1. Create a constructor for the `LocationJobService`.
2. Create a private read-only field for the `ILocationRepository` interface with the name `locationRepository`.
3. Use the `Resolver` in the constructor to create an instance of the `ILocationRepository`, as shown in the following code:

```
private ILocationRepository locationRepository;
public LocationJobService()
{
    locationRepository = Resolver.Resolve<ILocationRepository>();
}
```

Before we subscribe to location updates, we will add a listener. To do this, we will use the `Android.Locations.ILocationListener` interface by going through the following steps:

1. Add the `Android.Locations.ILocationListener` to the `LocationJobService`.
2. Implement the interface.
3. Remove all instances of `throw new NotImplementedException();`, which is added to the methods, if you let Visual Studio generate the implementation of the interface.
4. In the `OnLocationChanged` method, map the `Android.Locations.Location` object to the `Model.Location` object.
5. Use the `Save` method on the `LocationRepository` class, as shown in the following code:

```
public void OnLocationChanged(Android.Locations.Location location)
{
    var newLocation = new Models.Location(location.Latitude,
    location.Longitude);
    locationRepository.Save(newLocation);
}
```

When we have created a listener, we can subscribe for location updates by going through the following steps:

1. Go to the `StartJob` method in the `LocationJobService`.
2. Create a static field of the `LocationManager` type.
3. Get the `LocationManager` by using the `GetSystemService` on the `ApplicationContext`.
4. To subscribe for location updates, use the `RequestLocationUpdates` method, as shown in the following code:

```
public override bool OnStartJob(JobParameters @params)
{
    locationManager =
    (LocationManager)ApplicationContext.GetSystemService
    (Context.LocationService);
    locationManager.RequestLocationUpdates
    (LocationManager.GpsProvider, 1000L, 0.1f, this);

    return true;
}
```

The first argument that we pass to the `RequestLocationUpdates` method ensures that we get locations from the GPS. The second ensures that at least `1000` milliseconds will elapse between location updates. The third argument ensures that the user has to move at least `0.1` meters to get a location update. The last one specifies which listener we should use. Because the current class implements the `Android.Locations.ILocationListener` interface, we will pass `this`.

Creating a heat map

To visualize the data that we have collected, we will create a heat map. We will add lots of dots to a map and make them different colors, based on how much time a user spends in a particular place. The most popular places will have a warm color and the least popular places will have a cold color.

Adding a GetAll method to the LocationRepository

In order to visualize the data, we need to write code so that is can be read from the database. Let's set this up by going through the following steps:

1. In the `MeTracker` project, open the `ILocationRepository.cs` file.
2. Add a `GetAll` method, which returns a list of `Location` objects using the following code:

   ```
   Task<List<Location>> GetAll() ;
   ```

3. In the `MeTracker` project, open the `LocationRepository.cs` file, which implements the `ILocationRepository`.
4. Implement the new `GetAll` method and return all the saved locations in the database, as shown in the following code:

   ```
   public async Task<List<Location>> GetAll()
   {
       await CreateConnection();
       var locations = await connection.Table<Location>
       ().ToListAsync();

       return locations;
   }
   ```

Preparing the data for visualization

Before we can visualize the data on the map, we need to prepare the data. The first thing we will do is create a new model that we can use for the prepared data. Let's set this up by going through the following steps:

1. In the `Models` folder in the `MeTracker` project, create a new class and name it `Point`.

2. Add properties for the `Location`, the `Count`, and the `Heat`, as shown in the following code:

```
namespace MeTracker.Models
{
    public class Point
    {
        public Location Location { get; set; }
        public int Count { get; set; } = 1;
        public Xamarin.Forms.Color Heat { get; set; }
    }
}
```

The `MainViewModel` will store the locations that we will find later on. Let's add a property for storing the `Points` by going through the following steps:

1. In the `MeTracker` project, open the `MainViewModel` class.
2. Add a `private` field with the name `points`, which has the `List<Point>` type.
3. Create a property with the name `Points` that has the `List<Point>` type.
4. In the `get` method, return the value of the `points` field.
5. In the `set` method, set the `points` field to the new value and call `RaisePropertyChanged` with the name of the property as an argument.
6. At the end of the `LoadData` method, assign the `pointList` variable to the `Points` property, as shown in the following code:

```
private List<Models.Point> points;
public List<Models.Point> Points
{
    get => points;
    set
    {
        points = value;
        RaisePropertyChanged(nameof(Points));
    }
}
```

Now that we have the storage for our points, we must add code to add locations. We will do this by implementing the `LoadData` method of the `MainViewModel` class and making sure that it is called on the main thread right after the location tracking has started.

The first thing we will do is to group the saved locations so that all locations within 200 meters will be handled as one point. We will track how many times we have logged a position within that point so we can later decide which color the point will be on the map. Let's set this up using the following steps:

1. Add an `async` method with the name LoadData, which returns a `Task` to the `MainViewModel`.

2. Call the `LoadData` method from the constructor after the call to the `StartTracking` method on the `ILocationTrackingService`, as shown in the following code:

```
public MainViewModel(ILocationTrackingService
                     locationTrackingService,
                     ILocationRepository locationRepository)
{
    this.locationTrackingService = locationTrackingService;
    this.locationRepository = locationRepository;
    MainThread.BeginInvokeOnMainThread(async() =>
    {
        locationTrackingService.StartTracking();
        await LoadData();
    });
}
```

The first step in the `LoadData` method is to read all tracked locations from the SQLite database. When we have all the locations, we will loop through them and create the points. To calculate the distance between a location and a point, we will use the `CalculateDistance` method from `Xamarin.Essentials.Location`, as shown in the following code:

```
private async Task LoadData()
{
    var locations = await locationRepository.GetAll();
    var pointList = new List<Models.Point>();

    foreach (var location in locations)
    {
        //If no points exist, create a new one an continue to the next
        location in the list
        if (!pointList.Any())
        {
```

```
        pointList.Add(new Models.Point() { Location = location });
        continue;
    }

    var pointFound = false;

    //try to find a point for the current location
    foreach (var point in pointList)
    {
        var distance =
        Xamarin.Essentials.Location.CalculateDistance(
        new Xamarin.Essentials.Location(
        point.Location.Latitude, point.Location.Longitude),
        new Xamarin.Essentials.Location(location.Latitude,
        location.Longitude), DistanceUnits.Kilometers);

        if (distance < 0.2)
        {
            pointFound = true;
            point.Count++;
            break;
        }
    }

    //if no point is found, add a new Point to the list of points
    if (!pointFound)
    {
        pointList.Add(new Models.Point() { Location = location });
    }

    // Next section of code goes here
    }
}
```

When we have a list of points, we can calculate the heat color for each point. We are going to use the **hue, saturation, and lightness** (**HSL**) representation of a color, as described in the following list:

- **Hue**: Hue is a degree on the color wheel that goes from 0 to 360, 0 being red and 240 being blue. Because we want our most popular places to be red (hot) and our least popular places to be blue (cold), we will calculate a value between 0 and 240 for each point, based on how many times the user has been to that point. This means that we will only use two-thirds of the scale.
- **Saturation**: Saturation is a percentage value: 0% is a shade of gray, while 100% is full color. In our app, we will always use 100% (this will be represented as 1 in the code).

- **Lightness**: Lightness is a percentage value of the amount of light: 0% is black and 100% is white. We want it to be neutral, so we will use 50% (this will be represented as 0.5 in the code).

The first thing that we need to do is find out how many times the user has been in the most popular and least popular places. We find this out by going through the following steps:

1. First, check that the list of points is not empty.
2. Get the Min and Max values for the Count property in the list of points.
3. Calculate the difference between the minimum and the maximum values.
4. The code should be added at the // Next section of code goes comment at the bottom of the LoadData method, as shown in the following code:

```
private async Task LoadData()
{
    // The rest of the method has been commented out for brevity

    // Next section of code goes here
    if (pointList == null || !pointList.Any())
    {
        return;
    }

    var pointMax = pointList.Select(x => x.Count).Max();
    var pointMin = pointList.Select(x => x.Count).Min();
    var diff = (float)(pointMax - pointMin);

    // Last section of code goes here
}
```

We will now be able to calculate the heat for each point by going through the following steps:

1. Loop through all the points.
2. Use the following calculation to calculate the heat for each point.
3. The code should be added at the // Last section of code goes here comment at the bottom of the LoadData() method, as shown in bold in the following code:

```
private async Task LoadData()
{
    // The rest of the method has been commented out for brevity
```

```
// Next section of code goes here
if (pointList == null || !pointList.Any())
{
    return;
}

var pointMax = pointList.Select(x => x.Count).Max();
var pointMin = pointList.Select(x => x.Count).Min();
var diff = (float)(pointMax - pointMin);

// Last section of code goes here
foreach (var point in pointList)
{
    var heat = (2f / 3f) - ((float)point.Count / diff);
    point.Heat = Color.FromHsla(heat, 1, 0.5);
}

Points = pointList;
}
```

That's it for setting up location tracking in the `MeTracker` project. Let's turn our attention to visualizing the data we get.

Creating custom renderers

Custom renderers are a powerful way to extend Xamarin.Forms. As mentioned in `Chapter 1`, *Introduction to Xamarin*, Xamarin.Forms is built with renderers, so for each Xamarin.Forms control there is a renderer that creates a native control. By overriding an existing renderer or creating a new one, we can extend and customize how Xamarin.Forms controls are rendered to native controls. We can also use renderers to create new Xamarin.Forms controls from scratch.

Renderers are platform specific, so when we create custom renderers, we have to create one for each platform that we want to change or use to extend the behavior of a control. To make our renderers visible for Xamarin.Forms, we will use the assembly attribute `ExportRenderer`. This contains information about which control the renderer is for and which renderer will be used.

Creating a custom control for the map

In order to show the heat map on our map, we will create a new control, for which we will use a custom renderer. We set this up by going through the following steps:

1. In the `MeTracker` project, create a new folder with the name `Controls`.
2. Create a new class with the name `CustomMap`.
3. Add the `Xamarin.Forms.Maps.Map` as a base class to the new class, as shown in the following code:

```
using System.Collections.Generic;
using Xamarin.Forms;
using Xamarin.Forms.Maps;

namespace MeTracker.Controls
{
    public class CustomMap : Map
    {
    }
}
```

If we want to have properties that we want to bind data to, we need to create a `BindableProperty`. This should be a `public static` field in the class. We also need to create a *regular* property. The naming of the properties is really important. The name of the `BindableProperty` needs to be `{NameOfTheProperty}Property`; for example, the name of the `BindableProperty` that we will create in the following steps will be `PointsProperty`, because the name of the property is `Points`. A `BindableProperty` is created using the static `Create` method on the `BindableProperty` class. This requires at least four arguments, as shown in the following list:

- `propertyName`: This is the name of the property as a string.
- `returnType`: This is the type that will be returned from the property.
- `declaringType`: This is the type of the class in which the `BindableProperty` is declared.
- `defaultValue`: This is the default value that will be returned if no value is set. This is an optional argument. If it is not set, Xamarin.Forms will use `null` as a default value.

The set and get methods for the property will call methods in the base class to set or get values from the BindableProperty:

1. In the MeTracker project, create a BindableProperty with the name PointsProperty, as shown in the following code.

2. Create a property of the List<Models.Point> type with the name Points. Remember to cast the result of the GetValue as the same type as the property, because the GetValue will return the value as the type object:

```
public static BindableProperty PointsProperty =
    BindableProperty.Create(nameof(Points),
    typeof(List<Models.Point>), typeof(CustomMap), new
    List<Models.Point>());

public List<Models.Point> Points
{
        get => GetValue(PointsProperty) as List<Models.Point>;
        set => SetValue(PointsProperty, value);
}
```

When we have created a custom map control, we will use it to replace the Map control in the MainView by going through the following steps:

1. In the MainView.xaml file, declare the namespace for the custom control.

2. Replace the Map control with the new control that we have created.

3. Add a binding to the Points property in the MainViewModel, as shown in the following code:

```
<ContentPage xmlns="http://xamarin.com/schemas/2014/forms"
xmlns:x="http://schemas.microsoft.com/winfx/2009/xaml"
                xmlns:map="clr-namespace:MeTracker.Controls;"
                x:Class="MeTracker.Views.MainView">
        <ContentPage.Content>
        <map:CustomMap x:Name="Map" Points="{Binding Points}" />
        </ContentPage.Content>
</ContentPage>
```

Creating a custom renderer to extend the map in the iOS app

First, we will create a custom renderer for iOS by going through the following steps. Because we want to extend the functionality, we will use the MapRenderer as a base class:

1. Create a folder with the name Renderers in the MeTracker.iOS project.

2. Create a new class in this folder and name it CustomMapRenderer.

3. Add `MapRenderer` as a base class.

4. Add the `ExportRenderer` attribute, as shown in the following code:

```
using System.ComponentModel;
using System.Linq;
using MapKit;
using MeTracker.Controls;
using MeTracker.iOS.Renderers;
using Xamarin.Forms;
using Xamarin.Forms.Maps.iOS;
using Xamarin.Forms.Platform.iOS;

[assembly:ExportRenderer(typeof(CustomMap),
typeof(CustomMapRenderer))]
namespace MeTracker.iOS.Renderers
{
    public class CustomMapRenderer : MapRenderer
    {
    }
}
```

When a property changes for the control that we are writing a custom renderer for, the `OnElementPropertyChanged` method is called. The method is a virtual method, which means that we can override it. We want to listen to any changes to the `Points` property in our `CustomMap` control.

To do this, go through the following steps:

1. Override the `OnElementPropertyChanged` method. This method will run every time a property value is changed in the element (the Xamarin.Forms control).

2. Add an `if` statement to check that it is the `Points` property that has changed, as shown in the following code:

```
protected override void OnElementPropertyChanged(object sender,
    PropertyChangedEventArgs e)
{
    base.OnElementPropertyChanged(sender, e);

    if (e.PropertyName == CustomMap.PointsProperty.PropertyName)
    {
        //Add code here
    }
}
```

To create the heat map, we will add circles as overlays to the map, one circle for each point. Before we do this, however, we need to add some code to specify how an overlay should be rendered. Let's set this up by going through the following steps:

1. Create a `mapView` variable. Cast the `Control` property to `MKMapView` and assign it to the variable.
2. Create a `customMap` variable. Cast the `Element` property to the `CustomMap` and assign it to the variable.
3. Create an action using an expression with parameters for `MKMapView` and `IMKOverlay` and assign it to the `OverlayRenderer` property on the `map` view.
4. Cast the `overlay` parameter to `MKCircle` and assign it to a new variable called `circle`.
5. Verify that the circle variable is not `null`.
6. Find the point object from the point list on the `CustomMap` object using coordinates.
7. Create a new `MKCircleRenderer` object and pass the circle variable to the constructor.
8. Set the `FillColor` property to the heat color of the point. Convert it to `UIColor` using the extension method `ToUIColor`.
9. Set the `Alpha` property to `1.0f` to make sure that the circle not will be transparent.
10. Return the `circleRenderer` variable.
11. Return `null` if the circle variable is `null`.
12. The code should look like the bold code in the following fragment:

```
protected override void OnElementPropertyChanged(object sender,
    PropertyChangedEventArgs e)
{
    base.OnElementPropertyChanged(sender, e);

    if (e.PropertyName == CustomMap.PointsProperty.PropertyName)
    {
        var mapView = (MKMapView)Control;
        var customMap = (CustomMap)Element;

        mapView.OverlayRenderer = (map, overlay) =>
        {
            var circle = overlay as MKCircle;

            if (circle != null)
            {
```

```
var point = customMap.Points.Single
(x => x.Location.Latitude ==
circle.Coordinate.Latitude &&
x.Location.Longitude ==
circle.Coordinate.Longitude);

var circleRenderer = new MKCircleRenderer(circle)
{
    FillColor = point.Heat.ToUIColor(),
    Alpha = 1.0f
};

    return circleRenderer;
}

return null;
};

// Next section of code goes here
}
}
```

We have implemented how we want each overlay of the map to be rendered. What we need to do now is to go through all the points we have gathered so far and create an `Overlay` for each one. Let's set this up by going through the following steps:

1. Loop through all the points.
2. Create a circle overlay with the `static` method `Circle` on the `MKCircle` class, as shown in the following code. The first argument is the position of the `Circle` and the second one is the radius of the `Circle`.
3. Add the overlay to the map using the `AddOverlay` method.
4. The code should now look like the bold code in the following fragment:

```
// Next section of code goes here
foreach (var point in customMap.Points)
{
        var overlay = MKCircle.Circle(
        new CoreLocation.CLLocationCoordinate2D
        (point.Location.Latitude, point.Location.Longitude), 100);

    mapView.AddOverlay(overlay);
}
```

This concludes the section on how to extend the `Maps` control for iOS. Let's do the same for Android.

Creating a custom renderer to extend the map in the Android app

We will now create a custom renderer for Android. The structure is the same as the one we used for iOS. We will use the `ExportRenderer` attribute in the same way and we will also add the `MapRenderer` class as the base class. This, however, is the Android-specific `MapRenderer`.

We start by creating a custom renderer for our `CustomMap` control. The renderer will inherit from the `MapRenderer` base class so that we can extend any existing functionality. To do this, go through the following steps:

1. Create a folder with the name `Renderers` in the `MeTracker.Android` project.
2. Create a new class in this folder and name it `CustomMapRenderer`.
3. Add `MapRenderer` as a base class.
4. Add the `ExportRenderer` attribute.
5. Add a constructor that has `Context` as a parameter. Pass the parameter to the constructor of the base class.
6. Resolve all the references, as shown in the following code:

```
using System.ComponentModel;
using Android.Content;
using Android.Gms.Maps;
using Android.Gms.Maps.Model;
using MeTracker.Controls;
using MeTracker.Droid.Renderers;
using Xamarin.Forms;
using Xamarin.Forms.Maps;
using Xamarin.Forms.Maps.Android;
using Xamarin.Forms.Platform.Android;

[assembly: ExportRenderer(typeof(CustomMap),
typeof(CustomMapRenderer))]
namespace MeTracker.Droid.Renderers
{
    public class CustomMapRenderer : MapRenderer
    {
        public CustomMapRenderer(Context context) : base(context)
        {
        }
    }
}
```

To get a map object to work with, we need to request it. We do this by overriding the `OnElementChanged` method that all custom renderers have. This method is called each time an element changes, such as when it's set for the first time when parsing the XAML, or when it's replaced in code. Let's set this up by going through the following steps:

1. Override the `OnElementChanged` method.
2. If the `NewElement` property of the `ElementChangedEventArgs` is not `null`, request the map object with the `GetMapAsync` method on the `Control` property, as shown in the following code:

```
protected override void OnElementChanged
                        (ElementChangedEventArgs<Map> e)
{
    base.OnElementChanged(e);

    if (e.NewElement != null)
    {
        Control.GetMapAsync(this);
    }
}
```

When we have a map to work with, the virtual `OnMapReady` method will be called. To add code of our own to handle this, we override this method by going through the following steps:

1. Create a private field of the `GoogleMap` type and name it `map`.
2. Override the `OnMapReady` method.
3. Assign the new field with the parameter from the method body, as shown in the following code:

```
protected override void OnMapReady(GoogleMap map)
{
    this.map = map;

    base.OnMapReady(map);
}
```

Just as we did with the iOS renderer, we need to handle changes in the `Points` property of our custom map. To do this, we override the `OnElementPropertyChanged` method that is called each time a property on the control we are writing our renderer for changes. Let's do this by going through the following steps:

1. Override the `OnElementPropertyChanged` method. This method will run every time a property value is changed in the `Element` (the Xamarin.Forms control).

2. Add an `if` statement to check that it is the `Points` property that has changed, as shown in the following code:

```
protected override void OnElementPropertyChanged(object sender,
    PropertyChangedEventArgs e)
{
    base.OnElementPropertyChanged(sender, e);

    if(e.PropertyName == CustomMap.PointsProperty.PropertyName)
    {
    }
}
```

We can now add code to handle the specific event of the `Points` property being set by drawing the location out on the map. To do this, go through the following steps:

1. For each point, create an instance of the `CircleOptions` class.
2. Use the `InvokeStrokeWidth` method to set the stroke width of the circle to `0`.
3. Use the `InvokeFillColor` method to set the color of the circle. Use the `ToAndroid` extension method to convert the color to an `Android.Graphics.Color`.
4. Use the `InvokeRadius` method to set the size of the circle to `200`.
5. Use the `InvokeCenter` method to set where on the map the circle should be.
6. Add the circle to the `map` using the `AddCircle` method on the `map` object.
7. The code should look the same as the bold code in the following fragment:

```
protected override void OnElementPropertyChanged(object sender,
    PropertyChangedEventArgs e)
{
    base.OnElementPropertyChanged(sender, e);

    if(e.PropertyName ==
CustomMap.PointsProperty.PropertyName)
    {
        var element = (CustomMap)Element;
```

```
foreach (var point in element.Points)
{
    var options = new CircleOptions();
    options.InvokeStrokeWidth(0);
    options.InvokeFillColor(point.Heat.ToAndroid());
    options.InvokeRadius(200);
    options.InvokeCenter(new
    LatLng(point.Location.Latitude,
    point.Location.Longitude));
    map.AddCircle(options);
}
    }
}
```

Refreshing the map when resuming the app

The last thing we will do is to make sure that the map is up to date with the latest points when the app is resumed. The easiest way to do this is to set the MainPage property in the App.xaml.cs file to a new instance of MainView, in the same way as the constructor, as shown in the following code:

```
protected override void OnResume()
{
    MainPage = Resolver.Resolve<MainView>();
}
```

Summary

In this chapter, we built an app for iOS and Android that tracked the location of a user. When we built the app, we learned how to use maps in Xamarin.Forms and how to use location tracking running in the background. We also learned how to extend Xamarin.Forms with custom controls and custom renderers. With this knowledge, we can create applications that perform other tasks in the background. We also learned how to extend most controls in Xamarin.Forms.

The next project will be a real-time chat app. In the next chapter, we will set up a serverless backend based on services in Microsoft Azure. We will use that backend in a later chapter once we have built the app.

Building a Weather App for Multiple Form Factors

5

Xamarin.Forms isn't only be used for creating apps for phones; it can also be used for creating apps for tablets and desktop computers. In this chapter, we will build an app that will work on all of these platforms. As well as using three different form factors, we are also going to be working on three different operating systems: iOS, Android, and Windows.

The following topics will be covered in this chapter:

- How to use `FlexLayout` in Xamarin.Forms
- How to use `VisualStateManager`
- How to use different views for different form factors
- How to use behaviors

Technical requirements

To work on this project, we need to have Visual Studio for Mac or PC installed, as well as the Xamarin components. See `Chapter 1`, *Introduction to Xamarin*, for more details on how to set up your environment.

Project overview

Applications for iOS and Android can run on both phones and tablets. Very often, apps are just optimized for phones. In this chapter, we will build an app that will work on different form factors, but we aren't going to stick to just phones and tablets—we are going to target desktop computers as well. The desktop version will be for the **Universal Windows Platform (UWP)**.

The app that we are going to build is a weather app that displays the weather forecast based on the location of the user.

Getting started

We can use either Visual Studio 2017 for PC or Visual Studio for Mac to work on this project. To build an iOS app using Visual Studio for PC, you have to have a Mac connected. If you don't have access to a Mac at all, you can choose to just work on the Windows and Android parts of this project. Similarly, if you only have a Mac, you can choose to work on only the iOS and Android parts of this project.

Building the weather app

It's time to start building the app. Create a new blank Xamarin.Forms app using **.NET Standard** as the **Code Sharing Strategy**, and select **iOS**, **Android**, and **Windows (UWP)** as the platforms. We will name the project `Weather`.

As the data source for this app, we will use an external weather API. This project will use `OpenWeatherMap`, a service that offers a couple of free APIs. You can find this service at `https://openweathermap.org/api`. We will use the service called `5 day / 3 hour forecast` in this project, which provides a five-day forecast in three-hour intervals. To use the `OpenWeather` API, we have to create an account to get an API key. If you don't want to create an API key, we can mock the data instead.

Creating models for the weather data

Before we write the code to fetch data from the external weather service, we will create models in order to deserialize the results from the service so that we have a common model that we can use to return data from the service.

The easiest way to generate models to use when we are deserializing results from the service is to make a call to the service either in the browser or with a tool (such as Postman) to see the structure of the JSON. We can either create classes manually or use a tool that can generate C# classes from the JSON. One tool that can be used is **quicktype**, which can be found at `https://quicktype.io/`.

If you generate them manually, make sure to set the namespace to `Weather.Models`.

As stated, you can also create these models manually. We will describe how to do this in the next section.

Adding the weather API models manually

If you choose to add the models manually, then go through the following instructions. We will be adding a single code file called `WeatherData.cs` that will contain multiple classes:

1. In the `Weather` project, create a folder named `Models`.
2. Add a file called `WeatherData.cs`.
3. Add the following code:

```csharp
using System.Collections.Generic;

namespace Weather.Models
{
    public class Main
    {
        public double temp { get; set; }
        public double temp_min { get; set; }
        public double temp_max { get; set; }
        public double pressure { get; set; }
        public double sea_level { get; set; }
        public double grnd_level { get; set; }
        public int humidity { get; set; }
        public double temp_kf { get; set; }
    }

    public class Weather
    {
        public int id { get; set; }
        public string main { get; set; }
        public string description { get; set; }
        public string icon { get; set; }
    }

    public class Clouds
    {
        public int all { get; set; }
    }

    public class Wind
    {
        public double speed { get; set; }
        public double deg { get; set; }
```

```
        }

        public class Rain
        {
        }

        public class Sys
        {
            public string pod { get; set; }
        }

        public class List
        {
            public long dt { get; set; }
            public Main main { get; set; }
            public List<Weather> weather { get; set; }
            public Clouds clouds { get; set; }
            public Wind wind { get; set; }
            public Rain rain { get; set; }
            public Sys sys { get; set; }
            public string dt_txt { get; set; }
        }

        public class Coord
        {
            public double lat { get; set; }
            public double lon { get; set; }
        }

        public class City
        {
            public int id { get; set; }
            public string name { get; set; }
            public Coord coord { get; set; }
            public string country { get; set; }
        }

        public class WeatherData
        {
            public string cod { get; set; }
            public double message { get; set; }
            public int cnt { get; set; }
            public List<List> list { get; set; }
            public City city { get; set; }
        }
    }
```

As you can see, there are quite a lot of classes. These map directly to the response we get from the service.

Adding the app-specific models

In this section, we will create the models that our app will translate the Weather API models into. Let's start by adding the WeatherData class (unless you created this manually in the preceding section), using the following steps:

1. Create a new folder with the name Models in the Weather project.
2. Add a new file with the name WeatherData.
3. Paste or write the code for the classes based on the JSON. If code other than the properties is generated, ignore it and just use the properties.
4. Rename MainClass (this is what quicktype names the root object) as WeatherData.

We will now create models based on the data we are interested in. This will make the rest of the code more loosely coupled to the data source.

Adding the ForecastItem model

The first model we are going to add is ForecastItem, which represents a specific forecast for a point in time. We do this by going through the following steps:

1. In the Weather project, create a new class called ForecastItem.
2. Add the following code:

```
using System;
using System.Collections.Generic;

namespace Weather.Models
{
    public class ForecastItem
    {
        public DateTime DateTime { get; set; }
        public string TimeAsString => DateTime.ToShortTimeString();
        public double Temperature { get; set; }
        public double WindSpeed { get; set; }
        public string Description { get; set; }
        public string Icon { get; set; }
    }
}
```

Adding the Forecast model

Next, we'll create a model called `Forecast` that will keep track of a single forecast for a city. The `Forecast` keeps a list of multiple `ForeCastItem` objects, each representing a forecast for a specific point in time. Let's set this up by going through the following steps:

1. In the `Weather` project, create a new class called `Forecast`.
2. Add the following code:

```
using System;
using System.Collections.Generic;

namespace Weather.Models
{
    public class Forecast
    {
        public string City { get; set; }
        public List<ForecastItem> Items { get; set; }
    }
}
```

Now that we have our models for both the Weather API and the app, we need to fetch data from the Weather API.

Creating a service for fetching the weather data

To make it easier to change the external weather service and to make the code more testable, we will create an interface for the service. Here's how we go about it:

1. In the `Weather` project, create a new folder and name it `Services`.
2. Create a new `public interface` and name it `IWeatherService`.
3. Add a method for fetching data based on the location of the user, as shown in the following code. Name the method `GetForecast`:

```
public interface IWeatherService
{
    Task<Forecast> GetForecast(double latitude, double
longitude);
}
```

When we have an interface, we can create an implementation for it by going through the following steps:

1. In the `Services` folder, create a new class with the name `OpenWeatherMapWeatherService`.
2. Implement the interface and add the `async` keyword to the `GetForecast` method.
3. The code should look as follows:

```
using System;
using System.Globalization;
using System.Linq;
using System.Net.Http;
using System.Threading.Tasks;
using Newtonsoft.Json;
using Weather.Models;

namespace Weather.Services
{
    public class OpenWeatherMapWeatherService : IWeatherService
    {
        public async Task<Forecast> GetForecast(double latitude,
        double longitude)
        {
        }
    }
}
```

Before we call the `OpenWeatherMap` API, we need to build a URI for the call to the Weather API. It will be a `GET` call and the latitude and longitude will be added as query parameters. We will also add the API key and the language in which we would like the response. Let's set this up by going through the following steps:

1. In the `WeatherProject`, open the `OpenWeatherMapWeatherService` class.
2. Add the code marked in bold in the following code fragment:

```
public class OpenWeatherMapWeatherService : IWeatherService
{
    public async Task<Forecast> GetForecast(double latitude, double
    longitude)
    {
        var language =
        CultureInfo.CurrentUICulture.TwoLetterISOLanguageName;
        var apiKey = "{AddYourApiKeyHere}";
        var uri =
        $"https://api.openweathermap.org/data/2.5/forecast?
```

```
            lat={latitude}&lon={longitude}&units=metric&lang=
            {language}&appid={apiKey}";
    }
}
```

In order to deserialize the JSON that we will get from the external service, we will use `Json.NET`, the most popular NuGet package for serializing and deserializing JSON in .NET applications. We can install it using the following steps:

1. Open the **NuGet Package Manager**.
2. Install the `Json.NET` package. The ID of the package is `Newtonsoft.Json`.

To make the call to the `Weather` service, we will use the `HttpClient` class and the `GetStringAsync` method using the following steps:

1. Create a new instance of the `HttpClient` class.
2. Call `GetStringAsync` and pass the URL as the argument.
3. Use the `JsonConvert` class and the `DeserializeObject` method from `Json.NET` to convert the JSON string in to an object.
4. Map the `WeatherData` object to a `Forecast` object.
5. The code should look like the bold code in the following fragment:

```
public async Task<Forecast> GetForecast(double latitude, double
                                                longitude)
{
    var language =
    CultureInfo.CurrentUICulture.TwoLetterISOLanguageName;
    var apiKey = "{AddYourApiKeyHere}";
    var uri = $"https://api.openweathermap.org/data/2.5/forecast?
    lat={latitude}&lon={longitude}&units=metric&lang=
    {language}&appid={apiKey}";

    var httpClient = new HttpClient();
    var result = await httpClient.GetStringAsync(uri);

    var data = JsonConvert.DeserializeObject<WeatherData>(result);

    var forecast = new Forecast()
    {
        City = data.city.name,
        Items = data.list.Select(x => new ForecastItem()
        {
            DateTime = ToDateTime(x.dt),
            Temperature = x.main.temp,
            WindSpeed = x.wind.speed,
```

```
        Description = x.weather.First().description,
        Icon =
$"http://openweathermap.org/img/w/{x.weather.First().icon}.png"
    }).ToList()
    };
    return forecast;
}
```

To optimize the performance, we can use `HttpClient` as a singleton and reuse it for all network calls in the application. The following information is from Microsoft's documentation: *HttpClient is intended to be instantiated once and reused throughout the life of an application. Instantiating an HttpClient class for every request will exhaust the number of sockets available under heavy loads. This will result in SocketException errors.* This can be found at: `https://docs.microsoft.com/en-gb/dotnet/api/system.net.http.httpclient?view=netstandard-2.0`.

In the previous code, we have a call to a `ToDateTime` method, which is a method that we will need to create. This method converts the date from a Unix timestamp in to a `DateTime` object, as shown in the following code:

```
private DateTime ToDateTime(double unixTimeStamp)
{
    DateTime dateTime = new DateTime(1970, 1, 1, 0, 0, 0, 0,
    DateTimeKind.Utc);
    dateTime = dateTime.AddSeconds(unixTimeStamp).ToLocalTime();
    return dateTime;
}
```

By default, `HttpClient` uses the Mono implementation of `HttpClient` (iOS and Android). To increase performance, we can use a platform-specific implementation instead. For iOS, use `NSUrlSession`. This can be set in the project settings of the iOS project under the **iOS Build** tab. For Android, use **Android**. This can be set in the project settings of the Android project under **Android Options | Advanced**.

Configuring the applications to use location services

To be able to use location services, we need to carry out some configurations on each platform. We will use Xamarin.Essentials and the classes it contains. Ensure that you have installed Xamarin.Essentials from NuGet into all projects in the solution before going through the steps in the following sections.

Configuring the iOS app to use location services

To use location services in an iOS app, we need to add a description to indicate why we want to use the location in the `info.plist` file. In this app, we only need to get the location when we are using the app, so we only need to add a description for this. Let's set this up by going through the following steps:

1. Open `info.plist` in `Weather.iOS` with the **XML (Text) Editor**.
2. Add the key, which is `NSLocationWhenInUseUsageDescription`, using the following code:

   ```
   <key>NSLocationWhenInUseUsageDescription</key>
   <string>We are using your location to find a forecast for
   you</string>
   ```

Configuring the Android app to use location services

For Android, we need to set the app to require the following two permissions:

- **ACCESS_COARSE_LOCATION**
- **ACCESS_FINE_LOCATION**

We can set this in the `AndroidManifest.xml` file that can be found in the `Properties` folder in the `Weather.Android` project, but we can also set it in the project properties under the **Android Manifest** tab as well, as shown in the following screenshot:

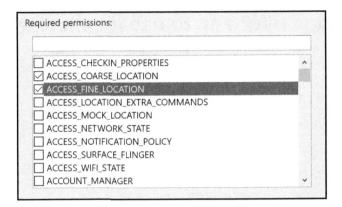

When we request permissions in an Android app, we also need to add the following code to `MainActivity.cs` file in the Android project:

```
public override void OnRequestPermissionsResult(int requestCode, string[]
permissions,
[GeneratedEnum] Android.Content.PM.Permission[] grantResults)
{
    Xamarin.Essentials.Platform.OnRequestPermissionsResult(requestCode,
permissions, grantResults); base.OnRequestPermissionsResult(requestCode,
permissions, grantResults);
}
```

For Android, we also need to initialize Xamarin.Essentials. We will do this in the `OnCreate` method of the `MainActivity`:

```
protected override void OnCreate(Bundle savedInstanceState)
{
    TabLayoutResource = Resource.Layout.Tabbar;
    ToolbarResource = Resource.Layout.Toolbar;

    base.OnCreate(savedInstanceState);
    global::Xamarin.Forms.Forms.Init(this, savedInstanceState);
    Xamarin.Essentials.Platform.Init(this, savedInstanceState);
    LoadApplication(new App());
}
```

Configuring the UWP app to use location services

Since we will use location services in the UWP app, we need to add the **Location** capability under **Capabilities** in the `Package.appxmanifest` file of the `Weather.UWP` project, as shown in the following screenshot:

Application	Visual Assets	Capabilities	Declarations	Content URIs	Packaging

Use this page to specify system features or devices that your app can use.

Capabilities:

- ☐ AllJoyn
- ☐ Appointments
- ☐ Background Media Playback
- ☐ Blocked Chat Messages
- ☐ Bluetooth
- ☐ Chat Message Access
- ☐ Code Generation
- ☐ Contacts
- ☐ Enterprise Authentication
- ☐ Internet (Client & Server)
- ☑ Internet (Client)
- ☑ Location
- ☐ Low Level
- ☐ Low Level Devices
- ☐ Microphone
- ☐ Music Library
- ☐ Objects 3D
- ☐ Offline Maps Management
- ☐ Phone Call

Description:

Provides access to the current location, which is obtained from dedicated hardware like a GPS sensor in the PC or derived from available network information.

More information

Creating the ViewModel class

We now have a service that is responsible for fetching weather data from the external weather source. It's time to create a `ViewModel`. First, however, we will create a base view model, where we can put the code that can be shared between all view models of the app. Let's set this up by going through the following steps:

1. Create a new folder with the name `ViewModels`.
2. Create a new class with the name `ViewModel`.
3. Make the new class `public` and `abstract`.

4. Add and implement the `INotifiedPropertyChanged` interface. This is necessary because we want to use data bindings.

5. Add a `Set` method that will make it easier to raise the `PropertyChanged` event from the `INotifiedPropertyChanged` interface, as shown in the following code. The method will check whether the value has changed. If it has, it will raise the event:

```
public abstract class ViewModel : INotifyPropertyChanged
{
    public event PropertyChangedEventHandler PropertyChanged;
    protected void Set<T>(ref T field, T newValue,
    [CallerMemberName] string propertyName = null)
    {
        if (!EqualityComparer<T>.Default.Equals(field,
        newValue))
        {
            field = newValue;
            PropertyChanged?.Invoke(this, new
            PropertyChangedEventArgs(propertyName));
        }
    }
}
```

The `CallerMemberName` attribute can be used in a method body if you want the name of the method or the property that made the call to the method to be a parameter. We can always override this, however, by simply passing a value to it. The default value of the parameter is required when you are using the `CallerMember` attribute.

We now have a base view model. We can use this for the view model that we are creating now, as well as for all of the other view models that we will add later.

It's now time to create `MainViewModel`, which will be `ViewModel` for our `MainView` in the app. We do this by going through the following steps:

1. In the `ViewModels` folder, create a new class called `MainViewModel`.

2. Add the abstract `ViewModel` class as a base class.

3. Because we are going to use constructor injection, we will add a constructor with the `IWeatherService` interface as a parameter.

4. Create a read-only `private` field that we will use to store the `IWeatherService` instance using the following code:

```
public class MainViewModel : ViewModel
{
```

```
private readonly IWeatherService weatherService;

public MainViewModel(IWeatherService weatherService)
{
    this.weatherService = weatherService;
}
}
```

MainViewModel takes any object that implements IWeatherService and stores a reference to that service in a field. We will be adding functionality to fetch weather data in the next section.

Getting the weather data

We will now create a new method for loading the data. This will be a three-step process. First, we will get the location of the user. Once we have this, we can fetch data related to that location. The final step is to prepare the data that the views can consume to create a user interface for the user.

To get the location of the user, we will use Xamarin.Essentials, which we installed earlier as a NuGet package, and the Geolocation class, which exposes methods to fetch the location of the user. We do this by going through the following steps:

1. Create a new method called LoadData. Make it an asynchronous method that returns a Task.
2. Use the GetLocationAsync method on the Geolocation class to get the location of the user.
3. Pass the latitude and longitude from the result of the GetLocationAsync call and pass it to the GetForecast method on the object that implements IWeatherService using the following code:

```
public async Task LoadData()
{
    var location = await Geolocation.GetLocationAsync();
    var forecast = await weatherService.GetForecast
    (location.Latitude, location.Longitude);
}
```

Grouping the weather data

When we present the weather data, we will group it by day so that all of the forecasts for one day will be under the same header. To do this, we will create a new model that we will name ForecastGroup. To make it possible to use this model with the Xamarin.Forms ListView, it has to have an IEnumerable type as the base class. Let's set this up by going through the following steps:

1. Create a new class called ForecastGroup in the Models folder.
2. Add List<ForecastItem> as the base class for the new model.
3. Add an empty constructor and a constructor that has a list of ForecastItem instances as a parameter.
4. Add a Date property.
5. Add a property, DateAsString, that returns the Date property as a short date string.
6. Add a property, Items, that returns the list of ForecastItem instances, as shown in the following code:

```
using System;
using System.Collections.Generic;

namespace Weather.Models
{
    public class ForecastGroup : List<ForecastItem>
    {
        public ForecastGroup() { }
        public ForecastGroup(IEnumerable<ForecastItem> items)
        {
            AddRange(items);
        }

        public DateTime Date { get; set; }
        public string DateAsString => Date.ToShortDateString();
        public List<ForecastItem> Items => this;
    }
}
```

When we have done this, we can update MainViewModel with two new properties by going through the following steps:

1. Create a property called City for the name of the city for which we are fetching the weather data.
2. Create a property called Days that will contain the grouped weather data.

3. The `MainViewModel` class should look like the bold code in the following fragment:

```
public class MainViewModel : ViewModel
{
    private string city;
    public string City
    {
        get => city;
        set => Set(ref city, value);
    }

    private ObservableCollection<ForecastGroup> days;
    public ObservableCollection<ForecastGroup> Days
    {
        get => days;
        set => Set(ref days, value);
    }

    // Rest of the class is omitted for brevity
}
```

We are now ready to do the actual grouping of the data. We will do this in the `LoadData` method. We will loop through the data from the service and add items to groups by going through the following steps:

1. Create a `itemGroups` variable of the `List<ForecastGroup>` type .
2. Create a `foreach` loop that loops through all items in the `forecast` variable.
3. Add an `if` statement that checks whether the `itemGroups` property is empty. If it is empty, add a new `ForecastGroup` to the variable and continue to the next item in the item list.
4. Use the `SingleOrDefault` method (this is an extension method from System.Linq) on the `itemGroups` variable to get a group based on the date of the current `ForecastItem`. Add the result to a new variable, `group`.
5. If the group property is `null`, then there is no group with the current day in the list of groups. If this is the case, a new `ForecastGroup` should be added to the list in the `itemGroups` variable, and the execution of the code will continue to the next `forecast` item in the `forecast.Items` list. If a group is found, it should be added to the list in the `itemGroups` variable.
6. After the `foreach` loop, set the `Days` property with a new `ObservableCollection<ForecastGroup>` and use the `itemGroups` variable as an argument in the constructor.

7. Set the `City` property to the `City` property of the `forecast` variable.

8. The `LoadData` method should now look as follows:

```
public async Task LoadData()
{
    var itemGroups = new List<ForecastGroup>();

    foreach (var item in forecast.Items)
    {
        if (!itemGroups.Any())
        {
            itemGroups.Add(new ForecastGroup(
            new List<ForecastItem>() { item })
            { Date = item.DateTime.Date});
            continue;
        }

        var group = itemGroups.SingleOrDefault(x => x.Date ==
        item.DateTime.Date);

        if (group == null)
        {
            itemGroups.Add(new ForecastGroup(
            new List<ForecastItem>() { item })
            { Date = item.DateTime.Date });

                    continue;
        }

        group.Items.Add(item);
    }

    Days = new ObservableCollection<ForecastGroup>(itemGroups);
    City = forecast.City;
}
```

Don't use the `Add` method on `ObservableCollection` when you want to add more than a couple of items. It is better to create a new instance of `ObservableCollection` and pass a collection to the constructor. The reason for this is that every time you use the `Add` method, you will have a binding to it from the view, and it will trigger a rendering of the view. We will get a better performance if we avoid using the `Add` method.

Creating a Resolver

We will create a helper class for **Inversion of Control (IoC)**. This will help us to create types based on a configured IoC container. In this project, we will use Autofac as the IoC library. Let's set this up by going through the following steps:

1. Install the NuGet package **Autofac** in the `Weather` project.
2. Create a new class called `Resolver` in the `Weather` project.
3. Add a `private static` field called `container` of the `IContainer` type (from Autofac).
4. Add a `public static` method called `Initialize` with `IContainer` as a parameter. Set the value of the parameter to the `container` field.
5. Add a generic `public static` method called `Resolve<T>`, which will return an instance of an object of the type specified with the `T` parameter. The `Resolve<T>` method will then call the `Resolve<T>` method on the `IContainer` instance that was passed to it during initialization.
6. The code should now look like the following:

```
using Autofac;

namespace Weather
{
    public class Resolver
    {
        private static IContainer container;

        public static void Initialize(IContainer container)
        {
            Resolver.container = container;
        }

        public static T Resolve<T>()
        {
            return container.Resolve<T>();
        }
    }
}
```

Creating a bootstrapper

In this section, we will create a `Bootstrapper` class that we will use to set up the common configurations that we need in the startup phase of the app. Usually, there is one part of the bootstrapper for each target platform and one that is shared for all platforms. In this project, we only need the shared part. Let's set this up by going through the following steps:

1. In the `Weather` project, create a new class called `Bootstrapper`.
2. Add a new `public static` method called `Init`.
3. Create a new `ContainerBuilder` and register the types to `container`.
4. Create a `Container` by using the `Build` method of the `ContainerBuilder`. Create a variable called `container` that contains the instance of `Container`.
5. Use the `Initialize` method on `Resolver` and pass `container` variable as an argument.
6. The `Bootstrapper` class should now look like the following code:

```
using Autofac;
using TinyNavigationHelper.Forms;
using Weather.Services;
using Weather.ViewModels;
using Weather.Views;
using Xamarin.Forms;

namespace Weather
{
    public class Bootstrapper
    {
        public static void Init()
        {
            var containerBuilder = new ContainerBuilder();
            containerBuilder.RegisterType
            <OpenWeatherMapWeatherService>().As
            <IWeatherService>();
            containerBuilder.RegisterType<MainViewModel>();

            var container = containerBuilder.Build();

            Resolver.Initialize(container);
        }
    }
}
```

Call the `Init` method of `Bootstrapper` in the constructor in the `App.xaml.cs` file after the call to the `InitializeComponent` method. Also, set the `MainPage` property to `MainView`, as shown in the following code:

```
public App()
{
    InitializeComponent();
    Bootstrapper.Init();
    MainPage = new NavigationPage(new MainView());
}
```

Creating a RepeaterView based on a FlexLayout

In Xamarin.Forms, we can use `ListView` if we want to show a collection of data. Using `ListView` is great, and we will use it later in this chapter, but it can only show data vertically. In this app, we want to show data in both directions. In the vertical direction, we will have the days (we group forecasts based on days), while in the horizontal direction, we will have the forecasts within a particular day. We also want the forecasts within a day to wrap if there is not enough space for all of them in one row. With `FlexLayout`, we are able to add items in both directions. However, `FlexLayout` is a layout, which means that we can't bind items to it, so we have to extend its functionality. We will name our extended `FlexLayout RepeaterView`. The `RepeaterView` class will render content based on a `DataTemplate` and the items added to it will appear as if you have used `ListView`.

Let's create `RepeaterView` by following these steps:

1. Create a new folder called `Controls` in the `Weather` project.
2. Add a new class called `RepeaterView` to the `Controls` folder.
3. Create an empty method called `Generate`. We will add code to this method later.
4. Create a new private field called `itemsTemplate` of the `DataTemplate` type.
5. Create a new property called `ItemsTemplate` of the `DataTemplate` type. The `get` method will just return the `itemsTemplate` field. The `set` method will set the `itemsTemplate` field to the new value. However, it will also call the `Generate` method to trigger a regeneration of the data when we have a new template that needs to be generated. The generation has to be done on the main thread, as shown in the following code:

```
using System.Collections.Generic;
using Xamarin.Essentials;
using Xamarin.Forms;
```

```
namespace Weather.Controls
{
    public class ReperaterView : FlexLayout
    {
        private DataTemplate itemsTemplate;
        public DataTemplate ItemsTemplate
        {
            get => itemsTemplate;
            set
            {
                itemsTemplate = value;
                MainThread.BeginInvokeOnMainThread(() =>
                Generate());
            }
        }

        public void Generate()
        {
        }
    }
}
```

In order to bind to a property, we need to add `BindableProperty` by going through the following steps:

1. Add a `public static BindableProperty` field called `ItemsSourceProperty` that returns `null` as a default value.
2. Add a `public` property called `ItemsSource`.
3. Add a setter to the `ItemSource` that sets the value of `ItemsSourceProperty`.
4. Add a getter to the `ItemsSource` property that returns the value of `ItemsSourceProperty`, as shown in the following code:

```
public static BindableProperty ItemsSourceProperty =
BindableProperty.Create(nameof(ItemsSource),
typeof(IEnumerable<object>), typeof(RepeaterView), null);

public IEnumerable<object> ItemsSource
{
    get => GetValue(ItemsSourceProperty) as
IEnumerable<object>;
    set => SetValue(ItemsSourceProperty, value);
}
```

In a bindable property declaration like the one in the preceding code, we can take action on different actions. The one we are interested in is the `propertyChanged` action. If we assign a delegate to this property, then it will get called any time that property changes in value and we can take action on that change. In this case, we will regenerate the content of `RepeaterView`. We do this by going through the following steps:

1. Add a property-changed delegate (as shown in the following code) as an argument to the `Create` method of `BindableProperty` to regenerate the UI when the `ItemsSource` property changes.

2. Check that `DateTemplate` is not `null` before regenerating the UI on the main thread, as shown in the following code:

```
public static BindableProperty ItemsSourceProperty =
BindableProperty.Create(nameof(ItemsSource),
typeof(IEnumerable<object>), typeof(RepeaterView), null,
        propertyChanged: (bindable, oldValue, newValue) =>
    {

            var repeater = (RepeaterView)bindable;

            if(repeater.ItemsTemplate == null)
            {
                return;
            }

            MainThread.BeginInvokeOnMainThread(() =>
            repeater.Generate());

    });
```

The last step of `RepeaterView` is to generate content in the `Generate` method.

Let's implement the `Generate` method by going through the following steps:

1. Clear all child controls with `Children.Clear();`.
2. Verify that `ItemSource` is not `null`. If it is `null`, do an empty `return`.
3. Loop through all items and generate content from `DataTemplate`. Set the current item as `BindingContext` and add it as a child of `FlexLayout`, as shown in the following code:

```
private void Generate()
{
    Children.Clear();

    if(ItemsSource == null)
```

```
    {
        return;
    }

    foreach(var item in ItemsSource)
    {
        var view = itemsTemplate.CreateContent() as View;

        if(view == null)
        {
            return;
        }

        view.BindingContext = item;

        Children.Add(view);
    }
}
```

Creating the view for tablets and desktop computers

The next step is to create the view that we will use when the app is running on a tablet or a desktop computer. Let's set this up by going through the following steps:

1. Create a new folder in the `Weather` project and name it `Views`.
2. Create a new **Content Page** with **XAML** and name it `MainView`.
3. Use the `Resolver` in the constructor of the view to set`BindingContext` to `MainViewModel`, as shown in the following code:

```
public MainView ()
{
    InitializeComponent ();
    BindingContext = Resolver.Resolve<MainViewModel>();
}
```

To trigger `LoadData` method in `MainViewModel`, call the `LoadData` method by overriding the `OnAppearing` method on the main thread. We need to make sure that the call gets marshaled to the UI thread since it will interact directly with the user interface.

To do this, follow these steps:

1. In the `Weather` project, open the `MainView.xaml.cs` file.
2. Create an override of the `OnAppearing` method.
3. Add the code in bold in the following fragment:

```
protected override void OnAppearing()
{
    base.OnAppearing();

    if (BindingContext is MainViewModel viewModel)
    {
        MainThread.BeginInvokeOnMainThread(async () =>
        {
            await viewModel.LoadData();
        });
    }
}
```

In the XAML, add a binding for the `Title` property of `ContentPage` to the `City` property in `ViewModel` by going through the following steps:

1. In the `Weather` project, open the `MainView.xaml` file.
2. Add the `Title` binding to the `ContentPage` element, as highlighted in bold in the following code fragment:

```
<ContentPage xmlns="http://xamarin.com/schemas/2014/forms"
    xmlns:x="http://schemas.microsoft.com/winfx/2009/xaml"
    xmlns:controls="clr-namespace:Weather.Controls"
    x:Class="Weather.Views.MainView"
    Title="{Binding City}">
```

Using RepeaterView

To add a custom control to a view, we need to import a namespace to the view. If the view is in another assembly, we also need to specify the assembly, but in this case, we have both the view and the control in the same namespace, as shown in the following code:

```
<ContentPage xmlns="http://xamarin.com/schemas/2014/forms"
    xmlns:x="http://schemas.microsoft.com/winfx/2009/xaml"
    xmlns:controls="clr-namespace:Weather.Controls"
    x:Class="Weather.Views.MainView"
```

Follow the steps below to build the view:

1. Add a `Grid` as the root view of the page.
2. Add a `ScrollView` to `Grid`. We need this to be able to scroll if the content is higher than the height of the page.
3. Add `RepeaterView` to `ScrollView` and set the direction to `Column` so the content will be in a vertical direction.
4. Add a binding to the `Days` property in `MainViewModel`.
5. Set a `DataTemplate` to the content of `ItemsTemplate`, as shown in the following code:

```
<Grid>
    <ScrollView BackgroundColor="Transparent">
        <controls:RepeaterView ItemsSource="{Binding Days}"
                Direction="Column">
            <controls:RepeaterView.ItemsTemplate>
                <DataTemplate>
                  <!--Content will be added here -->
                </DataTemplate>
            </controls:RepeaterView.ItemsTemplate>
        </controls:RepeaterView>
    </ScrollView>
</Grid>
```

The content for each item will be a header with the date and a horizontal `RepeaterView` with the forecasts for the day. Let's set this up by going through the following steps:

1. In the `Weather` project, open the `MainView.xaml` file.
2. Add `StackLayout` so that the children we are adding to it will be placed in a vertical direction.
3. Add `ContentView` to `StackLayout` with `Padding` set to `10` and `BackgroundColor` set to `#9F5010`. This will be the header. The reason that we need `ContentView` is that we want to have padding around the text.
4. Add `Label` to `ContentView` with the `TextColor` set to `White` and `FontAttributes` set to `Bold`.
5. Add a binding to `DateAsString` for the `Text` property of `Label`.
6. The code should be placed at the `<!-- Content will be added here -->` comment, and should look like the following code:

```
<StackLayout>
    <ContentView Padding="10" BackgroundColor="#9F5010">
        <Label Text="{Binding DateAsString}" TextColor="White"
```

```
                    FontAttributes="Bold" />
            </ContentView>
        </StackLayout>
```

Now that we have the date in the user interface, we need to add a `RepeaterView` that will repeat through `Items` in `MainViewModel` by going through the following steps. `RepeaterView` is the control we created earlier that inherits from `FlexLayout`:

1. Add a `RepeaterView` after the `</ContentView>` tag, but before the `</StackLayout>` tag.

2. Set `JustifyContent` to `Start` to set the `Items` to be added from the left side without distributing them over the available space.

3. Set `AlignItems` to `Start` to set the content to the left of each item in `FlexLayout` that `RepeaterView` is based on, as shown in the following code:

```
<controls:RepeaterView ItemsSource="{Binding Items}" Wrap="Wrap"
    JustifyContent="Start" AlignItems="Start">
```

After defining `RepeaterView`, we need to provide an `ItemsTemplate` that defines how each item in the list should be rendered. Continue adding the XAML directly under the `<controls:RepeaterView>` tag you just added by going through the following steps:

1. Set the `ItemsTemplate` property to `DataTemplate`.

2. Fill the `DataTemplate` with elements, as shown in the following code:

> If we want to add formatting to a binding, we can use `StringFormat`. In this case, we want to add the degree symbol after the temperature. We can do this by using the `{Binding Temperature, StringFormat='{0}° C'}` phrase. With the `StringFormat` property of the binding, we can format data with the same arguments that we would use if we did it in C#. This is the same as `string.Format("{0}° C", Temperature)` in C#. We can also use it to format a date—for example `{Binding Date, StringFormat='yyyy'}`. In C#, this would look like `Date.ToString("yyyy")`.

```
<controls:RepeaterView.ItemsTemplate>
    <DataTemplate>
        <StackLayout Margin="10" Padding="20" WidthRequest="150"
            BackgroundColor="#99FFFFFF">
            <Label FontSize="16" FontAttributes="Bold" Text="{Binding
                TimeAsString}" HorizontalOptions="Center" />
            <Image WidthRequest="100" HeightRequest="100"
                Aspect="AspectFit" HorizontalOptions="Center" Source="
```

```
        {Binding Icon}" />
    <Label FontSize="14" FontAttributes="Bold" Text="{Binding
        Temperature, StringFormat='{0}° C'}"
        HorizontalOptions="Center" />
    <Label FontSize="14" FontAttributes="Bold" Text="{Binding
        Description}" HorizontalOptions="Center" />
    </StackLayout>
    </DataTemplate>
</controls:RepeaterView.ItemsTemplate>
```

The `AspectFill` phrase, as a value of the `Aspect` property for `Image`, means that the whole image will always be visible and that aspects will not be changed. The `AspectFit` phrase will also keep the aspect of an image, but the image can be zoomed and cropped to fill the whole `Image` element. The last value that `Aspect` can be set to, `Fill`, means that the image can be stretched or compressed to match the `Image` view without ensuring that the aspect is kept.

Adding a toolbar item to refresh the weather data

To be able to refresh the data without restarting the app, we will add a **Refresh** button to the toolbar. `MainViewModel` is responsible for handling any logic that we want to perform, and we must expose any action as an `ICommand` that we can bind to.

Let's start by creating the `Refresh` command property on `MainViewModel` by going through the following steps:

1. In the `Weather` project, open the `MainViewModel` class.
2. Add an `ICommand` property with the name `Refresh` and a `get` method that returns a new `Command`
3. Add an action as an expression to the constructor of the `Command` that calls the `LoadData` method, as shown in the following code:

```
public ICommand Refresh => new Command(async() =>
{
    await LoadData();
});
```

Now that we have defined `Command`, we need to bind it to the user interface so that when the user clicks the toolbar button, the action will be executed.

To do this, follow these steps:

1. In the `Weather` app, open the `MainView.xaml` file.
2. Add a new `ToolbarItem` with the `Text` property set to `Refresh` to the `ToolbarItems` property of `ContentPage` and set the `Icon` property to `refresh.png` (the icon can be downloaded from GitHub; see `https://github.com/PacktPublishing/Xamarin.Forms-Projects/tree/master/Chapter-5`).
3. Bind the `Command` property to the `Refresh` property in `MainViewModel`, as shown in the following code:

```
<ContentPage.ToolbarItems>
    <ToolbarItem Icon="refresh.png" Text="Refresh"
Command="{Binding
    Refresh}" />
</ContentPage.ToolbarItems>
```

That's all for refreshing the data. Now we need some kind of indicator that data is loading.

Adding a loading indicator

When we refresh the data, we want to show a loading indicator so the user will know that something is happening. To do this, we will add `ActivityIndicator`, which is what this control is called in Xamarin.Forms. Let's set this up by going through the following steps:

1. In the `Weather` project, open the `MainViewModel` class.
2. Add a Boolean property with the name `IsRefreshing` to the `MainViewModel`.
3. Set the `IsRefreshing` property to `true` at the beginning of the `LoadData` method.
4. At the end of the `LoadData` method, set the `IsRefreshing` property to `false`, as shown in the following code:

```
private bool isRefreshing;
public bool IsRefreshing
{
    get => isRefreshing;
    set => Set(ref isRefreshing, value);
}

public async Task LoadData()
{
    IsRefreshing = true;
    .... // The rest of the code is omitted for brevity
    IsRefreshing = false;
}
```

Now that we have added some code in the `MainViewModel`, we need to bind the `IsRefreshing` property to a user interface element that will be displayed when the `IsRefreshing` property is `true`, as shown in the following code:

1. In the `MainView.xaml`, add a `Frame` after the `ScrollView` as the last element in the `Grid`.
2. Bind the `IsVisible` property to the `IsRefreshing` method that we created in the `MainViewModel`.
3. Set the `HeightRequest` and the `WidthRequest` to `100`.
4. Set the `VerticalOptions` and the `HorizontalOptions` to `Center` so that the `Frame` will be in the middle of the view.
5. Set the `BackgroundColor` to `#99000000` to set the background to white with a little bit of transparency.
6. Add `ActivityIndicator` to the `Frame` with the `Color` set to `Black` and `IsRunning` set to `True`, as shown in the following code:

```
<Frame IsVisible="{Binding IsRefreshing}"
    BackgroundColor="#99FFFFFF"
    WidthRequest="100" HeightRequest="100"
    VerticalOptions="Center"
    HorizontalOptions="Center">
    <ActivityIndicator Color="Black" IsRunning="True" />
</Frame>
```

This will create a spinner that will be visible while data is loading, a really good practice when creating any user interface. Now we'll add a background image to make the app look a bit nicer.

Setting a background image

The last thing we will do to this view for the moment is to add a background image. The image we are using in this example is a result of a Google search for images that are free to use. Let's set this up by going through the following steps:

1. In the `Weather` project, open the `MainView.xaml` file.
2. Wrap the `ScrollView` in a `Grid`. Using a `Grid` is great if we want to have our elements in layers.
3. Set the `Background` property of the `ScrollView` to `Transparent`.
4. Add an `Image` element in the `Grid` with `UriImageSource` as the value of the `Source` property.

5. Set the `CachingEnabled` property to `true` and the `CacheValidity` to 5. This means that the image will be cached in five days.

6. The XAML should now look like the following code:

```
<ContentPage xmlns="http://xamarin.com/schemas/2014/forms"
             xmlns:x="http://schemas.microsoft.com/winfx/2009/xaml"
             xmlns:controls="clr-namespace:Weather.Controls"
             x:Class="Weather.Views.MainView" Title="{Binding
                                                           City}">
    <ContentPage.ToolbarItems>
        <ToolbarItem Icon="refresh.png" Text="Refresh" Command="
        {Binding Refresh}" />
    </ContentPage.ToolbarItems>

    <Grid>
        <Image Aspect="AspectFill">
          <Image.Source>
           <UriImageSource
Uri="https://upload.wikimedia.org/wikipedia/commons/7/79/
Solnedg%C3%A5ng_%C3%B6ver_Laholmsbukten_augusti_2011.jpg"
            CachingEnabled="true" CacheValidity="1" />
          </Image.Source>
        </Image>
        <ScrollView BackgroundColor="Transparent">
            <!-- The rest of the code is omitted for brevity -->
```

We can also set the URL directly in the `Source` property by using `<Image Source="https://ourgreatimage.url" />`. However, if we do this, we can't specify the caching for the image.

Creating the view for phones

Structuring content on a tablet and on a desktop computer is very similar in many ways. On phones, however, we are much more limited in what we can do. Therefore, in this section, we will create a specific view for this app when used on phones by going through the following steps:

1. Create a new **XAML**-based **Content Page** in the `Views` folder.

2. Name the new view called `MainView_Phone`.

3. Use the `Resolver` in the constructor of the view to set the `BindingContext` to the `MainViewModel`, as shown in the following code:

```
public MainView_Phone ()
{
    InitializeComponent ();
    BindingContext = Resolver.Resolve<MainViewModel>();
}
```

To trigger the `LoadData` method in the `MainViewModel`, call the `LoadData` method by overriding the `OnAppearing` method on the main thread. To do this, go through the following steps:

1. In the `Weather` project, open the `MainView_Phone.xaml.cs` file.
2. Add the override of the `OnAppearing` method, as shown in the following code:

```
protected override void OnAppearing()
{
    base.OnAppearing();

    if (BindingContext is MainViewModel viewModel)
    {
        MainThread.BeginInvokeOnMainThread(async () =>
        {
            await viewModel.LoadData();
        });
    }
}
```

In the XAML, add a binding for the `Title` property of the `ContentPage` to the `City` property in the `ViewModel`, as shown in the following code:

1. In the `Weather` project, open the `MainView_Phone.xaml` file.
2. Add the `Title` property with a binding to the `City` property of the `MainViewModel`, as shown in the following code:

```
<ContentPage xmlns="http://xamarin.com/schemas/2014/forms"
    xmlns:x="http://schemas.microsoft.com/winfx/2009/xaml"
    xmlns:controls="clr-namespace:Weather.Controls"
    x:Class="Weather.Views.MainView_Phone"
    Title="{Binding City}">
```

Using a grouped ListView

We could use `RepeaterView` for the phone's view, but because we want our user experience to be as good as possible, we will use `ListView` instead. To get the headers for each day, we will use grouping for the `ListView`. For `RepeaterView`, we had `ScrollView`, but for `ListView`, we don't need that because `ListView` can handle scrolling by default.

Let's continue to create the user interface for the phone's view by going through the following steps:

1. In the `Weather` project, open the `MainView_Phone.xaml` file.
2. Add `ListView` to the root of the page.
3. Set a binding to the `Days` property in `MainViewModel` for the `ItemSource` property.
4. Set the `IsGroupingEnabled` to `True` to enable grouping in the `ListView`.
5. Set `HasUnevenRows` to `True` so the height of each cell will be calculated for each item in the `ListView`.
6. Set the `CachingStrategy` to `RecycleElement` to reuse cells that are not on the screen.
7. Set the `BackgroundColor` to `Transparent`, as shown in the following code:

```
<ListView ItemsSource="{Binding Days}" IsGroupingEnabled="True"
          HasUnevenRows="True" CachingStrategy="RecycleElement"
          BackgroundColor="Transparent">
</ListView>
```

 Set the `CachingStrategy` to `RecycleElement` to get better performance from the `ListView`. This means it will reuse cells that are not shown on the screen, so it will use less memory and we will get a smoother scrolling experience if we have many items in the `ListView`.

To format how each header will look, we will create a `DataTemplate` by going through the following steps:

1. Add a `DataTemplate` to the `GroupHeaderTemplate` property of the `ListView`.
2. Add `ViewCell` to the `DataTemplate`.
3. Add the content for the row to the `ViewCell`, as shown in the following code:

```
<ListView ItemsSource="{Binding Days}" IsGroupingEnabled="True"
          HasUnevenRows="True"
          CachingStrategy="RecycleElement"
```

```
                    BackgroundColor="Transparent">
        <ListView.GroupHeaderTemplate>
          <DataTemplate>
            <ViewCell>
                <ContentView Padding="15,5"
                BackgroundColor="#9F5010">
              <Label FontAttributes="Bold" TextColor="White"
              Text="{Binding DateAsString}"
              VerticalOptions="Center"/>
                </ContentView>
            </ViewCell>
          </DataTemplate>
        </ListView.GroupHeaderTemplate>
      </ListView>
```

To format how each forecast will look, we will create a `DataTemplate`, as we did with the group header. Let's set this up by going through the following steps:

1. Add a `DataTemplate` to the `ItemTemplate` property of the `ListView`.
2. Add `ViewCell` to the `DataTemplate`.
3. In the `ViewCell`, add a `Grid` that contains four columns. Use the `ColumnDefinition` property to specify the width of the columns. The second column should be `50` and the other three will share the rest of the space. We will do this by setting the `Width` to `*`.
4. Add content to the `Grid`, as shown in the following code:

```
    <ListView.ItemTemplate>
        <DataTemplate>
            <ViewCell>
                <Grid Padding="15,10" ColumnSpacing="10"
                    BackgroundColor="#99FFFFFF">
                    <Grid.ColumnDefinitions>
                        <ColumnDefinition Width="*" />
                        <ColumnDefinition Width="50" />
                        <ColumnDefinition Width="*" />
                        <ColumnDefinition Width="*" />
                    </Grid.ColumnDefinitions>
                    <Label FontAttributes="Bold" Text="{Binding
                      TimeAsString}" VerticalOptions="Center" />
                    <Image Grid.Column="1" HeightRequest="50"
                      WidthRequest="50" Source="{Binding Icon}"
                      Aspect="AspectFit" VerticalOptions="Center" />
                    <Label Grid.Column="2" Text="{Binding Temperature,
                    StringFormat='{0}°  C'}" VerticalOptions="Center"
        />

                    <Label Grid.Column="3" Text="{Binding Description}"
```

```
                    VerticalOptions="Center" />
            </Grid>
        </ViewCell>
    </DataTemplate>
</ListView.ItemTemplate>
```

Adding pull to refresh functionality

For the tablet and desktop version of the view, we added a button to the toolbar to refresh the weather forecast. In the phone version of the view, however, we will instead add pull to refresh, which is a common way to refresh content in a list of data. The `ListView` in Xamarin.Forms has built-in support for pull to refresh. Let's set this up by going through the following steps:

1. Go to the `MainView_Phone.xaml`.
2. Set the `IsPullToRefreshEnabled` property to `True` to enable pull-to-refresh for the `ListView`.
3. Bind the `Refresh` property in the `MainViewModel` to the `RefreshCommand` property of the `ListView` to trigger a refresh when the user performs a pull-to-refresh gesture.
4. To show a loading icon when the refresh is in progress, bind the `IsRefreshing` property in the `MainViewModel` to the `IsRefreshing` property of the `ListView`. When we are setting this, we will also get a loading indicator when the initial load is running, as shown in the following code:

```
<ListView ItemsSource="{Binding Days}" IsGroupingEnabled="True"
          HasUnevenRows="True" CachingStrategy="RecycleElement"
          BackgroundColor="Transparent"
          IsPullToRefreshEnabled="True"
          RefreshCommand="{Binding Refresh}"
          IsRefreshing="{Binding
          IsRefreshing}">
```

Navigating to different views based on the form factor

We now have two different views that should be loaded in the same place in the app. `MainView` should be loaded if the app is running on a tablet or on a desktop and `MainView_Phone` should be loaded if the app is running on a phone.

The `Device` class in Xamarin.Forms has a static `Idiom` property that we can use to check which form factor the app is running on. The value of `Idiom` can be `Phone`, `Table`, `Desktop`, `Watch`, or `TV`. Because we only have one view in this app, we could have used an `if` statement when we were setting `MainPage` in `App.xaml.cs` and checked what the `Idiom` value was. Instead, however, we are going to build a solution that we can also use for a bigger app.

One solution is to build a navigation service that we can use to navigate to different views based on a key. Which view will be loaded for which key will be configured upon starting the app. With this solution, we can configure different views on the same key on different types of devices. An open source navigation service that we can use for this purpose is `TinyNavigationHelper`, which can be found at `https://github.com/TinyStuff/` `TinyNavigationHelper` and was created by the authors of this book.

There is also an MVVM library called `TinyMvvm` that includes `TinyNavigationHelper` as a dependency. The `TinyMvvm` library is a library that contains helper classes to get started quicker with MVVM in a Xamarin.Forms app. We created `TinyMvvm` because we want to avoid writing the same code again and again. You can read more at `https://` `github.com/TinyStuff/TinyMvvm`.

Follow the steps below to add `TinyNavigationHelper` to the app:

1. Install the `TinyNavigationHelper.Forms` NuGet package in the `Weather` project.
2. Go to `Bootstrapper.cs`.
3. At the start of the `Execute` method, create a `FormsNavigationHelper` and pass the current application to the constructor.
4. Add an `if` statement to check whether the `Idiom` is `Phone`. If this is true, the `MainView_Phone` view should be registered for the `MainView` key.
5. Add an `else` statement that registers the `MainView` for the `MainView` key.
6. The `Bootstrapper` class should now look as shown in the following code, with the new code marked in bold:

```
public class Bootstrapper
{
    public static void Init()
    {
        var navigation = new
        FormsNavigationHelper(Application.Current);

        if (Device.Idiom == TargetIdiom.Phone)
```

```
    {
        navigation.RegisterView("MainView",
        typeof(MainView_Phone));
    }
    else
    {
        navigation.RegisterView("MainView", typeof(MainView));
    }

    var containerBuilder = new ContainerBuilder();
    containerBuilder.RegisterType<OpenWeatherMapWeatherService>
    ().As<IWeatherService>();
    containerBuilder.RegisterType<MainViewModel>();

    var container = containerBuilder.Build();

    Resolver.Initialize(container);
    }
}
```

Now, we can use the `NavigationHelper` class to set the root view of the app in the constructor of the `App` class by going through the following steps:

1. In the `Weather` app, open the `App.xaml.cs` file.
2. Locate the constructor of the `App` class.
3. Remove the assignment of the `MainPage` property.
4. Add the code to set the root view via the `NavigationHelper`.
5. The constructor should now look like the bold code in the following fragment:

```
public App()
{
    InitializeComponent();
    Bootstrapper.Execute();
    NavigationHelper.Current.SetRootView("MainView", true);
}
```

If we want to load different views on different operating systems, we can use the static `RuntimePlatform` method on the Xamarin.Forms `Device` class—for example, `if(Device.RuntimePlatform == Device.iOS)`.

Handling states with VisualStateManager

`VisualStateManager` was introduced in Xamarin.Forms 3.0. It is a way to make changes in the UI from the code. We can define states and set values for selected properties to apply for a specific state. `VisualStateManager` can be really useful in cases where we want to use the same view for devices with different screen resolutions. It was first introduced in UWP to make it easier to create Windows 10 applications for multiple platforms because Windows 10 could run on Windows Phone as well as on desktops and tablets (the OS was called Windows 10 Mobile). However, Windows Phone has now been depreciated. `VisualStateManager` is really interesting for us as Xamarin.Forms developers, especially when both iOS and Android can run on both phones and tablets.

In this project, we will use it to make a forecast item bigger when the app is running in landscape mode on a tablet or on a desktop. We will also make the weather icon bigger. Let's set this up by going through the following steps:

1. In the `Weather` project, open the `MainView.xaml` file.
2. In the first `RepeaterView` and in the `DataTemplate`, insert a `VisualStateManager.VisualStateGroups` element in the first `StackLayout`:

```
<StackLayout Margin="10" Padding="20" WidthRequest="150"
    BackgroundColor="#99FFFFFF">
    <VisualStateManager.VisualStateGroups>
        <VisualStateGroup>
        </VisualStateGroup>
    </VisualStateManager.VisualStateGroups>
</StackLayout>
```

To the `VisualStateGroup`, we should add two states, we will do that by following these steps:

1. Add a new `VisualState` called `Portrait` to the `VisualStateGroup`.
2. Create a setter in the `VisualState` and set the `WidthRequest` to `150`.
3. Create another `VisualState` called `Landscape` to the `VisualStateGroup`.
4. Create a setter in the `VisualState` and set the `WidthRequest` to `200`, as shown in the following code:

```
<VisualStateGroup>
    <VisualState Name="Portrait">
        <VisualState.Setters>
            <Setter Property="WidthRequest" Value="150" />
        </VisualState.Setters>
```

```
        </VisualState>
        <VisualState Name="Landscape">
            <VisualState.Setters>
                <Setter Property="WidthRequest" Value="200" />
            </VisualState.Setters>
        </VisualState>
    </VisualStateGroup>
```

We also want the icons in a forecast item to be bigger when the item itself is bigger. To do this, we will use the VisualStateManager again. Let's set this up by going through the following steps:

1. Insert a VisualStateManager.VisualStateGroups element in the second RepeaterView and in the Image element in the DataTemplate.
2. Add VisualState for both Portrait and Landscape.
3. Add setters to the states to set the WidthRequest and the HeightRequest. The value should be 100 in the Portrait state and 150 in the Landscape state, as shown in the following code:

```
<Image WidthRequest="100" HeightRequest="100" Aspect="AspectFit"
HorizontalOptions="Center" Source="{Binding Icon}">
    <VisualStateManager.VisualStateGroups>
        <VisualStateGroup>
            <VisualState Name="Portrait">
                <VisualState.Setters>
                    <Setter Property="WidthRequest" Value="100" />
                    <Setter Property="HeightRequest" Value="100" />
                </VisualState.Setters>
            </VisualState>
            <VisualState Name="Landscape">
                <VisualState.Setters>
                    <Setter Property="WidthRequest" Value="150" />
                    <Setter Property="HeightRequest" Value="150" />
                </VisualState.Setters>
            </VisualState>
        </VisualStateGroup>
    </VisualStateManager.VisualStateGroups>
</Image>
```

Creating a behavior to set state changes

With Behavior, we can add functionality to controls without having to subclass them. With behaviors, we can also create a more reusable code than we could if we subclassed a control. The more specific the Behavior we create, the more reusable it will be. For example, a Behavior that inherits from Behavior<View> could be used on all controls, but a Behavior that inherits from a Button can only be used for buttons. Because of this, we always want to create behaviors with a less specific base class.

When we create a Behavior, we need to override two methods: OnAttached and OnDetachingFrom. It is really important to remove event listeners in the OnDeattached method if we have added them in the OnAttached method. This will make the app use less memory. It is also important to set back values to the value that they had before the OnAppearing method ran; otherwise, we might see some strange behavior, especially if the behavior is in a ListView that is reusing cells.

In this app, we will create a Behavior for the RepeaterView. This is because we can't set the state of an item in the RepeaterView from the code behind. We could have added the code to check whether the app runs in portrait or landscape in the RepeaterView, but if we use Behavior instead, we can separate that code from the RepeaterView so that it will be more reusable. Instead, we will add a Property string to the RepeaterView, which will set the state for the RepeaterView and all children in it. Let's set this up by going through the following steps:

1. In the Weather project, open the RepeaterView.cs file.
2. Create a new private string field called visualState.
3. Create a new string property called VisualState.
4. Create a getter that uses an expression to return visualState.
5. In the setter, set the state of the RepeaterView and all children, as shown in the following code:

```
private string visualState;
public string VisualState
{
    get => visualState;
    set
    {
        visualState = value;

        foreach(var child in Children)
        {
            VisualStateManager.GoToState(child, visualState);
```

```
            }

            VisualStateManager.GoToState(this, visualState);
        }
    }
```

This will iterate through each `child` control and set the visual state. Now let's create the behavior that will trigger state changes by following these steps:

1. In the `Weather` project, create a new folder called `Behaviors`.
2. Create a new class called `RepeaterViewBehavior`.
3. Add the `Behavior<RepeaterView>` as a base class.
4. Create a `private` field of the `RepeaterView` type called `view`.
5. The code should look like the following:

```
using System;
using Weather.Controls;
using Xamarin.Essentials;
using Xamarin.Forms;

namespace Weather.Behaviors
{
    public class RepeaterViewBehavior : Behavior<RepeaterView>
    {
        private RepeaterView view;
    }
}
```

`RepeaterViewBehavior` is a class that inherits from the `Behavior<RepeaterView>` base class. This will give us the ability to override some virtual methods that will be called when we attach and detach the behavior from a `RepeaterView`.

But first, we need to create a method to handle the change in state by going through the following steps:

1. In the `Weather` project, open the `RepeaterViewBehavior.cs` file.
2. Create a `private` method called `UpdateState`.
3. Run the code on the `MainThread` to check whether the app is running in portrait or landscape mode.
4. Create a variable called `page` and set its value to `Application.Current.MainPage`.

5. Check whether the `Width` is larger than the `Height`. If this is true, set the `VisualState` property on the view variable to `Landscape`. If this is not true, set the `VisualState` property on the view variable to `Portrait`, as shown in the following code:

```
private void UpdateState()
{
    MainThread.BeginInvokeOnMainThread(() =>
    {
        var page = Application.Current.MainPage;

        if (page.Width > page.Height)
        {
            view.VisualState = "Landscape";
            return;
        }

        view.VisualState = "Portrait";
    });
}
```

The `UpdateState` method is now added. Now we need to override the `OnAttachedTo` method that will be called when the behavior is added to the `RepeaterView`. When it is, we want to update the state by calling this method and also hook up to the `SizeChanged` event of the `MainPage` so that when the size changes, we will update the state again.

Let's set this up by going through the following steps:

1. In the `Weather` project, open the `RepeaterViewBehavior.cs` file.
2. Override the `OnAttachedTo` method from the base class.
3. Set the `view` property to the parameter from the `OnAttachedTo` method.
4. Add an event listener to `Application.Current.MainPage.SizeChanged`. In the event listener, add a call to the `UpdateState` method, as shown in the following code:

```
protected override void OnAttachedTo(RepeaterView view)
{
    this.view = view;

    base.OnAttachedTo(view);

    UpdateState();

    Application.Current.MainPage.SizeChanged +=
    MainPage_SizeChanged;
```

```
        }

            void MainPage_SizeChanged(object sender, EventArgs e)
        {
            UpdateState();
        }
```

When we remove behaviors from a control, it's very important to also remove any event handlers from it in order to avoid memory leaks, and in the worst case, a crash of the app. Let's do this by going through the following steps:

1. In the `Weather` project, open the `RepeaterViewBehavior.cs` file.
2. Override `OnDetachingFrom` from the base class.
3. Remove the event listener from `Application.Current.MainPage.SizeChanged`.
4. Set the `view` field to `null`, as shown in the following code:

```
protected override void OnDetachingFrom(RepeaterView view)
{
    base.OnDetachingFrom(view);
    Application.Current.MainPage.SizeChanged -=
    MainPage_SizeChanged;
    this.view = null;
}
```

Follow the steps below to add the `behavior` to the view:

1. In the `Weather` project, open the `MainView.xaml` file.
2. Import the `Weather.Behaviors` namespace, as shown in the following code:

```
<ContentPage xmlns="http://xamarin.com/schemas/2014/forms"
             xmlns:x="http://schemas.microsoft.com/winfx/2009/xaml"
             xmlns:controls="clr-namespace:Weather.Controls"
             xmlns:behaviors="clr-
             namespace:Weather.Behaviors"
             x:Class="Weather.Views.MainView" Title="{Binding City}">
```

The last thing we will do is add the `RepeaterViewBehavior` to the second `RepeaterView`, as shown in the following code:

```
<controls:RepeaterView ItemsSource="{Binding Items}" Wrap="Wrap"
JustifyContent="Start" AlignItems="Start">
    <controls:RepeaterView.Behaviors>
    <behaviors:RepeaterViewBehavior />
    </controls:RepeaterView.Behaviors>
    <controls:RepeaterView.ItemsTemplate>
```

Summary

We have now successfully created an app for three different operating systems—iOS, Android, and Windows—and three different form factors—phones, tablets, and desktop computers. To create a good user experience on all platforms and form factors, we used `FlexLayout` and `VisualStateManager`. We also learned a way of handling when we want to use different views for different form factors, as well as how to use `Behaviors`.

The next app we will build is a chat app with real-time communication. In the next chapter, we will take a look at how we can use the SignalR service in Azure as the backend for the chat app.

6
Setting up a Backend for a Chat App Using Azure Services

In this chapter, we will build a chat app with real-time communication. To do this, we need a backend. We will create a backend that can scale up to handle a large number of users but also scale down when the number of users is reduced. To build that backend, we will use a serverless architecture based on services in Microsoft Azure.

The following topics will be covered in this chapter:

- Creating a SignalR service in Microsoft Azure
- Using Azure functions as an API
- Scheduling jobs with Azure functions
- Using blob storage to store photos
- Using Azure Cognitive Services to scan photos for adult content

Technical requirements

To be able to complete this project, you need to have Visual Studio for Mac or PC installed. See `Chapter 1`, *Introduction to Xamarin*, for more details on how to set up your environment. You also need an Azure account. If you have a Visual Studio subscription, there is a specific amount of Azure credits included each month. To activate your Azure benefits, go to the following link: `https://my.visualstudio.com`.

You can also create a free account, where you can use selected services for free over 12 months. You will get $200 worth of credit to explore any Azure service for 30 days and you can also use the free services at any time. Read more at the following link: `https://azure.microsoft.com/en-us/free/`.

Azure serverless services

Before we start to build a backend with a serverless architecture, we need to define what serverless actually means. In a serverless architecture, of course the code will run on a server, but we don't need to worry about that; the only thing we need to focus on is building our software. We let someone else handle everything to do with servers. We don't need to think about how much memory or CPU the server needs, or even how many servers we need. When we use services in Azure, Microsoft takes care of this for us.

Azure SignalR Service

The **Azure SignalR Service** is a service in **Microsoft Azure** for real-time communication between a server and clients. The service will push content to the clients without them having to poll the server to get content updates. SignalR can be used for multiple types of applications, including mobile applications, web applications, and desktop applications.

SignalR will use WebSockets if that option is available. If it is not, SignalR will use other techniques for communication, such as **Server-Sent Events** (**SSE**) or **long polling**. SignalR will detect which transport technology is available and use it without the developer having to think about it at all.

SignalR can be used in the following examples:

- **Chat applications**: Where the application needs updates from the server immediately when new messages are available
- **Collaborative applications**: For example, meeting applications or when users on multiple devices are working with the same document

- **Multiplayer games**: Where all users need live updates about other users
- **Dashboard applications**: Where users need live updates

Azure functions

Azure functions is a Microsoft Azure service that allows us to run code in a serverless way. We will deploy small pieces of code called **Functions**. Functions are deployed in groups, called **Function Apps**. When we are creating a Function App, we need to select whether we want it to run on a consumption plan or on an app service plan. We select a consumption plan if we want the application to be completely serverless, while with an app service plan, we have to specify the requirements of the server. With a consumption plan, we pay for the execution time and for how much memory the function uses. One benefit of the app service plan is that you can configure it to be **Always On** and you won't have any cold starts as long as you don't have to scale up to more instances. The big benefit of a consumption plan is that it will always scale according to which resources are needed at that time.

There are several ways in which a function can be triggered to run. Two examples are `HttpTrigger` and `TimeTrigger`. `HttpTrigger` will trigger the function to run when an HTTP request is calling the function. With `TimeTrigger`, functions will run at an interval that we can specify. There are also triggers for other Azure services. For example, we can configure a function to run when a file is uploaded to blob storage, when a new message is posted to an event hub or service bus, or when data is changed in an Azure CosmosDB.

Azure blob storage

Azure blob storage is used for storing unstructured data objects, such as images, videos, audio, and documents. Objects or blobs can be organized into containers. Blob storage can be redundant over multiple data centers in Azure. This to protect the data from unplanned events ranging from transient hardware failures to network or power outages, or even massive natural disasters. Blob storage in Azure can have different tiers, depending on how often we want to use the objects that we are storing. These include archive and cold tiers, and hot and premium tiers, which are used for applications in which we need to access data more often. As well as blob storage, we can add a **Content Delivery Network** (**CDN**) to make the content in our storage closer to our users. This is important if we have users around the globe. If we can deliver our content from a place that is closer to the user, we can reduce the loading time of content and we can give the users a better experience.

Azure Cognitive Services

The easiest way to describe **Azure Cognitive Services** is that it is **Machine Learning** as a service. With just a simple API call, we can use machine learning in our applications, without which we have to use complex data science techniques. When we use APIs, we are making predictions against the models that Microsoft has trained for us.

The services in Azure Cognitive Services have been organized into five categories:

- **Vision**: The vision services are about image processing. These include APIs for face recognition, detection of adult content, image classification, and **Optical Character Recognition** (OCR).
- **Knowledge**: An example of a knowledge service is the **Question and Answer** (**QnA**) makers that allow us to train a model with a knowledge base. When we have trained the model, we can use it for getting answers when we are asking questions.
- **Language**: The language services are about understanding text, such as text analytics, language understanding, and translations.
- **Speech**: Examples of speech APIs include speaker recognition, speech-to-text functionality, and speech translation.
- **Search**: The search services are about using the power of a web search engine to find an answer to your problems. These include knowledge acquisition from images, the auto-completion of search queries, and the identification of similar people.

Project overview

This project will be to set up the backend for a chat application. The biggest part of the project will be the configuration that we will carry out in the Azure portal. We will also write some code for the Azure Functions that will handle the SignalR connections. There will be one function to return information about the SignalR connection and one that posts messages to the SignalR service. The function that we will post messages to will also determine whether the message contains an image. If it does, it will be sent to the Vision API in Azure Cognitive Services to analyze whether it contains adult content. If it does, it won't be posted to the SignalR service and the other users will not get it. Because the SignalR service has a limitation about how big messages can be, we need to store images in blob storage and just post the URL of the image to the users. Because we don't save any chat history in this app, we also want to clear the blob storage at specific intervals. To do this, we will create a function that uses `TimeTrigger`.

The following diagram shows an overview of the architecture of this application:

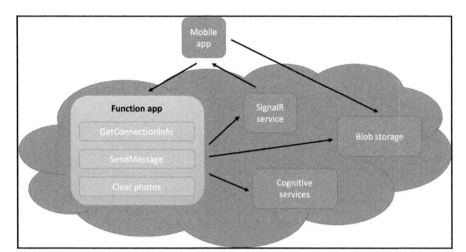

The estimated time to complete this project is about two hours.

Building the serverless backend

Let's start setting up the backend based on the services described in the preceding section.

Creating a SignalR service

The first service that we will set up is the one for SignalR:

1. Go to the Azure portal: `https://portal.azure.com`.
2. Create a new resource. The **SignalR Service** is in the web category.
3. Fill in a name for the resource in the form.
4. Select the subscription you want to use for this project.
5. We recommend that you create a new **Resource Group** and use it for all resources that we will create for this project. The reason that we want one resource group is that it is easier to track what resources are related to this project, and it is also easier to delete all the resources together.
6. Select a location that is close to your users.

7. Select a pricing tier. For this project, we can use the free tier. We can always use the free tier for development and later scale up to a tier that can handle more connections. Refer to the following screenshot:

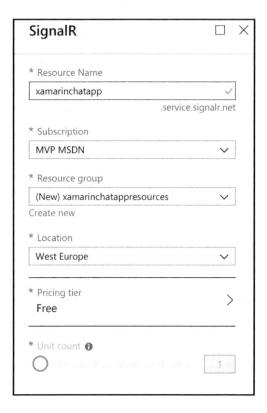

This is all we need to do to set up a SignalR Service. We will return to it in the Azure portal later to grab a connection string to it.

Creating a storage account

The next step is to set up a storage account in which we can store the images that are uploaded by the users:

1. Create a new **Storage Account** resource. **Storage Account** is found under the **Storage** category.
2. Select a subscription and a resource group. We recommend that you use the same as you did for the SignalR Service.

3. Give the storage account a name.
4. Select a location that is close to your users.
5. Select a performance option. If we use **Premium** storage, the data will be stored on **SSD** disks. Select **Standard** storage for this project.
6. Use **StorageV2** for the **Account kind**.
7. In replication, we can select how we want our data to be replicated across the data centers.
8. For the access tier, we will use **Hot**, because we will need to access the data frequently in this app.
9. Click **Create + review** to review the settings before creating the storage account.
10. Click **Create** to create the storage account:

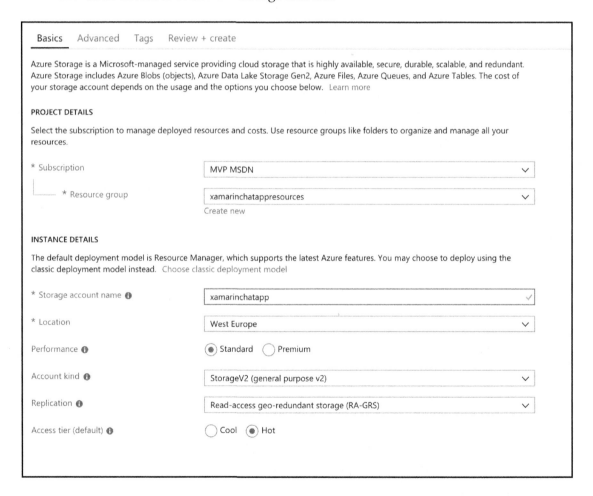

The last step of the configuration of the blob storage is to go to the resource and create a container for the chat images:

1. Go to the resource and select **Blobs**.
2. Create a **New container** with the name `chatimages`.
3. Set the **Public access level** to **Blob (anonymous read access for blobs only)**. This means that it will have public read access, but that you have to be authorized to upload content. Refer to the following screenshot:

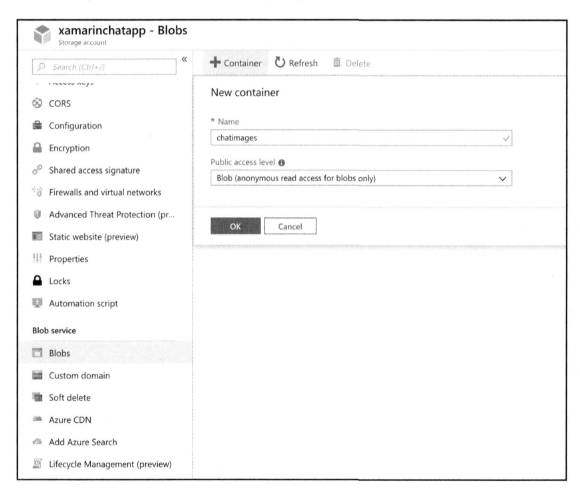

Creating a Cognitive Service

To be able to use **Cognitive Services** to scan images for adult content, we need to create a resource in the Azure portal. This will give us a key that we can use when making calls to the API:

1. Create a new **Custom Vision** resource.
2. Give the resource a name and select a subscription.
3. Select a location that is close to your users.
4. Select a pricing tier for prediction and training. This app will only use predictions because we will use a model that is already trained.
5. Select the same resource groups as you selected for the other resources.
6. Click **OK** to create the new resource. Refer to the following screenshot:

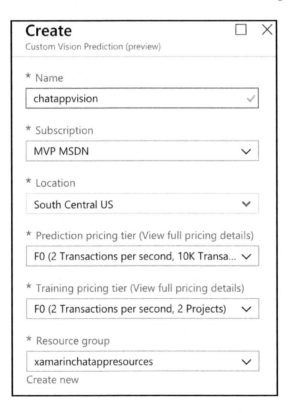

We have now finished creating the Cognitive Service. We will come back later to grab a key that we will use for the calls we will make against the API.

Creating functions

All the code we will write in the backend will be functions. We will use version 2 of Azure Functions, which will run on top of .NET Core. Version 1 ran on top of the full .NET framework.

Creating the Azure service for functions

Before we start to write any code, we will create the Function App. This will contain the functions in the Azure portal:

1. Create a new **Function App** resource. **Function App** is found under the **Compute** category.
2. Give the **Function App** a name. The name will also be the start of the URL of the function.
3. Select a subscription for the **Function App**.
4. Select a resource group for the **Function App**, which should be the same as the other resources we have created in this chapter.
5. Because we will use .NET Core as the runtime for the functions, we can run them in both Windows and Linux. In this case, however, we will run them in Windows.
6. We will use the **Consumption Plan** as our **Hosting Plan**, so we only pay for what we use. The **Function App** will scale both up and down according to our requirements, without us having to think about it at all, if we select a **Consumption Plan**.
7. Select a location that is close to your users.
8. Select **.NET** as the **Runtime stack**.
9. For storage, we can either create a new storage account or use the one we created earlier in this project.
10. Set **Application Insights** to be **On** so that we can monitor our functions.

11. Click **Create** to create the new resource:

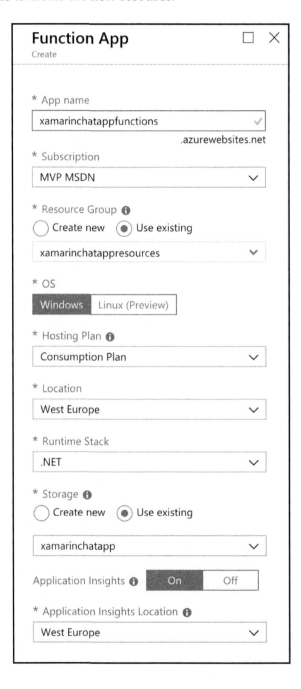

Creating a function to return the connection information for the SignalR service

If you want, you can create functions in the Azure portal. I prefer to use Visual Studio, however, because the code editing experience is much better and you can use version tracking for the source code:

1. Create a new project in Visual Studio of the **Azure Functions** type. This can be found under the **Cloud** tab of the new project dialog box.
2. Name the project Chat.Functions.
3. Click **OK** to continue:

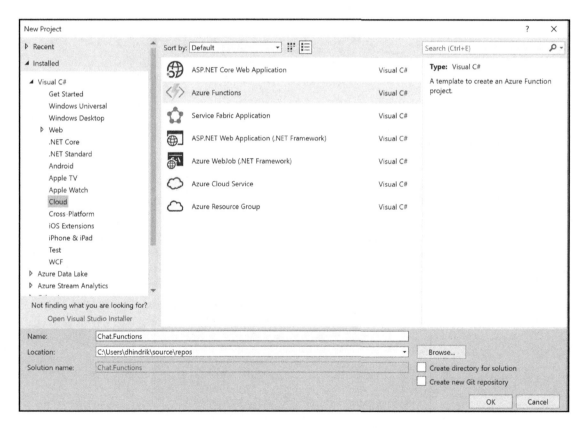

The next step is to create our first function:

1. Select **Azure Functions v2 (.NET Core)** at the top of the dialog box.
2. Select **Http trigger** as the trigger for our first function.

3. Change the **Access rights** from **Admin** to **Anonymous**.
4. Click **OK** to continue and our functions project will be created:

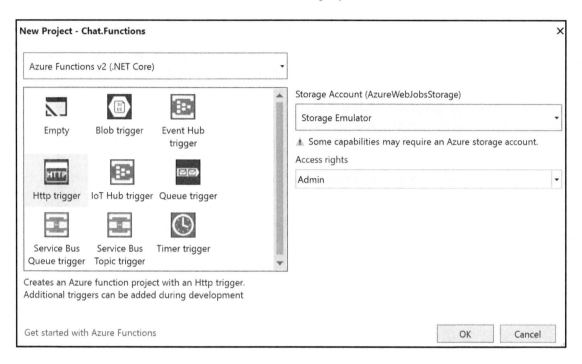

Our first function will return the connection information for the SignalR service. To do that, we need to connect the function by adding a connection string to the SignalR service:

1. Go to the SignalR Service resource in the Azure Portal.
2. Go to the **Keys** tab and copy the connection string.
3. Go to the **Function App** resource and add the connection string under **Application Settings**. Use AzureSignalRConnectionString as the name for the setting.
4. Add the connection string to the Values array in the local.settings.json file in the Visual Studio project to be able to run the function locally on the development machine:

```
{
    "IsEncrypted": false,
    "Values": {
    "AzureWebJobsStorage": "",
    "AzureWebJobsDashboard": ""
    "AzureSignalRConnectionString":
```

```
"{EnterTheConnectingStringHere}"
    }
}
```

Now, we can write the code for the function that will return the connection information. Go to Visual Studio and follow these instructions:

1. Install the `Microsoft.Azure.WebJobs.Extensions.SignalRService` NuGet package in the functions project. The package contains the classes we need to communicate with the SignalR service. It is a prerelease package so we have to check the **Include prerelease** checkbox. If an error occurs during this and you are not able to install the package, make sure that you have the latest version of all other packages in the project and try again.

2. Rename the function that was created when we created the functions project as `GetSignalRInfo`.

3. Also, rename the class as `GetSignalRInfo`.

4. To implement the binding to the SignalR service, we will add a parameter of the `SignalRConnectionInfo` type to the method of the function. The parameter will also have the `SignalRConnectionInfo` attribute, which specifies `HubName`, as in the following code.

5. Return the connection info parameter:

```
using Microsoft.AspNetCore.Http;
using Microsoft.Azure.WebJobs;
using Microsoft.Azure.WebJobs.Extensions.Http;
using Microsoft.Azure.WebJobs.Extensions.SignalRService;

[FunctionName("GetSignalRInfo")]
public static SignalRConnectionInfo GetSignalRInfo(
[HttpTrigger(AuthorizationLevel.Anonymous)] HttpRequest req,
[SignalRConnectionInfo(HubName = "chat")] SignalRConnectionInfo
connectionInfo)
{
    return connectionInfo;
}
```

Creating a message library

We will now define a couple of message classes that we will use to send the chat messages. We will create a base message class that will contain information that is shared between all types of messages. We will also create a separate project for the messages, which will be a .NET Standard library. The reason that we will create it as a separate .NET Standard library is that we then can reuse it in the app we will build in the next chapter.

1. Create a new **.NET Standard 2.0** project and name it `Chat.Messages`.
2. Add a reference to `Chat.Messages` in the `Chat.Functions` project.
3. Create a new class and name it `Message` in the `Chat.Messages` project.
4. Add a `TypeInfo` property to the `Message` class. We need this property later in *Chapter 7, Building a Real-Time Chat Application,* when we will carry out serialization of the messages.
5. Add a property for the `Id` of the `string` type.
6. Add a property for the `Timestamp` of the `DateTime` type.
7. Add a property for the `Username` of the `string` type.
8. Add an empty constructor.
9. Add a constructor that takes a username as a parameter.
10. Set the values of all properties as in the following code:

```
public class Message
{
    public Type TypeInfo { get; set; }
    public string Id {get;set;}
    public string Username { get; set; }
    public DateTime Timestamp { get; set; }

    public Message(){}
    public Message(string username)
    {
        Id = Guid.NewGuid().ToString();
        TypeInfo = GetType();
        Username = username;
        Timestamp = DateTime.Now;
    }
}
```

When a new client is connecting, a message will be sent to other users to indicate that they have connected:

1. Create a new class called `UserConnectedMessage`.
2. Set `Message` as the base class.
3. Add an empty constructor.
4. Add a constructor that takes the username as a parameter and sends it to the constructor of the base class, as shown in the following code:

```
public class UserConnectedMessage : Message
{
    public UserConnectedMessage() { }
    public UserConnectedMessage(string username) :
base(username) { }
}
```

When a client is sending a message with text, it will send a `SimpleTextMessage`:

1. Create a new class called `SimpleTextMessage`.
2. Add `Message` as the base class.
3. Add an empty constructor.
4. Add a constructor that takes the username as a parameter and sends it to the constructor of the base class.
5. Add a string property called `Text`. Refer to the following code:

```
public class SimpleTextMessage : Message
{
    public SimpleTextMessage(){}
    public SimpleTextMessage(string username) :
base(username){}
    public string Text { get; set; }
}
```

If a user uploads an image, it will be sent to the functions as a `base64` string:

1. Create a new class called `PhotoMessage`.
2. Add `Message` as the base class.
3. Add an empty constructor.
4. Add a constructor that takes the username as a parameter and sends it to the constructor of the base class.
5. Add a string property called `Base64Photo`.

6. Add a string property called `FileEnding` as shown in the following code snippet:

```
public class PhotoMessage : Message
{
    public PhotoMessage() { }
    public PhotoMessage(string username) : base(username) { }

    public string Base64Photo { get; set; }
    public string FileEnding { get; set; }
}
```

The last message we will create is used to send information about a photo to the user:

1. Create a new class called `PhotoUrlMessage`.
2. Add `Message` as the base class.
3. Add an empty constructor.
4. Add a constructor that takes the username as a parameter and sends it to the constructor of the base class.
5. Add a string property called `Url`. Refer to the following code:

```
public class PhotoUrlMessage : Message
{
    public PhotoUrlMessage() {}
    public PhotoUrlMessage(string username) : base(username){}

    public string Url { get; set; }
}
```

Creating a storage helper

We will create a helper to share some of the code that we will write for Azure Blob Storage between the send message function and the clear photos function that we will create. When we are creating the Function App in the Azure Portal, a setting for the connection string is created so we just have to add this to the `local.settings.json` file in order to be able to run it locally. The name for the connection string will be `StorageConnection`:

```
{
    "IsEncrypted": false,
    "Values": {
    "AzureWebJobsStorage": "",
    "AzureWebJobsDashboard": "",
    "AzureSignalRConnectionString": "{EnterTheConnectingStringHere}"
    "StorageConnection": "{EnterTheConnectingStringHere}"
```

```
        }
    }
```

For the helper, we will create a new static class, as given in the following steps:

1. Install the `WindowsAzure.Storage NuGet` package in the `Chat.Functions` project. This is to get the classes we need to work with storage.
2. Create a new class called `StorageHelper` in the `Chat.Functions` project.
3. Make the class `static`.
4. Create a new static method called `GetContainer`.
5. Use the static `GetEnviromentVariable` method on the `Environment` class to read the connection string for storage.
6. Create a `CloudStorageAccount` object of it using the static `Parse` method on `CloudStorageAccount`.
7. Create a new `CloudBlobClient` using the `CreateCloudBlobClient` method on the `CloudStorageAccount` class.
8. Get the container reference using the `GetContainerReference` method on the `CloudBlobClient` class and pass the name of the container we created earlier in the chapter as an argument:

```
using Microsoft.WindowsAzure.Storage;
using Microsoft.WindowsAzure.Storage.Blob;
using System;
using System.IO;
using System.Threading.Tasks;

public static class StorageHelper
{

    private static CloudBlobContainer GetContainer()
    {
        string storageConnectionString =
        Environment.GetEnvironmentVariable("StorageConnection");
        var storageAccount =
        CloudStorageAccount.Parse(storageConnectionString);
        var blobClient = storageAccount.CreateCloudBlobClient();

        var container =
        blobClient.GetContainerReference("chatimages");

        return container;
    }
}
```

To upload files to the blob storage, we will create a method that has the bytes of the photo and what type of photo it is as parameters. The photo type will be defined by its file ending:

1. Create a new `async static` method that returns `Task<string>`.
2. Add a `byte[]` and a `string` parameter to the method. Name the parameters `bytes` and `fileEnding`.
3. Call the `GetContainer` method to get a reference to the container.
4. Define a filename for the new blob and use it as an argument to `GetBlockBlobReference` in the `CloudBlobContainer` class. Use `GUID` as the filename to make sure that it is unique.
5. Create a `MemoryStream` of the bytes.
6. Use the `UploadFromStreamAsync` method on the `BlockBlobReference` class to upload the photo to the cloud.
7. Return the `AbsoluteUri` of the blob:

```
public static async Task<string> Upload(byte[] bytes, string
fileEnding)
{
  var container = GetContainer();
  var blob = container.GetBlockBlobReference($"
{Guid.NewGuid().ToString()}.{fileEnding}");

  var stream = new MemoryStream(bytes);
  await blob.UploadFromStreamAsync(stream);

  return blob.Uri.AbsoluteUri;
}
```

The second public method that we will add to the helper is a method to delete all photos that are older than an hour:

1. Create a new `async static` method called `Clear` that returns `Task`.
2. Use the `GetContainer` method to get a reference to the container.
3. Get all blobs in the container by calling the `ListBlobsSegmentedAsync` method with the arguments shown in the following code.
4. Loop through all blobs that are of the `CloudBlob` type.
5. Add an `if` statement to check whether the photos were created more than an hour ago. If so, the blob should be deleted:

```
public static async Task Clear()
{
    var container = GetContainer();
```

```
var blobList = await
container.ListBlobsSegmentedAsync(string.Empty, false,
BlobListingDetails.None, int.MaxValue, null, null, null);

foreach(var blob in blobList.Results.OfType<CloudBlob>())
{
    if(blob.Properties.Created.Value.AddHours(1) <
DateTime.Now)
    {
        await blob.DeleteAsync();
    }
}
}
```

Creating a function for sending messages

To handle messages that are sent by the user, we will create a new function:

1. Create a function with an `HttpTrigger` and with anonymous access rights.
2. Name the function `Messages`.
3. Add a collection of `SignalRMessage` as in the following code.
4. Use the `SignalR` attribute to specify the hub name:

```
[FunctionName("Messages")]
    public async static Task SendMessages(
        [HttpTrigger(AuthorizationLevel.Anonymous, "post")] object
        message,
        [SignalR(HubName = "chat")] IAsyncCollector<SignalRMessage>
        signalRMessages)
    {
```

The message parameter will be the message that the user sent. It will be of the `JObject` type (from `Newtonsoft.Json`). We need to convert it to the `Message` type that we created earlier. To do that, we need to add a reference to the `Chat.Messages` project. However, because the parameter is of an object type, we first need to cast it to `JObject`. Once we have done this, we can use the `ToObject` method to get a `Message`:

```
var jsonObject = (JObject)message;
var msg = jsonObject.ToObject<Message>();
```

If the message is a `PhotoMessage`, we will upload the photo to blob storage. All other messages will be sent directly to the SignalR service using the `AddAsync` method on the `signalRmessages` parameter:

```
if (msg.TypeInfo.Name == nameof(PhotoMessage))
{
    //ToDo: Upload the photo to blob storage.
}

await signalRMessages.AddAsync(new SignalRMessage
  {
    Target = "newMessage",
    Arguments = new[] { message }
  });
```

Before we upload the photo to blob storage with the helper we created, we need to convert the `base64` string to a `byte[]`:

1. Use the static `FromBase64String` method on the `Converter` class to convert the `base64` string to a `byte[]`.
2. Upload the photo to blob storage with the static `Upload` method on `StorageHelper`.
3. Create a new `PhotoUrlMessage`, pass the username to the constructor, and set it as the value for the `msg` variable.
4. Set the `Timestamp` property to the value of the original message, because we are interested in when the message was created by the user.
5. Set the `Id` property to the value of the original message so that it will be handled as the same message on the client.
6. Set the `Url` property to the URL that was returned by `StorageHelper` when we uploaded the photo.
7. Use the `AddAsync` method on the `signalRMessages` variable to send a message to the SignalR service.
8. Add an empty return statement:

```
if (msg.TypeInfo.Name == nameof(PhotoMessage))
{
    var photoMessage = jsonObject.ToObject<PhotoMessage>();
    var bytes = Convert.FromBase64String(photoMessage.Base64Photo);
    var url = await StorageHelper.Upload(bytes,
    photoMessage.FileEnding);
    msg = new PhotoUrlMessage(photoMessage.Username)
    {
        Id = photoMessage.Id,
```

```
                    Timestamp = photoMessage.Timestamp,
                    Url = url
            };

    await signalRMessages.AddAsync(new SignalRMessage
                                    {
                                        Target = "newMessage",
                                        Arguments = new[] { message }
                                    });
            return;
    }
```

Using the Computer Vision API to scan for adult content

To minimize the risk that offensive photos are shown in our chat, we will use machine learning to try to find problematic material and prevent it from being posted to the chat. For that, we will use the **Computer Vision API** in Azure, which is a part of the **Azure Cognitive services**. To use the API, we need a key. We will add it to the application settings of the Function App:

1. Go to the **Azure Portal**.
2. Go to the resource we created for the **Custom Vision API**.
3. The key can be found under the **Keys** tab. You can use either **Key 1** or **Key 2**.
4. Go to the resource for `Function App`.
5. Add the **Key** as an application setting named `ComputerVisionKey`. Also, add the key to `local.settings.json`.
6. Also, add the **Endpoint** as an application setting. Use the name `ComputerVisionEndpoint`. The **Endpoint** can be found under the **Overview** tab of the Function App resource. Also, add the **Endpoint** to `local.settings.json`.
7. Install the `Microsoft.Azure.CognitiveServices.Vision.ComputerVision` NuGet package in the `Chat.Functions` project in Visual Studio. This is to get the necessary classes to use the Computer Vision API.
8. The code for the call to the Computer Vision API will be added to the `Message` function. After that, we convert the `base 64` string to a `byte[]`.
9. Create a `MemoryStream` based on the byte array.

10. Create a `ComputerVisonClient` as shown in the following code and send the credentials to the constructor.

11. Create a list of which features we will use when we are analyzing the photo. In this case, we will use the `VisualFeatureTypes.Adult` feature.

12. Use the `AnalyzeImageInStreamAsync` method on `ComputerVisionClient` and pass the stream and feature list to the constructor to analyze the photo.

13. If the result is `IsAdultContent`, stop the execution of the function by using an empty return statement:

```
var stream = new MemoryStream(bytes);
  var subscriptionKey =
  Environment.GetEnvironmentVariable("ComputerVisionKey");
  var computerVision = new ComputerVisionClient(new
  ApiKeyServiceClientCredentials(subscriptionKey), new
  DelegatingHandler[] { });

  computerVision.Endpoint =
  Environment.GetEnvironmentVariable("ComputerVisionEndpoint");

  var features = new List<VisualFeatureTypes>() {
  VisualFeatureTypes.Adult };

  var result = await
  computerVision.AnalyzeImageInStreamAsync(stream, features);

if (result.Adult.IsAdultContent)
{
    return;
}
```

Creating a scheduled job to clear photos from storage

The last thing we will do is clean the blob storage at regular intervals and delete photos that are older than one hour. We will do that by creating a function that is triggered by `TimeTrigger`:

1. To create a new function, right-click the `Chat.Functions` project and click **New Azure Function**, which will be found under the **Add** menu.

2. Name the function `ClearPhotos`.

3. Select that the function will use a **Time trigger**, because we want it to run on a time interval.

4. Use a **chron** expression to set the **Schedule** to 0 */60 * * * * to make it run every 60 minutes:

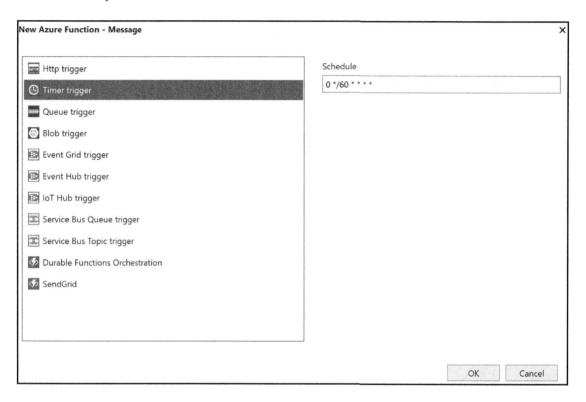

The only thing we will do in the ClearPhotos function is call the Clear method of the StorageHelper that we created earlier in this chapter:

```
[FunctionName("ClearPhotos")]
  public static async Task Run(
    [TimerTrigger("0 */60 * * * *")]TimerInfo myTimer, ILogger log)
{
    await StorageHelper.Clear();
}
```

Deploying the functions to Azure

The last step in this chapter is to deploy the functions to Azure. You can do that as a part of a CI/CD pipeline, for example with Azure DevOps. But the easiest way to deploy the functions in this case is to do it directly from Visual Studio. Follow these steps to deploy the functions:

1. Right-click on the `Chat.Functions` project and select **Publish**.
2. Select the **Select existing** option. Also, check the `Run from package` file option.
3. Click the **Create profile** button.
4. Sign in to the same Microsoft account that we used in the Azure portal when we were creating the Function App.
5. Select the subscription that contains the Function App. All Function Apps we have in the subscription will now be loaded.
6. Select the Function App and click **OK**.
7. When the profile is created, click the **Publish** button.

The following screenshot shows the last step. After that, the publishing profile is created:

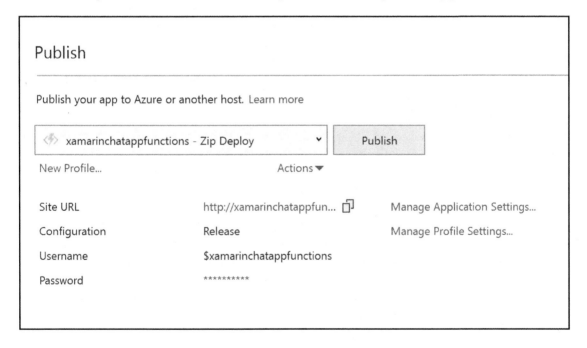

Summary

In this chapter, we have learned how to set up a serverless backend for real-time communication with Azure Functions and the Azure SignalR Service. We have also learned how to use blob storage and machine learning with the Azure Cognitive Services to scan for adult content in photos.

In the next chapter, we will build a chat app that will use the backend we have built in this project.

7
Building a Real-Time Chat Application

In this chapter, we will build a chat app with real-time communication. In the app, you will be able to send and receive messages and photos to and from other users, which will appear without the page needing to be refreshed. We will look at how we can use SignalR to implement a real-time connection with the server.

The following topics will be covered in this chapter:

- How to use SignalR in a Xamarin.Forms app
- How to use template selectors for a ListView
- How to use CSS-styling in a Xamarin.Forms app

Technical requirements

Before you can build the app for this project, you need to build the backend that we detailed in Chapter 6, *Setting up a Backend for a Chat App Using Azure Services*. You will also need to have Visual Studio for Mac or PC installed, as well as the Xamarin components. See Chapter 1, *Introduction to Xamarin*, for more details on how to set up your environment. The source code for this chapter is available in the GitHub repository, which is available at https://github.com/PacktPublishing/Xamarin.Forms-Projects/tree/master/Chapter-6-and-7.

Project overview

When building a chat app, it is really important to have real-time communication because the user expects messages to arrive more or less immediately. To achieve this, we will use SignalR, which is a library for real-time communication. SignalR will use WebSockets if they are available and, if not, it will have several fallback options it can use instead. In the app, a user will be able to send text and photos from the photo library on the device.

The build time for this project is about 180 minutes.

Getting started

We can use either Visual Studio 2017 on a PC or Visual Studio for Mac to do this project. To build an iOS app using Visual Studio for PC, you have to have a Mac connected. If you don't have a access to a Mac at all, you can choose to just build the Android part of the app.

Building the chat app

It's time to start building the app. We recommend that you use the same method as in Chapter 6, *Setting up a Backend for a Chat App Using Azure Services*, because this will make code sharing easier. In that solution, create a **Mobile App (Xamarin.Forms)** with the name Chat:

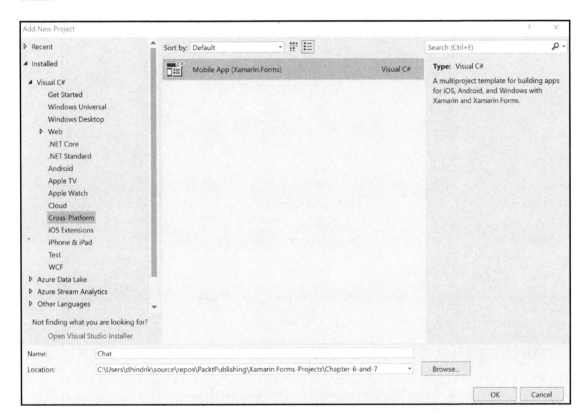

Select the **Blank** template and use **.NET Standard** as the **Code Sharing Strategy**. Select **iOS** and **Android** as the platforms. After we have created the project, we will update all NuGet packages to the latest versions because the project templates are not updated as often as the packages that are used inside the templates:

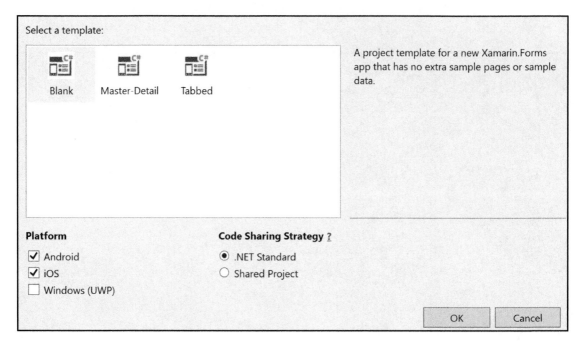

Creating the chat service

The first thing we will do is create a chat service that will be used by both the iOS and Android applications. To make the code more testable and to make it easier to replace the chat service if we want to use another provider in the future, we will follow these steps:

1. In the `Chat` project, add a reference to the `Chat.Messages` project.
2. Create a new folder in the `Chat` project called `Services`.
3. Create a new interface called `IChatService` in the `Services` folder.
4. Create a `bool` property called `IsConnected`.
5. Create a method called `SendMessage` that takes `Message` as an argument and returns `Task`.
6. Create a method called `CreateConnection` that returns `Task`. The method will create and start a connection to the SignalR service.

7. Create a method called `Dispose` that returns `Task`. The method will be used when the app goes to sleep to ensure that the connection to the SignalR service is properly closed:

```
using Chat.Events;
using Chat.Messages;
using System;
using System.Threading.Tasks;

namespace Chat.Services
{
    public interface IChatService
    {
        bool IsConnected { get; }

        Task CreateConnection();
        Task SendMessage(Message message);
        Task Dispose();
    }
}
```

The interface will also contain an event, but before we add the event to the interface, we will create an `EventArgs` class that the event will use. We will do this as follows:

1. In the `Chat` project, create a new folder called `Events`.
2. Create a new class called `NewMessageEventArgs` in the `Events` folder.
3. Add `EventArgs` as a base class.
4. Create a property called `Message` of the `Message` type with a public getter and a private setter.
5. Create an empty constructor.
6. Create a constructor with `Message` as a parameter.
7. Set the parameter of the constructor to the `Message` property.

The following code is the result of these steps:

```
using Chat.Messages;
using System;
namespace Chat.Events
{
    public class NewMessageEventArgs : EventArgs
    {
        public Message Message { get; private set; }

        public NewMessageEventArgs(Message message)
        {
```

```
                        Message = message;
                }
        }
}
```

Now that we have created a new `EventArgs` class, we can use it and add an event to the interface. We will name the event `NewMessage`:

```
public interface IChatService
{
    event EventHandler<NewMessageEventArgs> NewMessage;

    bool IsConnected { get; }

    Task CreateConnection();
    Task SendMessage(Message message);
    Task Dispose();
}
```

The first thing we will do in the service is to make a call to the `GetSignalRInfo` service that we created in `Chapter 6`, *Setting up a Backend for a Chat App Using Azure Services*, to obtain information about how to connect to the SignalR service. To serialize that information, we will create a new class:

1. In the `Chat` project, create a new folder called `Models`.
2. Create a new class called `ConnectionInfo`.
3. Add a string property called `Url` for the `string`.
4. Add a string property called `AccessToken` for the `string`:

   ```
   public class ConnectionInfo
   {
       public string Url { get; set; }
       public string AccessToken { get; set; }
   }
   ```

Now that we have the interface and a model to obtain the connection information, it is time to create an implementation of the `IChatService` interface. To use SignalR, we need to add a package for NuGet that will give us the necessary classes. Follow these steps:

1. In the `Chat` project, install the NuGet package, `Microsoft.AspNetCore.SignalR.Client`.
2. In the `Services` folder, create a new class called `ChatService`.
3. Add and implement the `IChatService` interface to the `ChatService`.

4. Add a private field for `HttpClient` called `httpClient`.

5. Add a private field for `HubConnection` called `hub`.

6. Add a private field for `SemaphoreSlim` called `semaphoreSlim` and create a new instance with an initial and maximum count of one in the constructor:

```
using Chat.Events;
using Chat.Messages;
using Microsoft.AspNetCore.SignalR.Client;
using Newtonsoft.Json;
using System;
using System.Net.Http;
using System.Text;
using System.Threading;
using System.Threading.Tasks;

public class ChatService : IChatService
{
    private HttpClient httpClient;
    private HubConnection hub;
    private SemaphoreSlim semaphoreSlim = new SemaphoreSlim(1, 1);

    public event EventHandler<NewMessageEventArgs> NewMessage;
    public bool IsConnected { get; set; }

    public async Task CreateConnection()
    {
    }

    public async Task SendMessage(Message message)
    {
    }
    public async Task Dispose()
    {
    }
}
```

We will start with the `CreateConnection`, which will call the `GetSignalRInfo` function. We will then use the information to connect to the SignalR service and start listening for messages. To do this, carry out the following steps:

1. Add a call to the `WaitAsync` method of `SemaphoreSlim` to make sure that only one thread can use the method at any one time.

2. Check weather `httpClient` is `null`. If it is, create a new instance. We will reuse the instance of the `httpClient` because this is better from a performance perspective.

3. Make a call to `GetSignalRInfo` and serialize the result to a `ConnectionInfo` object:

```
public async Task CreateConnection()
{
    await semaphoreSlim.WaitAsync();

    if(httpClient == null)
    {
     httpClient = new HttpClient();
    }

    var result = await
httpClient.GetStringAsync("https://{theNameOfTheFunctionApp}.azurew
ebsites.net/api/GetSignalRInfo");

    var info = JsonConvert.DeserializeObject<Models.ConnectionInfo>
    (result);
}
```

When we have the information about how to connect to the SignalR service, we can use the `HubConnectionBuilder` to create a connection. We can then start listening for messages:

1. Create a new `HubConnectionBuilder`.
2. Use the `WithUrl` method to specify the URL to the SignalR service as the first argument. The second argument is an `Action` of the `HttpConnectionObject` type. This means that you will get an object of the `HttpConnectionObject` type as a parameter.
3. In the action, set `AccessTokenProvider` to a `Func` that returns the value of the `AccessToken` property on the `ConnectionInfo` object.
4. Use the `Build` method of the `HubConnectionBuilder` to create a connection object.
5. Add an `Action` that will run when new messages arrive using the `On<object>` method on the `HubConnection` object. The action will be specified as the second argument. For the first argument, we will specify the name of the target (we specified the target in Chapter 6, *Setting up a Backend for a Chat App Using Azure Services*, when we sent the message), which is `newMessage`.
6. In the `Action`, convert the incoming message to a string using the `ToString` method and deserialize it to a `Message` object so we can read its `TypeInfo` property. To do this, use the `JsonConvert` class and the `DeserializeObject<Message>` method.

The reason we have to deserialize the object twice is that we only get the value of properties in the Message class the first time. When we know which subclass of Message we received, we can use this to deserialize that information for that class. We are casting it to Message so we can pass it to the NewMessageEventArgs object. In this case, we will not lose the properties of the subclass. To access the properties, we just cast the class back to the subclass.

7. When we know what type the message is, we can use this to deserialize the object to the actual type. Use the DeserializeObject method of JsonConvert and pass the JSON string and the TypeInfo to it and then cast it to Message.

8. Invoke the NewMessage event and pass the current instance of the ChatService and a new NewMessageEventArgs object to it. Pass the Message object to the constructor of NewMessageEventArgs.

9. Once we have a connection object and we have configured what will happen when a message arrives, we will start to listen to messages with the StartAsync method of the HubConnection.

10. Set the IsConnected property to true.

11. Use the Release method of SemaphoreSlim to let other threads go to the CreateConnection method:

```
var connectionBuilder = new HubConnectionBuilder();
connectionBuilder.WithUrl(info.Url,
(Microsoft.AspNetCore.Http.Connections.Client.HttpConnectionOpt
ions obj) =>
    {
        obj.AccessTokenProvider = () => Task.Run(() =>
        info.AccessToken);
    });

hub = connectionBuilder.Build();
hub.On<object>("newMessage", (message) =>
{
        var json = message.ToString();
        var obj = JsonConvert.DeserializeObject<Message>(json);
        var msg = (Message)JsonConvert.DeserializeObject(json,
        obj.TypeInfo);
        NewMessage?.Invoke(this, new NewMessageEventArgs(msg));
});

await hub.StartAsync();

IsConnected = true;
semaphoreSlim.Release();
```

The next method to implement is the `SendMessage` method. This will send a message to an Azure function, which will add the message to the SignalR service:

1. Use the `Serialize` method on the `JsonConvert` class to serialize the `Message` object to JSON.
2. Create a `StringContent` object and pass the JSON string as the first argument, `Encoding.UTF8` as the second argument, and the content-type `application/json` as the last argument to the constructor.
3. Use the `PostAsync` method on the `HttpClient` object with the URL as the first argument and the `StringContent` object as the second argument to post the message to the function:

```
public async Task SendMessage(Message message)
{
    var json = JsonConvert.SerializeObject(message);

    var content = new StringContent(json, Encoding.UTF8,
    "application/json");
    await
    httpClient.PostAsync
("https://{TheNameOfTheFunctionApp}.azurewebsites.net/api/messages"
    content);
}
```

The last method to implement is the `Dispose` method. This will close the connection when the app is entering the background state, for example when a user hits the home button or switches app:

1. Use the `WaitAsync` method to ensure that there is no thread that is trying to create a connection or to dispose of a connection when we are running the method.
2. Add an `if` statement to ensure that the hub field isn't `null`.
3. If it is not null, call the `StopAsync` method and the `DisposeAsync` method of the `HubConnection`.
4. Set the `httpClient` field to `null`.
5. Set `IsConnected` to `false`.
6. Release `SemaphoreSlim` with the `Release` method:

```
public async Task Dispose()
{
    await semaphoreSlim.WaitAsync();

    if(hub != null)
```

```
        {
            await hub.StopAsync();
            await hub.DisposeAsync();
        }

        httpClient = null;

        IsConnected = false;

        semaphoreSlim.Release();
    }
```

Initializing the app

We are now ready to write the initialization code for the app. We will set up **Inversion-of-Control (IoC)** and carry out the necessary configuration.

Creating a resolver

We will create a helper class that will ease the process of resolving object graphs through Autofac. This will help us to create types based on a configured IoC container. In this project, we will use `Autofac` as the IoC library:

1. Install the `NuGet` package, `Autofac`, in the `Chat` project.
2. Create a new class called `Resolver` in the `Chat` project.
3. Add a `private static` field called `container` of the `IContainer` type (from `Autofac`).
4. Add a public static method called `Initialize` with `IContainer` as a parameter. Set the value of the parameter to the container field.
5. Add a generic static public method called `Resolve`, which will return an instance that is based on the argument type with the `Resolve` method of `IContainer`:

   ```
   using Autofac;

   public class Resolver
   {
       private static IContainer container;

       public static void Initialize(IContainer container)
       {
           Resolver.container = container;
       }
   ```

```
public static T Resolve<T>()
{
    return container.Resolve<T>();
}
}
```

Creating a Bootstrapper

Here, we will create a `Bootstrapper` class that we will use to set up the common configurations that we need in the startup phase of the app. Usually, there is one part of the Bootstrapper for each target platform and one that is shared for all platforms. In this project, we only need the shared part:

1. Create a new class called `Bootstrapper` in the `Chat` project.
2. Add a new public static method called `Init`.
3. Create a new `ContainerBuilder` and register the types to the `container`.
4. Create a `Container` using the `Build` method of the `ContainerBuilder`. Create a variable called `container` that should contain the instance of the `Container`.
5. Use the `Initialize` method on the `Resolver` and pass the `container` variable as an argument, as shown in the following code:

```
using Autofac;
using Chat.Chat;
using System;
using System.Reflection;

public class Bootstrapper
{
    public static void Init()
    {
        var builder = new ContainerBuilder();

        builder.RegisterType<ChatService>().As<IChatService>
        ().SingleInstance();

        var currentAssembly = Assembly.GetExecutingAssembly();

        builder.RegisterAssemblyTypes(currentAssembly)
                .Where(x => x.Name.EndsWith("View",
                StringComparison.Ordinal));

        builder.RegisterAssemblyTypes(currentAssembly)
                .Where(x => x.Name.EndsWith("ViewModel",
                StringComparison.Ordinal));
```

```
                        var container = builder.Build();

                        Resolver.Initialize(container);
                }
        }
```

Call the `Init` method of the `Bootstrapper` in the constructor in the `App.xaml.cs` file after the call to `InitializeComponents`:

```
public App()
{
    InitializeComponent();
    Bootstrapper.Init();
    MainPage = new MainPage();
}
```

Creating a base ViewModel

We now have a service that is responsible for handling the communication with the backend. It's time to create a view model. First, however, we will create a base view model, where we can put the code that will be shared between all view models of the app:

1. Create a new folder called `ViewModels`.
2. Create a new class called `ViewModel`.
3. Make the new class public and abstract.
4. Add a static field called `Navigation` of the `INavigation` type. This will be used to store a reference to the navigation services provided by Xamarin.Forms.
5. Add a static field called `User` of the `string` type. The field will be used when connecting to the chat service so that messages you send will be displayed with your name attached.
6. Add and implement the `INotifiedPropertyChanged` interface. This is necessary because we want to use data bindings.
7. Add a `Set` method that will make it easier for us to raise the `PropertyChanged` event from the `INotifiedPropertyChanged` interface. The method will check if the value has changed. If it has, it will raise the event:

   ```
   using System.Collections.Generic;
   using System.ComponentModel;
   using System.Runtime.CompilerServices;
   using Xamarin.Forms;

   public abstract class ViewModel : INotifyPropertyChanged
   ```

```
        {
            public static INavigation Navigation { get; set; }
            public static string User { get; set; }

            public event PropertyChangedEventHandler PropertyChanged;
            protected void Set<T>(ref T field, T newValue,
                                  [CallerMemberName] string propertyName =
                                  null)
        {
            if (!EqualityComparer<T>.Default.Equals(field, newValue))
            {
                field = newValue;
                PropertyChanged?.Invoke(this, new
                PropertyChangedEventArgs(propertyName));
            }
        }
    }
}
```

Creating the Mainview

Now that we have our `ViewModel` base class set up and all of the code for receiving and sending messages, it's time to create the two views. These will act as the user interface of the app.

We are going to start by creating the main view. This is the view that will be displayed when the user starts the app. We will add an entry control (an input textbox) so that the user can enter a username and add a command to navigate to the chat view.

The main view will be composed of the following:

- A `ViewModel` file called `MainViewModel.cs`
- An XAML file called `MainView.xaml`, which contains the layout
- A code-behind file called `MainView.xaml.cs`, which will carry out the data-binding

Let's start by creating the `ViewModel` for the `MainView`.

Creating MainViewModel

The `MainViewModel` that we are about to create will hold a username that the user will enter in the UI. It will also contain a `Command` property called `Start` that will be bound to a `Button` that the user will click after entering their username:

1. In the `ViewModel` folder, create a class called `MainViewModel.cs`.
2. Inherit the class from `ViewModel`.
3. Make the class `public`.
4. Add a property called `Username` of the `string` type.
5. Add a property called `Start` of the `ICommand` type and implement it as shown as the following. The `Start` command will assign the `Username` from the `Username` property and assign it to the static `User` property in the base `ViewModel`. It then creates a new instance of `ChatView` by using the `Resolver` and pushing it onto the navigation stack.

`MainViewModel` should now look as follows:

```
using System.Windows.Input;
using Chat.Views;
using Xamarin.Forms;

namespace Chat.ViewModels
{
    public class MainViewModel : ViewModel
    {
        public string Username { get; set; }

        public ICommand Start => new Command(() =>
        {
            User = Username;

            var chatView = Resolver.Resolve<ChatView>();
            Navigation.PushAsync(chatView);
        });
    }
}
```

Now that we have the `MainViewModel`, we need a view that goes with it. It's time to create the `MainView`.

Creating the MainView

The `MainView` will display a user interface that allows the user to enter a name before starting the chat. This section will be about creating the `MainView` XAML file and the code behind that view.

We will start by removing the template-generated `MainPage` and replacing it with an MVVM-friendly `MainView`.

Replacing the MainPage

When we created the app, the template generated a page called `MainPage`. Since we are using MVVM as a pattern, we need to remove this page and replace it with a view called `MainView` instead:

1. In the root of the `Chat` project, delete the page called `MainPage`.
2. Create a new folder called `Views`.
3. Add a new XAML page called `MainView` in the `Views` folder.

Editing the XAML

It's now time to add some content to the newly created `MainView.xaml` file. The icons that are mentioned next can be found in the same folder that they should be added to if you go to the project on GitHub. The GitHub URL can be found at the beginning of this chapter. There is a lot going on here, so make sure to check what you write against the code:

1. Add the `chat.png` icon to the `Drawable` folder that is inside the `Resources` folder in the Android project.
2. Add the `chat@2x.png` icon to the `Resources` folder in the iOS project.
3. Open the `MainView.xaml` file.
4. Add a `Title` property in the `ContentPage` node. This will be the title displayed in the navigation bar of the app.
5. Add a `Grid` and define two rows in it. The first one should have a height of `"*"` and the second one of `"2*"`. This will partition the space in two rows, of which the first will take up 1/3 of the space and the second will take up 2/3 of the space.
6. Add an `Image` with the `Source` set to `"chat.png"` and its `VerticalOptions` and `HorizontalOptions` set to `"Center"`.

7. Add `StackLayout` with the `Grid.Row` set to `"1"`, the `Padding` set to `"10"`, and the `Spacing` set to `"20"`. The `Grid.Row` property positions the `StackLayout` in the second row. The `Padding` adds 10 units of space around the `StackLayout` and the `Spacing` defines the amount of space between each element added in the `StackLayout`.

8. In the `StackLayout`, add an `Entry` node that has its `Text` property set to `"{Binding UserName}"` and a `Placeholder` property set to `"Enter a username"`. The binding of the Text node will make sure that, when the user enters a value in the `Entry` control, it's updated in the `ViewModel`.

9. In the `StackLayout`, add a `Button` control that will have the `Text` property set to `"Start"` and its `Command` property set to `"{Binding Start}"`. The `Command` property binding will execute when the user taps the button. It will run the code that we defined in the `MainViewModel` class.

When finished, the code should look as follows:

```xml
<?xml version="1.0" encoding="UTF-8"?>
<ContentPage xmlns="http://xamarin.com/schemas/2014/forms"
             xmlns:x="http://schemas.microsoft.com/winfx/2009/xaml"
             x:Class="Chat.Views.MainView" Title="Welcome">
    <Grid>
        <Grid.RowDefinitions>
            <RowDefinition Height="*" />
            <RowDefinition Height="2*" />
        </Grid.RowDefinitions>
        <Image Source="chat.png" VerticalOptions="Center"
                               HorizontalOptions="Center" />
        <StackLayout Grid.Row="1" Padding="10" Spacing="20">
            <Entry Text="{Binding Username}"
            Placeholder="Enter a username" />
            <Button Text="Start" Command="{Binding Start}" />
        </StackLayout>
    </Grid>
</ContentPage>
```

The layout is finished and we now need to turn our focus to the code behind this view to wire up some loose ends.

Fixing the code behind the view

As with all views, when using MVVM, we need to pass our view a `ViewModel`. Since we are using dependency injection in this project, we will pass it through the constructor and then assign it to the `BindingContext` of the view itself. We will also make sure that we enable safe areas to avoid controls being partially hidden behind the iPhone X notch at the top:

1. Open the `MainView.xaml.cs` file.
2. Add a parameter called `viewModel` of the `MainViewModel` type in the constructor of the `MainView` class. The argument for this parameter will be injected by `Autofac` at runtime.
3. Add a `platform-specific` statement that instructs the application to use safe areas on iOS. A safe area makes sure that the app does not use the space on the side of the notch at the top of the screen on an iPhone X.
4. Assign the `viewModel` argument to the `BindingContext` property of the view.

The changes made are marked in bold in the code, as follows:

```
using Chat.ViewModels;
using Xamarin.Forms;
using Xamarin.Forms.PlatformConfiguration.iOSSpecific;
using Xamarin.Forms.Xaml;

public partial class MainView : ContentPage
{
        public MainView(MainViewModel viewModel)
        {
            InitializeComponent();

            On<Xamarin.Forms.PlatformConfiguration.iOS>
            ().SetUseSafeArea(true);

            BindingContext = viewModel;
        }
    }
```

Our `MainView` is complete but we still need to tell the application to use it as the entry point view.

Setting the main view

The entry point view, also referred to as the application's `MainPage`, is set during the initialization of a Xamarin.Forms app. Usually, it is set in the constructor of the App class. We will be creating the `MainView` through the resolver we created earlier and wrapping it in `NavigationPage` to enable platform-specific navigation on the device that the app runs on:

1. Open the `App.xaml.cs` file.
2. Resolve an instance to a `MainView` class by using the `Resolver` and storing it in a variable called `mainView`.
3. Create a new instance of `NavigationPage` by passing the `mainView` variable as a constructor argument and assigning it to a variable called `navigationPage`.
4. Assign the `navigationPage.Navigation` property to the static `Navigation` property on the `ViewModel` type. This property will be used when navigating between pages later on.
5. Assign the `navigationPage` variable to the `MainPage` property on the App class. This sets the start view of our application:

```
public App()
{
    InitializeComponent();
    Boostrapper.Init();

    var mainView = Resolver.Resolve<MainView>();
    var navigationPage = new NavigationPage(mainView);
    ViewModel.Navigation = navigationPage.Navigation;
    MainPage = navigationPage;
}
```

That's it for the `MainView`; nice and easy. Let's now move on to something more interesting: the `ChatView` that will be used to send and receive messages.

Creating the ChatView

The `ChatView` is a standard chat client. It will have an area for displaying incoming and outgoing messages and a text field at the bottom in which the user can type a message. It will also have a button for taking a photo and a button for sending messages if the user doesn't hit return on the on-screen keyboard.

We will start by creating the ChatViewModel that contains all of the logic by acting as the glue between the view and the model. Our model, in this case, is represented by our ChatService.

After that, we will create the ChatView that handles the rendering of the **Graphical User Interface (GUI)**.

Creating the ChatViewModel

As stated previously, the ChatViewModel is the glue between the visual representation (the View) and the model (which is basically our ChatService). The ChatViewModel will handle the storing of messages and the communication with the ChatService by hooking up the functionality to send and receive messages.

Creating the class

The ChatViewModel is a simple class that inherits from the ViewModel base class we created earlier. In the first code exercise, we will create the class, adding relevant using statements and a property called Messages in which we will store the messages that we have received. The view will use the Message collection to display the messages in a ListView.

Since this is a large block of code, we recommend that you write it first and then go over the numbered list to get to grips with what has been added to the class:

1. Create a new class called ChatViewModel in the ViewModels folder of the Chat project.
2. Make the class public and inherit it from the ViewModel base class to gain the common base functionality from the base class.
3. Add a readonly property called chatService of the IChatService type. This will store a reference to an object that implements IChatService and make the concrete implementation of ChatService replaceable. It's good practice to expose any service as an interface.
4. Add a public property called Messages of the public ObservableCollection<Message> type with a private setter. This collection will hold all messages. The private setter makes the property inaccessible from outside this class. This maintains the integrity of the collection by ensuring messages are not inserted anywhere but inside the class.

5. Add a constructor parameter called `chatService` of the `IChatService` type. When we use dependency injection, this is where `Autofac` will inject an object that implements `IChatService`.

6. In the constructor, assign the `chatService` parameter to the `chatService` property. This will store the reference to the `ChatService` so that we can use it during the lifetime of the `ChatViewModel`.

7. In the constructor, instantiate the `Messages` property to a new `ObservableCollection<Message>`.

8. In the constructor, create a `Task.Run` statement that will call the `chatService.CreateConnection()` method if the `chatService.IsConnected` property is `false`. End the `Task.Run` statement by sending a new `UserConnected` message:

```
using System;
using System.Collections.ObjectModel;
using System.IO;
using System.Linq;
using System.Threading.Tasks;
using System.Windows.Input;
using Acr.UserDialogs;
using Chat.Messages;
using Chat.Services;
using Plugin.Media;
using Plugin.Media.Abstractions;
using Xamarin.Forms;

namespace Chat.ViewModels
{
    public class ChatViewModel : ViewModel
    {
        private readonly IChatService chatService;
        public ObservableCollection<Message> Messages { get;
        private set; }

        public ChatViewModel(IChatService chatService)
        {
            this.chatService = chatService;

            Messages = new ObservableCollection<Message>();

            Task.Run(async() =>
            {
                if(!chatService.IsConnected)
                {
                    await chatService.CreateConnection();
```

```
                                }
                                await chatService.SendMessage(new
                                UserConnectedMessage(User));
                        });
                    }
                }
            }
```

Now that we have our `ChatViewModel` instantiated, it's time to add a property that will hold whatever the user is typing at that moment.

Adding the text property

At the bottom of the GUI, there will be a text field (an entry control) that will allow the user to enter the message. This entry will be data-bound to a property that we will call `Text` in the `ChatViewModel`. Whenever the user changes the text, this property will be set. This is classic data binding:

1. Add a new private field called `text` of the `string` type.
2. Add a public property called `Text` that returns the private text field in the getter and makes a call to the `Set()` method of the base class in the setter. The `Set` method is defined in the `ViewModel` base class and will raise an event back to the view if the property changes in the `ChatViewModel`, effectively keeping them in sync:

```
private string text;
public string Text
{
    get => text;
    set => Set(ref text, value);
}
```

We now have a property ready for data-binding. Let's look at some code for receiving messages from the `ChatService`.

Receiving messages

When a message is sent from the server, over SignalR, the `ChatService` will parse this message and transform it into a Message object. It will then raise an event called `NewMessage`, which is defined in the ChatService.

What we will do in this section is implement an event handler to handle these events and add them to the Messages collection, unless a message with the same ID already exists in the collection.

Again, follow the steps and look at the code:

1. In the `ChatViewModel`, create a method called `ChatService_NewMessage`, which will be a standard event handler. This has two parameters: `sender`, which is of the `object` type, and e, which is of the `Events.NewMessageEventArgs` type.

2. Wrap the code in this method in a `Device.BeginInvokeOnMainThread()` since we are going to add messages to the Message collection. Items added to this collection will be modifying the view and any code that modifies the view must be run on the UI thread.

3. In the `Device.BeginInvokeOnMainThread`, add the incoming message from `e.Message` to the `Messages` collection if a message with the specific `Message.Id` isn't already present in the collection. This is to avoid message duplication.

The method should look as follows:

```
private void ChatService_NewMessage(object sender,
Events.NewMessageEventArgs e)
{
    Device.BeginInvokeOnMainThread(() =>
    {
        if (!Messages.Any(x => x.Id == e.Message.Id))
        {
            Messages.Add(e.Message);
        }
    });
}
```

When the event handler is defined, we need to hook it up in the constructor:

1. Locate the constructor of the `ChatViewModel` class.

2. Wire up a `chatService.NewMessage` event to the `ChatService_NewMessage` handler we just created. A good place to do this is under the instantiation of the `Messages` collection.

The code marked in bold is what we should add to the `ChatViewModel` class:

```
public ChatViewModel(IChatService chatService)
{
    this.chatService = chatService;

    Messages = new ObservableCollection<Message>();

    chatService.NewMessage += ChatService_NewMessage;

    Task.Run(async() =>
    {
        if(!chatService.IsConnected)
        {
            await chatService.CreateConnection();
        }

        await chatService.SendMessage(new UserConnectedMessage(User));
    });
}
```

The app will now be able to receive messages. How about sending them? Well, stay tuned!

Creating the LocalSimpleTextMessage class

To make it easier to recognize whether a message is coming from the server or whether it is sent by the user of the device that the code is executing on, we will create a `LocalSimpleTextMessage`:

1. Create a new class with the name `LocalSimpleTextMessage` in the `Chat.Messages` project.
2. Add `SimpleTextMessage` as the base class.
3. Create a constructor with `SimpleTextMessage` as the parameter.
4. Set the value to all of the base properties with the value from the parameter, as in the code that follows:

```
public class LocalSimpleTextMessage : SimpleTextMessage
{
    public LocalSimpleTextMessage(SimpleTextMessage message)
    {
        Id = message.Id;
        Text = message.Text;
        Timestamp = message.Timestamp;
        Username = message.Username;
        TypeInfo = message.TypeInfo;
```

```
    }
  }
```

Sending text messages

Sending text messages is also very straightforward. We need to create a command that we can data-bind for the GUI. The command will be executed either when the user hits return or when the user clicks the send button. When a user does either of these two things, the command will create a new `SimpleTextMessage` and pass in the current user to identify the message for other users. We will copy the text from the `ChatViewModel` text property, which, in turn, is in sync with the `Entry` control.

We will then add the message to the Messages collection, triggering the `ListView` that will be handling messages to update. After that, we will pass the message to the `ChatService` and clear the `ChatViewModel` text property. By doing this, we notify the GUI that it has changed and let the data-binding magic clear the field.

Refer to the following steps and look at the code:

1. Create a new property called `Send` of the `ICommand` type.
2. Assign it a new `Command` instance and follow these steps to implement it.
3. Create a new instance of a `SimpleTextMessage` class by passing the User property of the base class as an argument. Assign the instance to a variable called `message`.
4. Set the `Text` property of the message variable to the `Text` property of the `ChatViewModel` class. This copies the current text in the chat entry defined by the GUI later on.
5. Create a `LocalSimpleTextMessage` object and pass in the message variable as a constructor argument. The `LocalSimpleTextMessage` is a `SimpleTextMessage` and makes it possible for the view to recognize it as a message that the user of the app sent, effectively rendering it on the right side of the chat area. Add the `LocalSimpleTextMessage` instance to the Messages collection. This will display the message in the view.
6. Make a call to the `chatService.SendMessage()` method and pass the message variable as an argument.

7. Empty the `Text` property of the `ChatViewModel` to clear the entry control in the GUI:

```
public ICommand Send => new Command(async()=>
{
    var message = new SimpleTextMessage(User)
    {
        Text = this.Text
    };

    Messages.Add(new LocalSimpleTextMessage(message));

    await chatService.SendMessage(message);

    Text = string.Empty;
});
```

What good is a chat app if we can't send photos? Let's implement this in the next section.

Installing the Acr.UserDialogs plugin

`Acr.UserDialogs` is a plugin that makes it possible to use several standard user dialogs from code that are shared between platforms. To install and configure it, there are a few steps we need to follow:

1. Install the `Acr.UserDialogs` NuGet package to the `Chat-`, `Chat.iOS`, and `Chat.Android` projects.
2. In the `MainActivity.cs` file, add `UserDialogs.Init(this)` in the `OnCreate` method:

```
protected override void OnCreate(Bundle savedInstanceState)
{
    TabLayoutResource = Resource.Layout.Tabbar;
    ToolbarResource = Resource.Layout.Toolbar;
    base.OnCreate(savedInstanceState);
    UserDialogs.Init(this);

    global::Xamarin.Forms.Forms.Init(this, savedInstanceState);
    LoadApplication(new App());
}
```

Installing the Media plugin

We will use the `Xam.Plugin.Media` NuGet package to access the photo library of the device. We need to install the package to the `Chat-`, `Chat.iOS`, and `Chat.Android` projects in the solution. Before we can use the package, however, we need to do some configuration for each platform. We will start with Android:

1. The plugin needs the `WRITE_EXTERNAL_STORAGE` and `READ_EXTERNAL_STORAGE` permissions. The plugin will add these for us, but we need to override the `OnRequestPermissionResult` in the `MainActivity.cs`.

2. Call the `OnRequestPermissionsResult` method.

3. Add `CrossCurrentActivity.Current.Init(this, savedInstanceState)` after the initalizing of Xamarin.Forms in the `OnCreate` method in the `MainActivity.cs` file, as shown in the following code:

```
public override void OnRequestPermissionsResult(int requestCode,
string[] permissions, Android.Content.PM.Permission[] grantResults)
{
Plugin.Permissions.PermissionsImplementation.Current.OnRequestPermi
ssionsResult(requestCode, permissions, grantResults);
}
```

We also need to add some configuration for the file paths from which the users can pick photos:

1. Add a folder called `xml` to the `Resources` folder in the Android project.

2. Create a new XML file called `file_paths.xml` in the new folder.

3. Add the following code to `file_paths.xml`:

```
<?xml version="1.0" encoding="utf-8"?>
<paths xmlns:android="http://schemas.android.com/apk/res/android">
    <external-files-path name="my_images" path="Pictures" />
    <external-files-path name="my_movies" path="Movies" />
</paths>
```

The last thing we need to do to set up the plugin for the Android project is to add the code that follows in the `AndroidManifest.xml` field inside the application element:

```
<manifest xmlns:android="http://schemas.android.com/apk/res/android"
android:versionCode="1" android:versionName="1.0" package="xfb.Chat">
<uses-sdk android:minSdkVersion="21" android:targetSdkVersion="27" />
    <application android:label="Chat.Android">
        <provider
        android:name="android.support.v4.content.FileProvider"
```

```
        android:authorities="${applicationId}.fileprovider"
        android:exported="false" android:grantUriPermissions="true">
        <meta-data android:name="android.support.FILE_PROVIDER_PATHS"
        android:resource="@xml/file_paths"></meta-data>
        </provider>
    </application>
</manifest>
```

For the iOS project, the only thing we need to do is to add the following four usage descriptions to the `info.plist`:

```
<key>NSPhotoLibraryUsageDescription</key>
<string>This app needs access to photos.</string>
<key>NSPhotoLibraryAddUsageDescription</key>
<string>This app needs access to the photo gallery.</string>
```

Sending photos

To be able to send photos, we will have to use a source of photos. In our case, we will be using the camera as the source. The camera will return the photo as a stream after it has been taken. We need to convert that stream into a byte array and then finally Base64 encode it into a string that is easy to send over SignalR.

The method that we are about to create, called `ReadFully()`, takes a stream and turns it into a byte array, which is a step towards achieving the Base64-encoded string. This is a standard piece of code that creates a buffer that will be used when we are reading the `Stream` parameter and writing it to the `MemoryStream` in chunks until we have read the full stream, hence the name of the method.

Follow along and check out the code:

1. Create a method called `ReadFully` that takes a `stream` called `input` as a parameter and returns a `byte` array.
2. Declare a `buffer` variable of the `byte[]` type and initialize it as a 16 KB big byte array. (`16 * 1024`)
3. Inside a using statement, create a new `MemoryStream` called `ms`.
4. Read the input of the `Stream` into the `ms` variable:

```
private byte[] ReadFully(Stream input)
{
    byte[] buffer = new byte[16 * 1024];
    using (MemoryStream ms = new MemoryStream())
    {
        int read;
```

```
        while ((read = input.Read(buffer, 0, buffer.Length)) >
0)
        {
            ms.Write(buffer, 0, read);
        }
        return ms.ToArray();
    }
}
```

Following this, we have a large chunk of code. This code exposes a command that will be executed when the user clicks the photo button in the app. It starts by configuring `CrossMedia` (a media plugin), which indicates the quality the photo should be, and then it starts the photo picker. When the photo picker returns from the `async` call to `PickPhotoAsync()`, we start uploading the photo. To notify the user, we use `UserDialogs.Instance.ShowLoading` to create a loading overlay with a message to indicate that we are uploading the photo.

We will then get the stream of the photo, convert it into a byte array using the `ReadFully()` method, and Base64 encode it into a string. The string will be wrapped in a `PhotoMessage` instance, added to the local `Message` collection of the `ChatViewModel`, and then sent to the server.

Follow the steps and study the code:

1. Create a new property called `Photo` of the `ICommand` type. Assign it a new `Command` instance.
2. Create an anonymous `async` method (a lambda expression) and add the code defined in the upcoming steps into it. You can see the full code of the method in the code section following.
3. Create a new instance of the `PickMediaOptions` class and set the `CompressionQuality` property to 50.
4. Call `CrossMedia.Current.PickPhotoAsync` with an `async` method call and save the result to a local variable called `photo`.
5. Install the NuGet package.
6. Show a message dialog by calling `UserDialogs.Instance.ShowLoading()` with the text, "Uploading photo".
7. Get the photo stream by calling the `GetStream()` method of the photo variable and save it to a variable called `stream`.

8. Convert the stream in to a byte array by calling the `ReadFully()` method.

9. Convert the byte array in to a Base64-encoded string using the `Convert.ToBase64String()` method. Save the string to a variable called `base64photo`.

10. Create a new `PhotoMessage` instance and pass the `User` as the constructor argument. Set the `Base64Photo` property to the `base64photo` variable and the `FileEnding` property to the file ending of the `photo.Path` string, using the `Split` function of the string object. Store the new `PhotoMessage` instance in a variable called `message`.

11. Add the message object to the `Messages` collection.

12. Send the message to the server by calling the async `chatService.SendMessage()` method.

13. Hide the loading dialog by calling `UserDialogs.Instance.HideLoading()`.

The code that follows shows how this can be implemented:

```
public ICommand Photo => new Command(async() =>
{
    var options = new PickMediaOptions();
    options.CompressionQuality = 50;

    var photo = await CrossMedia.Current.PickPhotoAsync();

    UserDialogs.Instance.ShowLoading("Uploading photo");

    var stream = photo.GetStream();
    var bytes = ReadFully(stream);

    var base64photo = Convert.ToBase64String(bytes);

    var message = new PhotoMessage(User)
    {
        Base64Photo = base64photo,
        FileEnding = photo.Path.Split('.').Last()
    };

    Messages.Add(message);
    await chatService.SendMessage(message);

    UserDialogs.Instance.HideLoading();
});
```

The `ChatViewModel` is complete. It's now time to visualize our GUI.

Creating the ChatView

The `ChatView` is responsible for creating the user interface that the user will interact with. It will display local and remote messages, both text and photos, and also notify a user when a remote user has joined the chat. We'll start by creating a converter that will convert photos represented as a Base64-encoded string into an `ImageSource` that can be used as the source of the image control in XAML.

Creating Base64ToImageConverter

When we take a picture using the phone's camera, it will be handed to us as a byte array. In order to send this to the server, we will convert in it to a Base64-encoded string. To display that message locally, we will need to convert it back into a byte array and then pass that byte array to a helper method of the `ImageSource` class to create an instance of the `ImageSource` object. This object will make sense to the `Image` control and an image will be displayed.

Since there is a lot of code here, we suggest you follow the steps and look at each line of code in detail as you follow them:

1. Create a folder called `Converters` in the `Chat` project.
2. Create a new class called `Base64ImageConverter` in the `Converters` folder; let the class implement the `IValueConverter` interface.
3. In the `Convert()` method of the class, cast the object parameter called value to a string called `base64String`.
4. Convert the `base64String` to a byte array using the `System.Convert.FromBase64String()` method. Save the result to a variable called `bytes`.
5. Create a new `MemoryStream` by passing the byte array into its constructor. Save the stream to a variable called `stream`.
6. Call the `ImageSource.FromStream()` method and pass the stream as a lambda expression that returns the stream variable. Return the `ImageSource` object created.
7. The `ConvertBack()` method does not need to be implemented since we will never convert an image back into a Base64-encoded string via data-binding. We will just let it throw a `NotImplementedException`:

```
using System;
using System.Globalization;
using Xamarin.Forms;
using System.IO;
```

```
namespace Chat.Converters
{
    public class Base64ToImageConverter : IValueConverter
    {
        public object Convert(object value, Type targetType,
                              object parameter, CultureInfo
culture)
        {
            var base64string = (string)value;
            var bytes =
            System.Convert.FromBase64String(base64string);
            var stream = new MemoryStream(bytes);
            return ImageSource.FromStream(() => stream);
        }

        public object ConvertBack(object value, Type targetType,
                                  object parameter, CultureInfo
                                  culture)
        {
            throw new NotImplementedException();
        }
    }
}
```

Now it's time to start adding some actual XAML code to the view. We will start by creating the main layout skeleton that we will then gradually build on until we have the finished view.

Creating the skeleton ChatView

This XAML file will contain the view that lists messages we have sent and messages we have received. It's quite a large file to create, so for this part, I suggest that you copy the XAML and study every step carefully:

1. Create a new XAML Content Page in the Views folder called ChatView.
2. Add XML namespaces for Chat.Selectors and Chat.Converters and call them selectors and converters.
3. Add a ContentPage.Resources node that will, later on, contain resources for this view.
4. Add ScrollView as the page content.
5. Add Grid as the only child of the ScrollView and name it MainGrid by setting the x:Name property to MainGrid.

6. Create a `RowDefinitions` element that contains three rows. The first should have a height of `*`, the second a height of 1, and the third a platform-specific height based on the platform using an `OnPlatform` element.

7. Save some space for the `ListView` that will be inserted later on.

8. Add a `BoxView` that will act as a visual divider by setting the `HeightRequest` property to 1, the `BackgroundColor` property to `#33000000`, and the `Grid.Row` property to 1. This will position the `BoxView` in the one-unit-high row of the grid, effectively drawing a single line across the screen.

9. Add another `Grid` that will use the space of the third row by setting the `Grid.Row` property to 2. Also, add some padding by setting the `Padding` property to 10. Define three rows in the grid with heights of 30, `*`, and 30:

```xml
<?xml version="1.0" encoding="UTF-8"?>
<ContentPage xmlns="http://xamarin.com/schemas/2014/forms"
             xmlns:x="http://schemas.microsoft.com/winfx/2009/xaml"
             xmlns:selectors="clr-namespace:Chat.Selectors"
             xmlns:converters="clr-namespace:Chat.Converters"
             x:Class="Chat.Views.ChatView">
    <ContentPage.Resources>
        <!-- TODO Add resources -->
    </ContentPage.Resources>
    <ScrollView>
        <Grid x:Name="MainGrid">
            <Grid.RowDefinitions>
                <RowDefinition Height="*" />
                <RowDefinition Height="1" />
                <RowDefinition>
                    <RowDefinition.Height>
                        <OnPlatform x:TypeArguments="GridLength">
                            <On Platform="iOS" Value="50" />
                            <On Platform="Android" Value="100" />
                        </OnPlatform>
                    </RowDefinition.Height>
                </RowDefinition>
            </Grid.RowDefinitions>

            <!-- TODO Add ListView -->
            <BoxView Grid.Row="1" HeightRequest="1"
            BackgroundColor="#33000000" />
            <Grid Grid.Row="2" Padding="10">
                <Grid.ColumnDefinitions>
                    <ColumnDefinition Width="30" />
                    <ColumnDefinition Width="*" />
                    <ColumnDefinition Width="30" />
                </Grid.ColumnDefinitions>
```

```
            <!-- TODO Add buttons and entry controls -->
          </Grid>
        </Grid>
      </ScrollView>
    </ContentPage>
```

Now that we have completed the main skeleton of our page, we need to start adding some specific content. First, we will add `ResourceDictionary` to create a `DataTemplate` selector that will select the correct layouts for different chat messages. Then, we need to put the `Base64ToImageConverter` to use and, to do that, we need to define it in the view.

Adding ResourceDictionary

It's now time to add some resources to the view. In this case, we will be adding a template selector that we will create later on, and the `Base64ToImageConverter` that we created earlier. The template selector will look at each row that we will bind to the `ListView`, which will be presenting messages and selecting the best layout template that suits that message. To be able to use these pieces of code from XAML, we need to define a way for the XAML parser to find them:

1. Locate the `<!-- TODO Add resources -->` comment inside the `ContentPage.Resources` element.

2. Add the XAML in the sample as follows, right underneath this comment mentioned in *step 1*:

   ```
   <ResourceDictionary>
       <selectors:ChatMessageSelector
       x:Key="SelectMessageTemplate" />
       <converters:Base64ToImageConverter x:Key="ToImage" />
   </ResourceDictionary>
   ```

This will create one instance of each resource that we define and make it accessible to the rest of the view.

Adding ListView

We will be using a `ListView` to display the messages in the chat app. Again, follow the steps and take a look at the code to make sure you understand each step:

1. Locate the `<!-- TODO Add ListView -->` comment in the `ChatView.xaml` file.

2. Add a `ListView` and set the `x:Name` property to `MessageList`.

3. Data-bind the `ListView` by setting the `ItemsSource` property to `{Binding Messages}`. This will make the `ListView` aware of changes in the `ObservableCollection<Message>`, which is exposed through the `Messages` property. Any time a message is added or removed, the `ListView` will update to reflect this change.

4. Add the `SelectMessageTemplate` resource we defined in the previous section to the `ItemTemplate` property. This will run some code each time that an item is added to make sure that we programmatically select the correct visual template for a specific message. No worries, we will soon write that code.

5. Make sure that the `ListView` is able to create rows of uneven height by setting the `HasUnevenRows` property to `true`.

6. The last property we need to set is the `SeparatorVisibility`, and we set it to `None` to avoid a row in between each row.

7. We define a placeholder where we will add resources. The resources we will be adding are the different `DataTemplate` that we will be using to render different types of messages.

The XAML should look as follows:

```
<ListView x:Name="MessageList" ItemsSource="{Binding Messages}"
  ItemTemplate="{StaticResource SelectMessageTemplate}"
  HasUnevenRows="true" SeparatorVisibility="None">
    <ListView.Resources>
      <ResourceDictionary>
        <!-- Resources go here later on -->
      </ResourceDictionary>
    </ListView.Resources>
</ListView>
```

Adding templates

We will now be adding five different templates, each corresponding to a specific message type that the app either sends or receives. Each of these templates goes under the `<!-- Resources go here later on -->` comment from the code snippet in the previous section.

We will not be explaining each of these templates step by step, since the XAML that they contain should be starting to feel familiar at this point.

Each template starts the same way: the root element is a `DataTemplate` with a name set. The name is important because we will be referencing it in code very soon. The first child of the `DataTemplate` is always `ViewCell` with the `IsEnabled` property set to `false` to avoid the user being able to interact with the content. We simply want to display it. The content that follows after this element is the actual content that the row will be constructed from.

Bindings inside the `ViewCell` will also be local to each item or row that the `ListView` renders. In this case, this will be an instance of a `Message` class, since we are data binding the `ListView` to a collection of Message objects. You will see some `StyleClass` properties in the code. These will be used when we do the final styling of the app using **Cascading Style Sheets (CSS)**.

Our task here is to write each of these templates under the `<!-- Resources go here later on -->` comment.

The `SimpleText` is the `DataTemplate` that is selected when the Message is a remote message. It will be rendered on the left side of the list view, just as you might expect. It displays a `username` and a `text` message:

```
<DataTemplate x:Key="SimpleText">
    <ViewCell IsEnabled="false">
        <Grid Padding="10">
            <Grid.ColumnDefinitions>
                <ColumnDefinition Width="*" />
                <ColumnDefinition Width="*" />
            </Grid.ColumnDefinitions>
            <Frame StyleClass="remoteMessage" HasShadow="false">
                <StackLayout>
                 <Label Text="{Binding Username}"
                  StyleClass="chatHeader" />
                 <Label Text="{Binding Text}" StyleClass="chatText" />
                </StackLayout>
            </Frame>
        </Grid>
    </ViewCell>
</DataTemplate>
```

The `LocalSimpleText` template is the same as the `SimpleText` data template, except that it renders on the right side of the `ListView` by setting the `Grid.Column` property to 1, effectively using the right column:

```
<DataTemplate x:Key="LocalSimpleText">
    <ViewCell IsEnabled="false">
        <Grid Padding="10">
            <Grid.ColumnDefinitions>
                <ColumnDefinition Width="*" />
                <ColumnDefinition Width="*" />
            </Grid.ColumnDefinitions>
            <Frame Grid.Column="1" StyleClass="localMessage"
            HasShadow="false">
                <StackLayout>
                  <Label Text="{Binding Username}"
                  StyleClass="chatHeader" />
                  <Label Text="{Binding Text}" StyleClass="chatText" />
                </StackLayout>
            </Frame>
        </Grid>
    </ViewCell>
</DataTemplate>
```

This `DataTemplate` is used when a user connects to the chat:

```
<DataTemplate x:Key="UserConnected">
    <ViewCell IsEnabled="false">
        <StackLayout Padding="10" BackgroundColor="#33000000"
        Orientation="Horizontal">
            <Label Text="{Binding Username}" StyleClass="chatHeader"
            VerticalOptions="Center" />
            <Label Text="connected" StyleClass="chatText"
            VerticalOptions="Center" />
        </StackLayout>
    </ViewCell>
</DataTemplate>
```

A photo that is uploaded to the server is accessible via a URL. This `DataTemplate` displays an image based on a URL and is used for remote images:

```
<DataTemplate x:Key="Photo">
    <ViewCell IsEnabled="false">
        <Grid Padding="10">
            <Grid.ColumnDefinitions>
                <ColumnDefinition Width="*" />
                <ColumnDefinition Width="*" />
            </Grid.ColumnDefinitions>
            <StackLayout>
                <Label Text="{Binding Username}"
                 StyleClass="chatHeader" />
                <Image Source="{Binding Url}" Aspect="AspectFill"
                HeightRequest="150" HorizontalOptions="Fill" />
            </StackLayout>
        </Grid>
    </ViewCell>
</DataTemplate>
```

A message that contains a photo that is sent by the user and rendered directly based on the Base64-encoded image that we generate from the camera. Since we don't want to wait for the image to upload, we use this `DataTemplate`, which utilizes the `Base64ImageConverter` that we wrote earlier to transform the string into `ImageSource` that can be displayed by the Image control:

```
<DataTemplate x:Key="LocalPhoto">
    <ViewCell IsEnabled="false">
        <Grid Padding="10">
            <Grid.ColumnDefinitions>
                <ColumnDefinition Width="*" />
                <ColumnDefinition Width="*" />
            </Grid.ColumnDefinitions>
            <StackLayout Grid.Column="1">
                <Label Text="{Binding Username}"
                StyleClass="chatHeader" />
                <Image Source="{Binding Base64Photo, Converter=
                {StaticResource ToImage}}"
                Aspect="AspectFill" HeightRequest="150"
                HorizontalOptions="Fill" />
            </StackLayout>
        </Grid>
    </ViewCell>
</DataTemplate>
```

These are all of the templates we need. It's now time to add some code to make sure we select the right template for the message to display.

Creating a template selector

Using a template selector is a powerful way of injecting different layouts based on the items that are being data-bound. In this case, we will look at each message that we want to display and select the best `DataTemplate` for them. The code is somewhat repetitive, so we will be using the same approach as for the XAML—simply adding the code and letting you study it yourself:

1. Create a folder called `Selectors` in the `Chat` project.
2. Create a new class called `ChatMessagesSelector` in the `Selectors` folder and inherit it from `DataTemplateSelector`.
3. Add the following code, which will look at each object that is data-bound and pull the correct `DataTemplate` from the resources we just added:

```
using Chat.Messages;
using Xamarin.Forms;

namespace Chat.Selectors
{
    public class ChatMessagesSelector : DataTemplateSelector
    {
        protected override DataTemplate OnSelectTemplate(object
        item, BindableObject container)
        {
            var list = (ListView)container;

            if(item is LocalSimpleTextMessage)
            {
                return
            (DataTemplate)list.Resources["LocalSimpleText"];
            }
            else if(item is SimpleTextMessage)
            {
                return (DataTemplate)list.Resources["SimpleText"];
            }
            else if(item is UserConnectedMessage)
            {
                return
            (DataTemplate)list.Resources["UserConnected"];
            }
            else if(item is PhotoUrlMessage)
            {
```

```
                    return (DataTemplate)list.Resources["Photo"];
            }
            else if (item is PhotoMessage)
            {
                    return (DataTemplate)list.Resources["LocalPhoto"];
            }

            return null;
        }
    }
}
```

Adding the buttons and entry control

Now we will add the buttons and the entry that the user will use for writing chat messages. The icons that we are using can be found in the GitHub repository for this chapter. For Android, the icons will be placed in the `Drawable` folder inside the `Resource` folder and for iOS, they will be in the `Resource` folder. The icons are in the same folder on GitHub:

1. Locate the `<!-- TODO Add buttons and entry controls -->` comment in the `ChatView.xaml` file.

2. Add an `ImageButton`. The `Source` should be set to `photo.png`, the `Command` set to `{Binding Photo}`, and the `VerticalOptions` and `HorizontalOptions` set to `Center`. The `Source` is used to display an image; the `Command` will be executed when a user taps the image and the `HorizontalOptions` and `VerticalOptions` will be used to center the image in the middle of the control.

3. Add an `Entry` control to allow the user the enter a message to be sent. The `Text` property should be set to `{Binding Text}`. Set the `Grid.Column` property to 1 and the `ReturnCommand` to `{Binding Send}` to execute the send command in the `ChatViewModel` when a user hits *Enter*.

4. An `ImageButton` with the `Grid.Column` property set to 2, the `Source` set to `send.png`, and the `Command` set to `{Binding Send}` (the same as the return command). Center it horizontally and vertically:

```
<ImageButton Source="photo.png" Command="{Binding Photo}"
        VerticalOptions="Center" HorizontalOptions="Center" />
        <Entry Text="{Binding Text}" Grid.Column="1"
        ReturnCommand="{Binding Send}" />
<ImageButton Grid.Column="2" Source="send.png"
        Command="{Binding Send}"
        VerticalOptions="Center" HorizontalOptions="Center" />
```

Fixing the code behind

Now that the XAML is done, we have some work to do in the code behind. We'll start by modifying the class to be partial and then we'll be adding some using statements:

1. Open the `ChatView.xaml.cs` file.
2. Mark the class as `partial`.
3. Add a `private` field called `viewModel` of the `ChatViewModel` type, which will hold a local reference to the `ChatViewModel`.
4. Add `using statements` for `Chat.ViewModels`, `Xamarin.Forms`, and `Xamarin.Forms.PlatformConfiguration.iOSSpecific`.

The class should now look as follows. The bold code indicates what should have changed:

```
using System.Linq;
using Chat.ViewModels;
using Xamarin.Forms;
using Xamarin.Forms.PlatformConfiguration.iOSSpecific;

namespace Chat.Views
{
    public partial class ChatView : ContentPage
    {
        private ChatViewModel viewModel;
        public ChatView()
        {
            InitializeComponent();
        }
    }
}
```

When a new message arrives, this will be added to the Messages collection in the `ChatViewModel`. To make sure that the `MessageList` and `ListView` scroll appropriately so that the new message is visible, we need to write some additional code:

1. Create a new method called `Messages_CollectionChanged` that takes an object as the first parameter and `NotifyCollectionChangedEventArgs` as the second parameter.
2. Add a call to the `MessageList.ScrollTo()` method and pass the last Message in the `viewModel.Messages` collection by calling `viewModel.Messages.Last()`. The second parameter should be set to `ScrollPosition.End`, indicating that we want to make the entire messages `ListView` row visible. The third parameter should be set to `true` to enable animations.

The method should now look as follows:

```
private void Messages_CollectionChanged(object sender,
            System.Collections.Specialized.NotifyCollectionChangedEventArgs
e)
{
    MessageList.ScrollTo(viewModel.Messages.Last(),
    ScrollToPosition.End, true);
}
```

It's now time to extend the constructor so that it takes `ChatViewModel` as a parameter and sets the `BindingContext` in the way that we are used to. The constructor will also make sure that we use the safe area when rendering controls and that we hook up to the events necessary for handling changes in the `Messages` collection of the `ChatViewModel`:

1. Modify the constructor in the `ChatView` class so that it takes a `ChatViewModel` as the only parameter and name the parameter `viewModel`.
2. Assign the `viewModel` parameter from the constructor to the local `viewModel` field in the class.
3. The call to the `InitializeComponent()` method, add a platform-specific call to the `SetUseSafeArea(true)` method to ensure that the app will be visually safe to use on an iPhone X and not partially hidden behind the notch at the top:

```
public ChatView(ChatViewModel viewModel)
{
    this.viewModel = viewModel;

    InitializeComponent();
    On<Xamarin.Forms.PlatformConfiguration.iOS>
    ().SetUseSafeArea(true);

    viewModel.Messages.CollectionChanged +=
    Messages_CollectionChanged;
    BindingContext = viewModel;
}
```

Every time a view appears, the `OnAppearing()` method is called. This method is virtual and we can override it. We will use this feature to make sure that we will have the correct height on the `MainGrid`. This is because we have to wrap everything in a `ScrollView` because the view has to be able to scroll when the keyboard appears. If we don't calculate the width of the `MainGrid` it could be bigger than the screen because the `ScrollView` allows it to expand:

1. Override the `OnAppearing()` method.
2. Calculate the safe area to use by calling the platform-specific method, `On<Xamarin.Forms.PlatformConfiguration.iOS>().SafeAreaInsets()`. This will return a `Xamarin.Forms.Thickness` object that will contain the inset information we need in order to calculate the height of the `MainGrid`. Assign the `Thickness` object to a variable called `safeArea`.
3. Set the `MainGrid.HeightRequest` property to the height of the view (`this.Height`) and then subtract the `Top` and `Bottom` properties of the `safeArea`:

```
protected override void OnAppearing()
{
    base.OnAppearing();
    var safeArea = On<Xamarin.Forms.PlatformConfiguration.iOS>
    ().SafeAreaInsets();
    MainGrid.HeightRequest = this.Height - safeArea.Top -
    safeArea.Bottom;
}
```

Styling

Styling is an important part of an app. Just like with HTML, you can do styling by setting properties on each control directly, or by setting `Style` elements in the application's resource dictionary. Recently, however, a new way of styling has emerged in Xamarin.Forms, which is using Cascading Style Sheets, better known as CSS.

Since CSS doesn't cover all cases, we will fall back to standard application resource dictionary styling as well.

Styling with CSS

Xamarin.Forms supports styling via CSS files. It has a subset of the functionalities you would expect from normal CSS, but support is getting better with each version. We are going to use two different selectors to apply the styling.

First, let's create the style sheet and we'll discuss the content of it after that:

1. Create a folder called `Css` in the `Chat` project.
2. Create a new text file in the `Css` folder and name it `Styles.css`.
3. Copy the style sheet, shown as follows, into that file:

```css
button {
 background-color: #A4243B;
 color: white;
}

.chatHeader {
 color: white;
 font-style: bold;
 font-size: small;
}

.chatText {
 color: white;
 font-size: small;
}

.remoteMessage {
 background-color: #F04D6A;
 padding: 10;
}

.localMessage {
 background-color: #24A43B;
 padding: 10;
}
```

The first selector, button, applies to every button control in the entire application. It sets the background color to #A4243B and the foreground color to white. You can do this for almost every type of control in Xamarin.Forms.

The second selectors we use are class selectors, which are the ones beginning with a period, such as `.chatHeader`. The selectors are used in the XAML with the `StyleClass` property. Look back at the `ChatView.xaml` file we created earlier and you'll find these in the template resources.

Each property in the CSS is mapped to a property on the control itself. There are also some Xamarin.Forms specific properties that can be used, but those are out of the scope of this book. If you search for Xamarin.Forms and CSS on the internet, you'll find all of the information you need to dive deeper into this.

Applying the style sheet

A style sheet is no good on its own. We need to apply it to our application. We also need to set some styling on the NavigationPage here as well, since we can't gain access to it from the CSS directly.

We will be adding some resources and a reference to the style sheet. Copy the code and refer to the steps to study what each line does:

1. Open the `App.xaml` file in the `Chat` project.
2. In the `Application.Resources` node, add a `<StyleSheet Source="/Css/Styles.css" />` node to reference the style sheet.
3. Following is the `StyleSheet` node. Add a `Style` node with the `TargetType` set to `"NavigationPage"` and create a setter for the `BarBackgroundColor` property with a value of `"#273E47"` and a setter for the `BarTextColor` property with a value of `"White"`.

The `App.xaml` file should now look as follows:

```xml
<?xml version="1.0" encoding="utf-8"?>
<Application xmlns="http://xamarin.com/schemas/2014/forms"
             xmlns:x="http://schemas.microsoft.com/winfx/2009/xaml"
             x:Class="Chat.App">
    <Application.Resources>
        <StyleSheet Source="/Css/Styles.css" />
        <ResourceDictionary>
            <Style TargetType="NavigationPage">
                <Setter Property="BarBackgroundColor" Value="#273E47" />
                <Setter Property="BarTextColor" Value="White" />
            </Style>
        </ResourceDictionary>
    </Application.Resources>
</Application>
```

Handling life cycle events

Finally, we need to add some life cycle events that will take care of our SignalR connection in case the app goes to sleep or when it wakes up again:

1. Open the `App.Xaml.cs` file.
2. Add the code that follows somewhere in the class:

```
protected override void OnSleep()
{
    var chatService = Resolver.Resolve<IChatService>();
    chatService.Dispose();
}
protected override void OnResume()
{
    Task.Run(async() =>
    {
        var chatService = Resolver.Resolve<IChatService>();

        if (!chatService.IsConnected)
        {
            await chatService.CreateConnection();
        }
    });

    Page view = null;

    if(ViewModel.User != null)
    {
        view = Resolver.Resolve<ChatView>();
    }
    else
    {
        view = Resolver.Resolve<MainView>();
    }

    var navigationPage = new NavigationPage(view);
    MainPage = navigationPage;
}
```

The `OnSleep()` method will be called when the user minimizes the app and it will dispose of any active `chatService` that is running by closing the active connections. The `OnResume()` method has a little more content. It will recreate the connection if there isn't one already active and, depending on whether the user is set or not, it will resolve to the correct view. If a user isn't present, it will display the `MainView`; otherwise it will display the `ChatView`. Finally, it sets the selected view, wrapped in a navigation page.

Summary

That's that—good work! We have now created a chat app that connects to our backend. We have learned how to work with SignalR, how to style an app with CSS, how to use template selectors in a `ListView`, and how to use a value converter to convert a `byte[]` into a Xamarin.Forms `ImageSource`.

In the next chapter, we will dive into an augmented world! We will create an AR-game for iOS and Android using UrhoSharp together with ARKit (iOS) and ARCore (Android).

Creating an Augmented-Reality Game

8

In this chapter, we will be exploring **augmented reality (AR)** using Xamarin.Forms. We will be using custom renderers to inject platform-specific code, **UrhoSharp** to render the scene and handle input, and `MessagingCenter` to pass internal messages around in the app.

The following topics will be covered in this chapter:

- Setting up a project
- Using ARKit
- Using ARCore
- Learning how to use UrhoSharp to render graphics and handle input
- Using custom renderers to inject platform-specific code
- Using `MessagingCenter` to send messages

Technical requirements

To be able to complete this project, we need to have Visual Studio for Mac or PC installed, as well as the Xamarin components. See `Chapter 1`, *Introduction to Xamarin*, for more details on how to set up your environment.

You cannot run AR on an emulator. To run AR, you need a physical device, along with the following software:

- On iOS, you need iOS 11 or higher and a device that has an A9 processor or above
- On Android, you need Android 8.1 and a device that supports ARCore

Essential theory

This section will describe how AR works. The implementation differs slightly between platforms. Google's implementation is called **ARCore,** and Apple's implementation is called **ARKit**.

AR is all about superimposing computer graphics on top of a camera feed. This sounds like a simple thing to do, except that you have to track the camera position with great accuracy. Both Google and Apple have written some great APIs to do this magic for you, with the help of the motion sensors in your phone and data from the camera. The computer graphics that we add on top of the camera feed are synced to be in the same coordinate space as the surrounding real-life objects, making them appear as if they are part of the image you see on your phone.

An overview of the project

In this chapter, we are going to create a game that explores the fundamentals of AR. We are also going to learn how to integrate AR control in Xamarin.Forms. Android and iOS implement AR differently, so we will need to unify the platforms along the way. We will do this using UrhoSharp, an open source 3D game engine, which will do the rendering for us. This is simply made up of bindings to the **Urho3D** engine, which allows us to use Urho3D with .NET and C#.

The game will render boxes in AR that the user needs to tap to make disappear. You can then extend the game yourself by learning about the Urho3D engine.

The shared code will be placed in a shared project. This is different than the usual .NET Standard library approach we have taken so far. The reason for this is that UrhoSharp doesn't support .NET Standard (at the time of writing this book). It's also a good idea to learn how to create a shared project. The code in a shared library will not compile by itself. It needs to be linked to a platform project (such as iOS or Android) and then the compiler can compile all the source files along with the platform project. This is exactly the same thing as copying the files directly into that project. So, by defining a shared project, we don't need to write code twice.

This strategy also unlocks another powerful feature: **conditional compilation.** Consider the following example:

```
#if __IOS__
    // Only compile this code on iOS
#elif __ANDROID__
    // Only compile this code on Android
#endif
```

The preceding code shows how you can insert platform-specific code inside a shared code file. This will come in very handy in this project.

The estimated build time for this project is 90 minutes.

Beginning the project

It's time to start coding! First, however, make sure you have your development environment set up as described in `Chapter 1`, *Introduction to Xamarin*.

This chapter will be a classic **File | New Project** chapter, guiding you step-by-step through the process of creating the app. There will be no downloads required whatsoever.

Creating the project

Open Visual Studio and click on **File | New | Project**, as shown in the following screenshot:

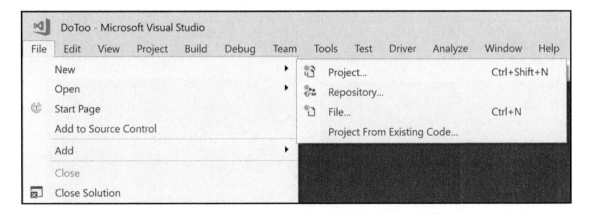

This will open the **New Project** dialog. Expand the **Visual C#** node and click on **Cross-Platform**. Select the **Mobile App (Xamarin.Forms)** item in the list. Complete the form by naming your project. We will be calling our application WhackABox in this example. Move on to the next dialog box by clicking **OK**, as shown in the following screenshot:

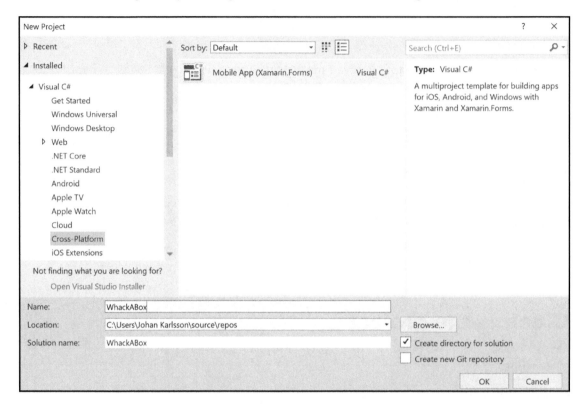

The next step is to select a project template and a **Code Sharing Strategy**. Select the **Blank** template option to create a bare minimum Xamarin.Forms app and make sure that the **Code Sharing Strategy** is set to **Shared Project**. Uncheck the **Windows (UWP)** checkbox under the **Platform** heading, since this app will only be supporting **iOS** and **Android**. Finish the setup wizard by clicking **OK** and let Visual Studio scaffold the project for you. This might take a couple of minutes. Please note that we will be using a **Shared Project** for this chapter—this is very important! You can see the aforementioned fields and options that you need to select in the following screenshot:

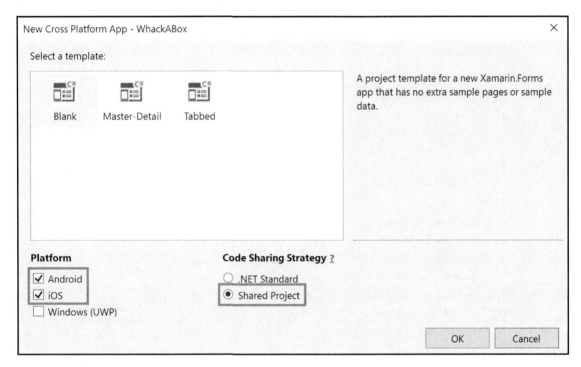

Just like that, the app has been created. Let's move on to updating Xamarin.Forms to the latest version.

Updating the Xamarin.Forms NuGet packages

Currently, the Xamarin.Forms version that your project has been created with is most likely a bit old. To rectify this, we need to update the NuGet packages. Please note that you should only update the Xamarin.Forms packages and not the Android packages; updating the Android packages might cause your packages to get out of sync with each other, resulting in the app not building at all. To update the NuGet packages, go through the following steps:

1. Right-click on our **Solution** in the **Solution Explorer**.
2. Click **Manage NuGet Packages for Solution...**, as shown in the following screenshot:

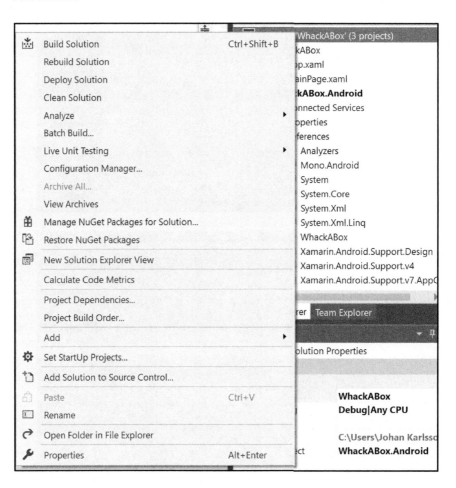

This will open the **NuGet Package Manager** in Visual Studio, as shown in the following screenshot:

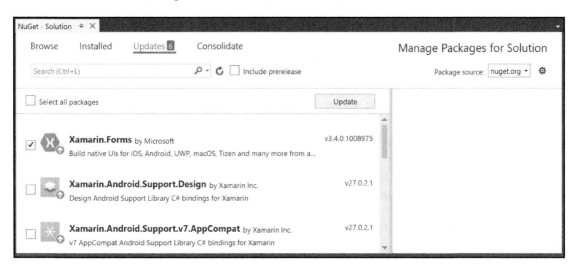

To update Xamarin.Forms to the latest version, go through the following steps:

1. Click the **Updates** tab.
2. Check the **Xamarin.Forms** checkbox and click **Update**.
3. Accept any license agreements.

The update takes at most a few minutes. Look at the output pane to find information about the update. At this point, we can run the app to make sure it works. We should see the text **Welcome to Xamarin.Forms!** in the middle of the screen.

Setting the Android target to 8.1

ARCore is available from Android version 8.1 and later. We will, therefore, verify the **Target Framework** for the Android project by going through the following steps:

1. Double-click on the **Properties** node under the Android project in the **Solution Explorer**.
2. Verify that the **Target Framework** version is at least **Android 8.0 (Oreo)**, as shown in the following screenshot:

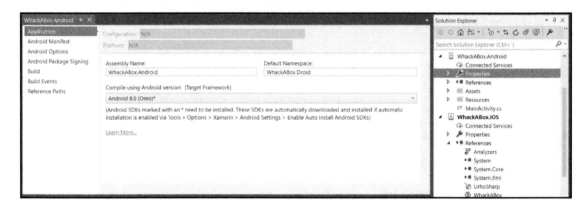

If it's not at least Android 8.0 (Oreo), you will need to select **Android 8.1** (or above). If there is an asterisk next to the **Target Framework** name, then you will need to install that SDK by going through the following steps:

1. Locate the **Android SDK Manager** in the toolbar.
2. Click the highlighted button to open the **SDK Manager**, as shown in the following screenshot:

This is the control center for all SDK versions of Android that are installed on the system:

1. Expand the SDK version you want to install. In our case, this should be at least **Android 8.1 - Oreo**.
2. Select the **Android SDK Platform <version number>** node. You can also to install emulator images that will be used by the emulator to run the selected version of Android.
3. Click **Apply Changes**, as shown in the following screenshot:

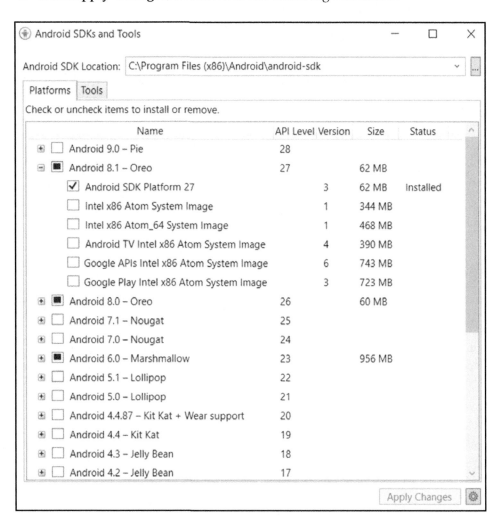

Adding the camera permission to Android

In order to get access to the camera in Android we must add a required permission in the Android manifest. This can be done by following these steps:

1. Open up the Android project node in the **Solution Explorer**.
2. Double-click the **Properties** node to open the properties for Android.
3. Click the **Android Manifest** tab on the left and scroll down until you see the **Required permissions** section.
4. Locate the **CAMERA** permission and check the box.
5. Save the file by clicking *Ctrl + S* or File and the Save.

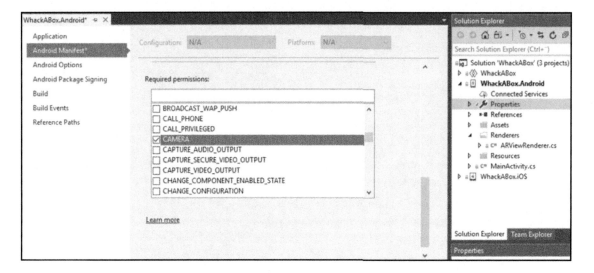

Now that we have configured Android, we only have one small change to make on iOS before we are ready to write some code.

Adding Camera Usage Description for iOS

In iOS, you need to specify why you need access to the camera. The way to do this is to add an entry to the `info.plist` file in the root folder of the iOS project. The `info.plist` file is an XML file that you can edit in any text editor. A simpler way to this, however, is by using the **Generic PList Editor** provided by Visual Studio.

Add the required **Camera Usage Description** using the **Generic PList Editor**, as follows:

1. Locate the `WhackABox.iOS` project.
2. Right-click on `info.plist` and click **Open With...**, as shown in the following screenshot:

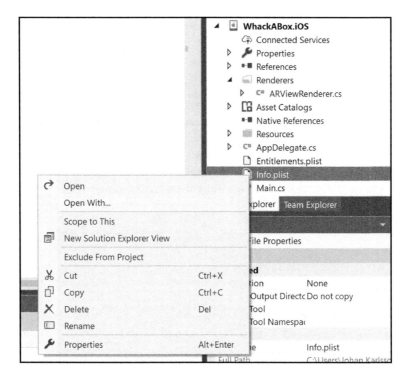

3. Select **Generic PList Editor** and click **OK**, as shown in the following screenshot:

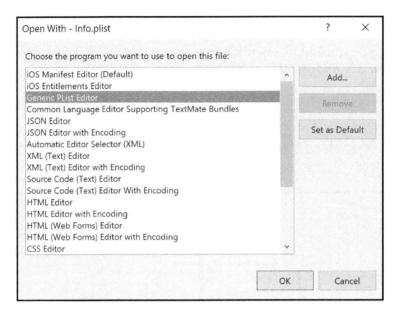

4. Locate the plus (+) icon at the bottom of the property list.
5. Click the plus (+) icon to add a new key. Make sure that the key is in the root of the document and not under another property, as shown in the following screenshot:

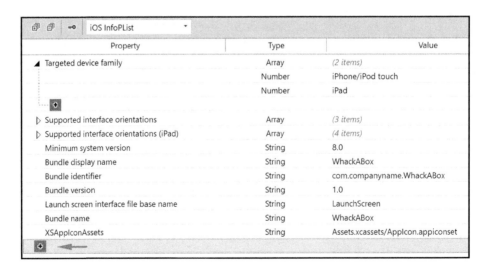

The **Generic PList Editor** helps you to find the right property by giving it a more user-friendly name. Let's add the value we need to describe why we want to use the camera:

1. Open the drop-down menu on the newly created row.
2. Select **Privacy - Camera Usage Description**.
3. Write a good reason in the values field to the right, as shown in the following screenshot. The field for the reason is a free-text field, so use plain English to describe why your app needs access to the camera:

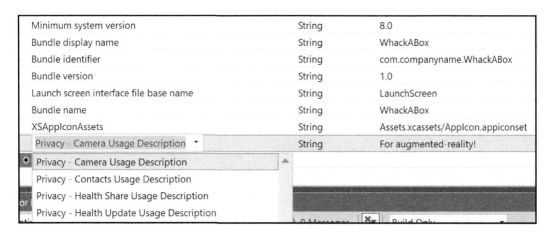

Minimum system version	String	8.0
Bundle display name	String	WhackABox
Bundle identifier	String	com.companyname.WhackABox
Bundle version	String	1.0
Launch screen interface file base name	String	LaunchScreen
Bundle name	String	WhackABox
XSAppIconAssets	String	Assets.xcassets/AppIcon.appiconset
Privacy - Camera Usage Description ▾	String	For augmented-reality!

- ⊕ Privacy - Camera Usage Description ▲
- Privacy - Contacts Usage Description
- Privacy - Health Share Usage Description
- Privacy - Health Update Usage Description

That's it. The setup of both Android and iOS is complete, and we can now focus on the fun part—writing code!

> You can also open the `Info.plist` file in any text editor, since it's an XML file. The key's name is `NSCameraUsageDescription`, and it must be added as a direct child of the root node.

Defining the user interface

We are going to start off by defining the user interface that will wrap the AR components. First, we will define a custom control that we will use as a placeholder for injecting an `UrhoSurface` that will contain the AR components. Then, we will add this control in a grid that will contain some statistics about how many planes we have found and how many boxes are active in the world. The goal of the game is to find boxes in AR using your phone and tapping on them to make them disappear.

Let's start by defining the custom `ARView` control.

Creating the ARView control

The `ARView` control belongs in the shared project, since it will be a part of both applications. It's a standard Xamarin.Forms control that inherits directly from `Xamarin.Forms.View`. It will not load any XAML (so it will simply be a single class), nor will it contain any functionality other than simply being defined, so we can add it to the main grid.

Go over to Visual Studio and go through the following three steps to create an `ARView` control:

1. In the `WhackABox` project, add a folder called `Controls`.
2. Create a new class called `ARView` in the `Controls` folder.
3. Add the following code to the `ARView` class:

```
using Xamarin.Forms;

namespace WhackABox.Controls
{
    public class ARView : View
    {
    }
}
```

What we have created here is a simple class, without implementation, that inherits from `Xamarin.Forms.View`. The point of this is to make use of custom renderers for each platform, allowing us to specify platform-specific code to be inserted at the place in the XAML where we put this control. Your project should now look as follows:

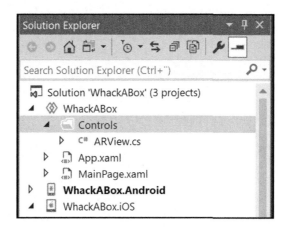

The `ARView` control is no good just sitting there. We need to add it to the `MainPage`.

Modifying the MainPage

We will be replacing the entire contents of the `MainPage` and adding a reference to the `WhackABox.Controls` namespace so that we can use the `ARView` control. Let's set this up by going through the following steps:

1. In the `WhackABox` project, open the `MainPage.xaml` file.
2. Edit the XAML to look like the following code. The XAML in bold represents the new elements that must be added:

```xml
<?xml version="1.0" encoding="utf-8">
<ContentPage xmlns="http://xamarin.com/schemas/2014/forms"
xmlns:x="http://schemas.microsoft.com/winfx/2009/xaml"
            xmlns:local="clr-namespace:WhackABox"
            xmlns:controls="clr-namespace:WhackABox.Controls"
            x:Class="WhackABox.MainPage">
    <Grid>
        <Grid.ColumnDefinitions>
            <ColumnDefinition Width="*" />
            <ColumnDefinition Width="*" />
        </Grid.ColumnDefinitions>
        <Grid.RowDefinitions>
            <RowDefinition Height="100" />
            <RowDefinition Height="*" />
        </Grid.RowDefinitions>
        <StackLayout Grid.Row="0" Padding="10">
            <Label Text="Plane count" />
            <Label Text="0" FontSize="Large"
             x:Name="planeCountLabel" />
        </StackLayout>
        <StackLayout Grid.Row="0" Grid.Column="1" Padding="10">
          <Label Text="Box count" />
          <Label Text="0" FontSize="Large"
          x:Name="boxCountLabel"/>
        </StackLayout>

    <controls:ARView Grid.Row="1" Grid.ColumnSpan="2" />
    </Grid>
</ContentPage>
```

Now that we have the code, let's go through it step by step:

- First, we define a controls namespace that points to the `WhackABox.Controls` namespace in code. This namespace is used at the end of the XAML to locate the `ARView` control.
- We then define the content element by setting it to a `Grid`. A page can only have one child, which, in this case, is a `Grid`. The `Grid` defines two columns and two rows. The columns split the `Grid` into two equal parts, where we have one row that is `100` units high at the top and one row that takes up all the available space below it.
- We use the top two cells to add instances of `StackLayout` that contain the information about the number of planes and the number of boxes in the game. The location of those instances of `StackLayout` in the grid is defined by the `Grid.Row=".."` and `Grid.Column=".."` attributes. Remember that the rows and columns are zero based. You don't actually have to add attributes for row or column `0`, but it can sometimes be a good practice to improve code readability.
- Finally, we have the `ARView` control, which resides in row `1` but spans both columns by specifying `Grid.ColumnSpan="2"`.

The next step is to install UrhoSharp, which will be our library for rendering graphics to represent the augmented part of our reality.

Adding Urhosharp

Urho is an open source 3D game engine. UrhoSharp is a package that contains bindings to iOS and Android binaries, enabling us to use Urho in .NET. It is a very competent piece of software, and we will only be using a very small part of it to do the heavy lifting when it comes to rendering planes and boxes in the app. We urge you to find out more about UrhoSharp to add your own cool features to the app.

All you have to do to install UrhoSharp is download a NuGet package for each platform. The iOS platform uses the UrhoSharp NuGet package, and Android uses the UrhoSharp.ARCore package. Also, in Android, we need to add some code to wire up life cycle events, but we will get to that later. Basically, we will set up an `UrhoSurface` on each platform. We will access this to add nodes to the node tree. These nodes will then be rendered based on their type and properties.

First, however, we need to install the packages.

Installing the UrhoSharp NuGet package for iOS

All we need to do for iOS is to add the UrhoSharp NuGet package. This contains everything we need for our AR app. You can add the package as follows:

1. Right-click on the `WhackABox.iOS` project.
2. Click **Manage NuGet Packages...**, as shown in the following screenshot:

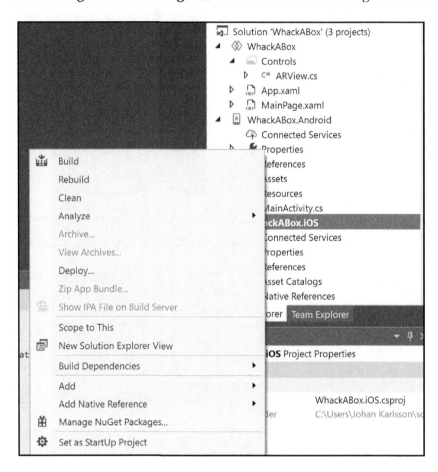

3. This opens the **NuGet Package Manager**. Click the **Browse** link on the top-left of the window.
4. Enter UrhoSharp in the search box and hit *Enter*.

5. Select the **UrhoSharp** package and click Install on the right side of the window, as shown in the following screenshot:

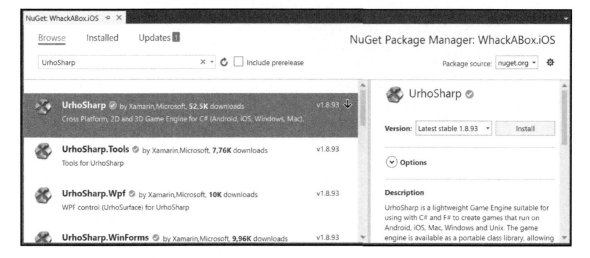

That's it for iOS. Android is a little bit trickier to set up, since it needs a special UrhoSharp package and some code to be written to wire everything up.

Installing the UrhoSharp.ARCore Nuget Package for Android

For Android, we will be adding the UrhoSharp.ARCore package, which contains extensions for ARCore. It has a dependency on UrhoSharp, so we don't have to add that package specifically. You can add the UrhoSharp.ARCore package as follows:

1. Right-click on the `WhackABox.Android` project.
2. Click **Manage NuGet Packages...**, as shown in the following screenshot:

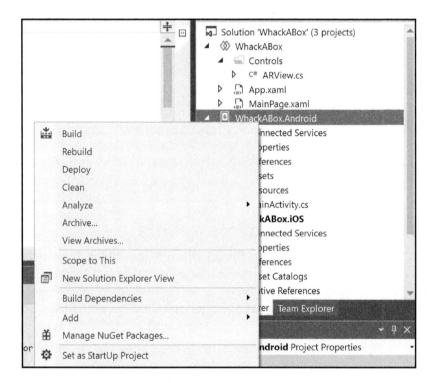

3. This opens the **NuGet Package Manager**. Click the **Browse** link on the top-left of the window.
4. Enter `UrhoSharp.ARCore` in the search box and hit *Enter*.

5. Select the **UrhoSharp.ARCore** package and click **Install** on the right side of the window, as shown in the following screenshot:

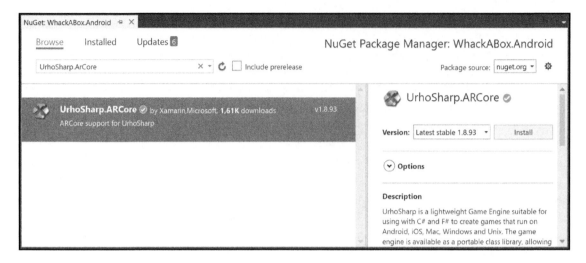

That's it—all your dependencies on UrhoSharp have been installed in the project. We now have to wire up some life cycle events.

Adding the Android life cycle events

In Android, `Urho` needs to know about some specific events and be able to respond to them accordingly. We also need to add an internal message using `MessagingCenter` so that we can react to the `OnResume` event later on in the app. We will get to that when we add the code to initialize ARCore. But for now, add the five required overrides for Android events, as follows:

1. In the Android project, open `MainActivity.cs`.
2. Add the five overrides from the following code anywhere in the `MainActivity` class.
3. Resolve the unresolved references by adding `using` statements for `Urho.Droid` and `Xamarin.Forms`, as shown in the following code:

```
protected override void OnResume()
{
    base.OnResume();
    UrhoSurface.OnResume();

    MessagingCenter.Send(this, "OnResume");
```

```
    }

    protected override void OnPause()
    {
        UrhoSurface.OnPause();
        base.OnPause();
    }

    protected override void OnDestroy()
    {
        UrhoSurface.OnDestroy();
        base.OnDestroy();
    }

    public override void OnBackPressed()
    {
        UrhoSurface.OnDestroy();
        Finish();
    }

    public override void OnLowMemory()
    {
        UrhoSurface.OnLowMemory();
        base.OnLowMemory();
    }
```

The events map one-on-one to internal UrhoSharp events, except for `OnBackPressed`, which calls `UrhoSharp.OnDestroy()`. The reason for this is memory management, so that UrhoSharp knows when to clean up.

The `MessagingCenter` library is a built-in Xamarin.Forms pub-sub library for passing internal messages in an app. It has a dependency on Xamarin.Forms. We have created a library of our own called `TinyPubSub` that breaks this dependency and has a slightly easier API (as well as some additional features). You can check it out on GitHub at `https://github.com/TinyStuff/TinyPubSub`.

Defining the PlaneNode

In `Urho`, you work with scenes that contain a tree of nodes. A node can be just about anything in the game, such as a renderer, a sound player, or simply a placeholder for subnodes.

As we talked about earlier when discussing AR fundamentals, planes are a common entity that is shared between the platforms. We need to create a common ground that represents a plane, which we can do by extending an `Urho` node. The position and the rotation will be tracked by the node itself, but we need to add a property to track the origin and the size of the plane, expressed by ARKit and ARCore as the extent of the plane.

We will add this class now and put it to use when we implement the AR-related code on each platform. The code to do this is straightforward, and can be set up by going through the following steps:

1. In the `WhackABox` project, create a new file called `PlaneNode.cs` in the root of the project.
2. Add the following implementation of the class:

```
using Urho;

namespace WhackABox
{
    public class PlaneNode :Node
    {
        public string PlaneId { get; set; }
        public float ExtentX { get; set; }
        public float ExtentZ { get; set; }
    }
}
```

The `PlaneId` will be an identifier that allows us to track which platform-specific plane this node represents. In iOS, this will be a string, while in Android, it will be the hashcode of the plane-object that is converted to a string. The `ExtentY` and `ExtentZ` properties represent the size of the plane in meters. We are now ready to start creating the game logic and hooking up our application to the AR SDKs.

Adding custom renderers for the ARView control

Custom renderers are a very smart way of extending platform-specific behaviors to custom controls. They can also be used to override behaviors on controls that are already defined. In fact, all of the controls in Xamarin.Forms use renderers to translate the Xamarin.Forms control into a platform-specific control.

We are going to create two renderers, one for iOS and one for Android, that initialize the `UrhoSurface` on which we are going to render. The instantiation of the `UrhoSurface` differs on each platform, which is why we need two different implementations.

For iOS

A custom renderer is a class that inherits from another renderer. It allows us to add custom code for important events, such as when an element in XAML is created when the XAML file is parsed. Since the `ARView` control inherits from the `View`, we will be using the `ViewRenderer` as a base class. Let's create the `ARViewRenderer` by going through the following steps:

1. In the iOS project, create a folder called `Renderers`.
2. Add a new class called `ARViewRenderer` to that folder.
3. Add the following code to the class:

```
using System.Threading.Tasks;
using Urho.iOS;
using WhackABox.Controls;
using WhackABox.iOS.Renderers;using Xamarin.Forms;
using Xamarin.Forms.Platform.iOS;

[assembly: ExportRenderer(typeof(ARView), typeof(ARViewRenderer))]
namespace WhackABox.iOS.Renderers
{
    public class ARViewRenderer : ViewRenderer<ARView, UrhoSurface>
    {
        protected async override void
        OnElementChanged(ElementChangedEventArgs<ARView> e)
        {
            base.OnElementChanged(e);

            if (Control == null)
            {
                await Initialize();
            }
        }

        private async Task Initialize()
        {
            var surface = new UrhoSurface();
            SetNativeControl(surface);
            await surface.Show<Game>();
        }
    }
}
```

The `ExportRenderer` attribute registers this renderer to Xamarin.Forms so that it knows that when it parses (or compiles) an `ARView` element, it should render it using this specific renderer. It takes two arguments: the first is the `Control` that we want to register a renderer to and the second is the type of the renderer. This attribute must be placed outside the namespace declarations.

The `ARViewRenderer` class inherits `ViewRenderer<ARView, UrhoSurface>`. This specifies which control this renderer is created for and which native control it should render. In this case, the `ARView` will be natively replaced by a `UrhoSurface` control that in itself is an iOS-specific `UIView`.

We override the `OnElementChanged()` method that is called every time the `ARView` element changes, either when it is created or when it is replaced. We can then check whether the `Control` property is set. The control is of the `UrhoSurface` type, since we declared that in the class definition. If it's `null`, then we make a call to `Initialize()` to create it.

The creation is straightforward. We simply create a new `UrhoSurface` control and set the native control to this newly created object. We then call the `Show<Game>()` method to start the game by specifying which class represents our `Urho` game. Note that the `Game` class is not defined yet, but it will be very soon, right after we create the custom renderer for Android.

For Android

The custom renderer for Android does the same thing as it does for iOS, but with the additional step of checking permissions. Let's create the `ARViewRenderer` for Android by going through the following steps:

1. In the Android project, create a folder called `Renderers`.
2. Add a new class called `ARViewRenderer` to that folder.
3. Add the following code to the class:

```
using System.Threading.Tasks;
using Android;
using Android.App;
using Android.Content;
using Android.Content.PM;
using Android.Support.V4.App;
using Android.Support.V4.Content;
using WhackABox.Droid.Renderers;
using WhackABox;
using WhackABox.Controls;
```

```
using WhackABox.Droid;
using Urho.Droid;
using Xamarin.Forms;
using Xamarin.Forms.Platform.Android;

[assembly: ExportRenderer(typeof(ARView),
typeof(ARViewRenderer))]
namespace WhackABox.Droid.Renderers
{
    public class ARViewRenderer : ViewRenderer<ARView,
    Android.Views.View>
    {
        private UrhoSurfacePlaceholder surface;
        public ARViewRenderer(Context context) : base(context)
        {
            MessagingCenter.Subscribe<MainActivity>(this,
            "OnResume", async (sender) =>
            {
                await Initialize();
            });
        }

        protected async override void
        OnElementChanged(ElementChangedEventArgs<ARView> e)
        {
            base.OnElementChanged(e);

            if (Control == null)
            {
                await Initialize();
            }
        }

        private async Task Initialize()
        {
            if (ContextCompat.CheckSelfPermission(Context,
                Manifest.Permission.Camera) != Permission.Granted)
            {
                ActivityCompat.RequestPermissions(Context as
                Activity, new[] { Manifest.Permission.Camera },
                42);
                return;
            }

            if (surface != null)
                return;

            surface = UrhoSurface.CreateSurface(Context as
```

```
            Activity);
            SetNativeControl(surface);
            await surface.Show<Game>();
        }
    }
}
```

This custom renderer also inherits from `ViewRenderer<T1, T2>`, where the first type is the type of the renderer itself and the second is the native control that the renderer will produce. In this case, the native control will be a control that inherits from `Android.Views.View`. The renderer creates a `UrhoSurfacePlaceholder` instance, which it assigns as the native control. The `UrhoSurfacePlaceholder` is a class that wraps some functionality of the **Simple DirectMedia Layer (SDL)** library that `Urho` uses on Android to access media functionality. The last thing it does is to start the game based on the soon-to-exist `Game` class. We will define this in the next section of this chapter.

Creating the game

To write an application that uses `Urho`, we need to create a class that inherits from `Urho.Application`. This class defines some virtual methods that we can use to set up the scene. The method we will use is `Start()`. Before that, however, we need to create the class. The class will be split into three files using partial classes, as described in the following list:

- The `Game.cs` file, which will contain code that is cross platform
- The `Game.iOS.cs` file, which will contain code that will only be compiled in the iOS version of the app
- The `Game.Android.cs` file, which will contain code that will only be compiled in the Android version of the app

We will be using a conditional compile to do so. We discussed conditional compiling in the introduction to this project. Simply put, this means that we can use something called **preprocessor directives** to determine at compile time whether the code should be included. In practice, this means that we will be compiling different code in Android and iOS by defining the same `InitializeAR()` method in both `Game.iOS.cs` and `Game.Android.cs`. During initialization, we will call this method, and, depending on which platform we run it on, it will be implemented differently. This can only be done with a shared project.

Visual Studio has excellent support for conditional compiling and will resolve the correct references depending on which project you have set as the startup project or what you select in the toolbar above the code file itself.

For this project, we could have moved the Game.iOS.cs file to the iOS project and the Game.Android.cs and removed the conditional compile preprocessor statements. The app would compile just fine, but for the purposes of learning how this works, we will include them in the shared project. This could also be a positive thing, since we are gathering related code in one place, making it easier to understand the architecture.

Adding the shared partial Game class

We start by creating the Game.cs file that will contain shared code. Let's set this up by going through the following steps:

1. In the WhackABox project, create a new file called Game.cs in the root of the project.
2. Add the following code to the class:

```
using System;
using System.Linq;
using Urho;
using Urho.Shapes;

namespace WhackABox
{
    public partial class Game : Application
    {
        private Scene scene;

        public Game(ApplicationOptions options) : base(options)
        {
        }
    }
}
```

The first thing to notice is the partial keyword in the class. This indicates to the compiler that this is not the entire implementation, and that more code will be present in other files. The code in those files will be treated as if it were in this file; it's a nice way to split large implementations into different files.

The Game inherits from Urho.Application, which will do most of the work regarding the game itself. We define a property called scene of the Scene type. A Scene in Urho represents one screen of the game (we could have different scenes for different parts of a game or for a menu, for example). In this game, we will only be defining one scene, which will be initialized later. A scene maintains a hierarchy of nodes that compose it, and each node can have any number of children and any number of components. It's the components that do the work. Later on, for example, we will be rendering boxes, which will be represented by a node that will have a Box component attached.

The Game class itself is instantiated from the custom renderers that we defined in the earlier section, and it takes an ApplicationOptions instance as a parameter in the constructor. This needs to be passed to the base class. We now need to write some methods that will be AR specific and used by the code we will write later on.

CreateSubPlane

The first method is the CreateSubPlane() method. When the application finds a plane on which we can place objects, it will create a node. We will write that code specifically for each platform soon. This node also defines a subplane that will position a box, representing the position and size of that plane. We have already defined the PlaneNode class earlier in this chapter.

Let's add the code by going through the following steps:

1. In the WhackABox project, open the Game.cs class.
2. Add the following CreateSubPlane() method to the class:

```
private void CreateSubPlane(PlaneNode planeNode)
{
    var node = planeNode.CreateChild("subplane");
    node.Position = new Vector3(0, 0.05f, 0);

    var box = node.CreateComponent<Box>();
    box.Color = Color.FromHex("#22ff0000");
}
```

Any class inheriting from Urho.Node, such as PlaneNode, has the CreateChild() method. This allows us to create a child node and specify a name for that node. That name will be used later on to find specific children to perform operations on. We position the node at the same position as the parent node, except that we raise it 0.05 meters (5 cm) above the plane.

To see the plane, we add a `box` component with a semitransparent red color. The `box` is a component that is created with a call to `CreateComponent()` on our node. The color is defined in the AARRGGBB pattern, where AA is the alpha component (the transparency) and RRGGBB is the standard red-green-blue format. We use hexadecimal representation of the colors.

UpdateSubPlane

Both ARKit and ARCore update planes continuously. What we are interested in are changes in the position of a subplane and the extent of it. By extension, we are referring to the size of the plane. Let's set this up by going through the following steps:

1. In the `WhackABox` project, open the `Game.cs` class.
2. Add the `UpdateSubPlane()` method in the code anywhere in the `Game.cs` class, as shown in the following code:

```
private void UpdateSubPlane(PlaneNode planeNode, Vector3 position)
{
    var subPlaneNode = planeNode.GetChild("subplane");
    subPlaneNode.Scale = new Vector3(planeNode.ExtentX, 0.05f,
    planeNode.ExtentZ);
    subPlaneNode.Position = position;
}
```

The method takes the `PlaneNode` that we want to update, along with a new position for it. We locate the subplane by querying the current node for any node called `"subplane"`. Remember that we named the subplane in the `AddSubPlane()` method. We can now easily access the node by name. We update the scale of the subplane node by taking the `ExtentX` and `ExtentZ` properties from the `PlaneNode`. The plane node will be updated by some platform-specific code before we call `UpdateSubPlane()`. Finally, we set the position of the subplane to the passed `position` parameter.

FindNodeByPlaneId

We need a method to quickly find nodes. Both ARKit and ARCore keep an internal track of their planes, and to map those internal representations of planes to our `PlaneNode`, we have to assign a custom ID to a plane when it's created. This will be done in the platform-specific code, but we can still write the function to query the scene for `PlaneNode`.

The `PlaneNode` is a `string`, since ARKit defines the plane ID in a form that resembles a **Global Unique Identifier (GUID)**. A GUID is a structured sequence of hexadecimal numbers that can be represented in a `string` format, as shown in the following code:

```
private PlaneNode FindNodeByPlaneId(string planeId) =>
              scene.Children.OfType<PlaneNode>()
              .FirstOrDefault(e => e.PlaneId == planeId);
```

The method queries the scene by using `Linq` and looks for the first child with the plane ID that it was given. If it can't find one, it returns `null`, since `null` is the default value of a reference type object.

These are all of the methods that we need in the shared code before dropping down into ARKit and ARCore.

Adding platform-specific partial classes

It's now time to take advantage of conditional compiling. We will create two partial classes, one for iOS and one for Android, that will be conditionally compiled into the `Game` class.

In this section, we will simply set up the skeleton code for these files.

Adding the iOS-specific partial class

Let's start by creating the `partial` class for `Game` on iOS and wrapping the whole code file within a preprocessor directive that specifies that this code will only be compiled on iOS:

1. In the `WhackABox` project, add a new file called `Game.iOS.cs`.
2. Rename the class `Game` in the code, if Visual Studio doesn't do it automatically.
3. Make the class `public` and `partial`.
4. Add the `#if` and `#endif` preprocessor directives to allow for conditional compiling, as shown in the following code:

```
#if __IOS__
namespace WhackABox
{
    public partial class Game
    {
    }
}
#endif
```

The first line of code is a preprocessor directive that the compiler will use to determine whether the code within the `#if` and `#endif` directives should be included in the compilation. If it is included, a `partial` class will be defined. The code in this class can be iOS specific, even though we are defining it in the shared project. Visual Studio is smart enough to treat any code within this section as if it were present directly in the iOS project. There will be no problem with instantiating a `UIView` here, since the code will never be compiled for any platform other than iOS.

Adding the Android-specific partial class

The same goes for Android: only the name of the file and the preprocessor directive changes. Let's set this up by going through the following steps:

1. In the `WhackABox` project, add a new file called `Game.Android.cs`.
2. Rename the class `Game` in the code, if Visual Studio doesn't do it automatically.
3. Make the class `public` and `partial`.
4. Add the `#if` and `#endif` conditional compile statements, as shown in the following code:

```
#if __ANDROID__
namespace WhackABox
{
    public partial class Game
    {
    }
}
#endif
```

As with iOS, only code for Android will ever be compiled between the `#if` and `#endif` statements.

Let's now start adding some platform-specific code.

Writing the ARKit-specific code

In this section, we will write the platform-specific code for iOS that will initialize ARKit, find planes, and create nodes for UrhoSharp to render on the screen. We will be taking advantage of an Urho component that wraps ARKit in iOS. We will also be writing all the functions that will position, add, and remove nodes. ARKit uses anchors, which act as virtual points that glue the overlaid graphics to the real world. We are specifically looking for ARPlaneAnchor, which represents a plane in the AR world. There are other types of anchors available, but for this app, we only need to find horizontal planes.

Let's start off by defining the ARKitComponent so that we can use it later.

Defining the ARKitComponent

We start by adding a private field to an ARKitComponent that will be initialized later on. Let's set this up by going through the following steps:

1. In the WhackABox project, open Game.iOS.cs.
2. Add a private field that holds an ARKitComponent, as shown in bold in the following code :

```
#if __IOS__
using System;
using System.Collections.Generic;
using System.Text;
using System.Linq;
using ARKit;
using Urho;
using Urho.iOS;

namespace WhackABox
{
    public partial class Game
    {
        private ARKitComponent arkitComponent;
    }
}
#endif
```

Make sure that you add all the using statements to ensure that all the code we later use resolves the correct types.

Writing handlers for adding and updating anchors

We will now add the necessary code that will add and update anchors. We will also add some methods to help set the orientation of the nodes after ARKit updates the anchors.

SetPositionAndRotation

The `SetPositionAndRotation()` method will be used by both the add and update anchors, so we need to define it before creating the handlers for the events that will be raised by ARKit. Let's set this up by going through the following steps:

1. In the `WhackABox` project, open the `Game.iOS.cs` file.
2. Add the `SetPositionAndRotation()` method to the class, as shown in the following code:

```
private void SetPositionAndRotation(ARPlaneAnchor anchor, PlaneNode
                                    node)
{
    arkitComponent.ApplyOpenTkTransform(node, anchor.Transform,
                                        true);

    node.ExtentX = anchor.Extent.X;
    node.ExtentZ = anchor.Extent.Z;

    var position = new Vector3(anchor.Center.X, anchor.Center.Y, -
                               anchor.Center.Z);
    UpdateSubPlane(node, position);
}
```

The method takes two parameters. The first is an `ARPlaneAnchor` defined by ARKit and the second is the `PlaneNode` that we have in the scene. The purpose of the method is to make sure that the `PlaneNode` is in sync with the `ARPlaneAnchor` object passed by ARKit. The `arkitComponent` has a helper method called `ApplyOpenTkTransform()` to translate the position and rotation of the `ARPlaneAnchor` object into the position and rotation objects used by Urho. We then update the `Extent` (size) of the plane to the `PlaneNode` and get the `anchor` center position from the `ARPlaneAnchor`. Finally, we call a method that we defined earlier to update the subplane node that holds the `Box` component that will do the actual rendering of the plane as a semitransparent red box.

We need one more method to handle the update and add functionality.

UpdateOrAddPlaneNode

The UpdateOrAddPlaneNode() does exactly what the name implies: it takes an ARPlaneAnchor as an argument and either updates or adds a new PlaneNode to the scene. Let's set this up by going through the following steps:

1. In the WhackABox project, open the Game.iOS.cs file.
2. Add the UpdateOrAddPlaneNode() method, as described in the following code:

```
private void UpdateOrAddPlaneNode(ARPlaneAnchor anchor)
{
    var node = FindNodeByPlaneId(anchor.Identifier.ToString());

    if (node == null)
    {
        node = new PlaneNode()
        {
            PlaneId = anchor.Identifier.ToString(),
            Name = $"plane{anchor.GetHashCode()}"
        };

        CreateSubPlane(node);
        scene.AddChild(node);
    }

    SetPositionAndRotation(anchor, node);
}
```

A node is either already present in the scene or it needs to be added. The first line of code calls the FindNodeByPlaneId() to query the scene for an object with the given PlaneId. For iOS, we use the anchor.Identifier property to track planes defined by iOS. If this call returns null, it means that the plane is not present in the scene and we need to create it. To do this, we instantiate a new PlaneNode, giving it a PlaneId and a user-friendly name for debugging purposes. We then create the subplane to visualize the plane itself by calling CreateSubPlane(), which we defined earlier, and add the node to the scene. Lastly, we update the position and rotation. We do this for every call to the UpdateOrAddPlaneNode() method, since it's the same for both new and existing nodes. It's now time to write the handlers that we will eventually hook up to ARKit directly.

OnAddAnchor

Let's add some code. The `OnAddAnchor()` method will be called each time ARKit updates its collection of anchors that describe points that we will use to relate to within our virtual world. We are specifically looking for anchors of the `ARPlaneAnchor` type.

Add the `OnAddAnchor()` method to the `Game.iOS.cs` class by going through the following two steps:

1. In the `WhackABox` project, open the `Game.iOS.cs` file.
2. Add the `OnAddAnchor()` method anywhere in the class, as shown in the following code:

```
private void OnAddAnchor(ARAnchor[] anchors)
{
    foreach (var anchor in anchors.OfType<ARPlaneAnchor>())
    {
        UpdateOrAddPlaneNode(anchor);
    }
}
```

The method takes an array of `ARAnchors` as a parameter. We filter out the anchors that are of the `ARPlaneAnchor` type and iterate through the list. For each `ARPlaneAnchor`, we call the `UpdateOrAddPlaneNode()` method that we created earlier to add a node to the scene. Let's now do the same for when ARKit wants to update anchors.

OnUpdateAnchors

Each time ARKit receives new information about an anchor, it will call this method. We do the same as we did with the previous code and iterate through the list to update the extent and position of the `anchor` in the scene:

1. In the `WhackABox` project, open the `Game.iOS.cs` file.
2. Add the `OnUpdateAnchors()` method anywhere in the class, as shown in the following code:

```
private void OnUpdateAnchors(ARAnchor[] anchors)
{
    foreach (var anchor in anchors.OfType<ARPlaneAnchor>())
    {
        UpdateOrAddPlaneNode(anchor);
    }
}
```

The code is a copy of the `OnAddAnchors()` method. It updates all nodes in the scene based on the information provided by ARKit.

We also need to write some code to remove the anchors that ARKit has removed.

Writing a handler for removing anchors

When ARKit decides that an anchor is invalid, it will remove it from the scene. This does not happen very often, but it's a good practice to handle this call anyway.

OnRemoveAnchors

Let's add a method to handle the removal of an `ARPlaneAnchor` by going through the following steps:

1. In the `WhackABox` project, open the `Game.iOS.cs` file.
2. Add the `OnRemoveAnchors()` method anywhere in the class, as shown in the following code:

```
private void OnRemoveAnchors(ARAnchor[] anchors)
{
    foreach (var anchor in anchors.OfType<ARPlaneAnchor>())
    {
        FindNodeByPlaneId(anchor.Identifier.ToString())?.Remove();
    }
}
```

As with the `Add` and `Remove` functions, this method accepts an array of `ARAnchor`. We iterate through this array, looking for anchors of the `ARPlaneAnchor` type. We then look for a node that represents this plane by calling the `FindNodeByPlaneId()` method. If it's not `null`, then we call for that node to be removed. Note the null-check operator before the `Remove()` call.

Initializing ARKit

We've now come to the last part of the iOS-specific code, which is where we initialize ARKit. This method is called `InitializeAR()`, and takes no parameters. It is the same as the method for Android, but since they are never compiled simultaneously because of the use of conditional compiling, the code calling this method will not know the difference.

The code to initialize ARKit is straightforward, and the `ARKitComponent` does a lot of work for us. Let's set it up by going through the following steps:

1. In the `WhackABox` project, open the `Game.iOS.cs` file.
2. Add the `InitializeAR()` method anywhere in the class, as shown in the following code:

```
private void InitializeAR()
{
    arkitComponent = scene.CreateComponent<ARKitComponent>();
    arkitComponent.Orientation =
    UIKit.UIInterfaceOrientation.Portrait;
    arkitComponent.ARConfiguration = new
    ARWorldTrackingConfiguration
    {
        PlaneDetection = ARPlaneDetection.Horizontal
    };
    arkitComponent.DidAddAnchors += OnAddAnchor;
    arkitComponent.DidUpdateAnchors += OnUpdateAnchors;
    arkitComponent.DidRemoveAnchors += OnRemoveAnchors;
    arkitComponent.RunEngineFramesInARKitCallbakcs =
    Options.DelayedStart;
    arkitComponent.Run();
}
```

The code starts by creating an `ARKitComponent`. We then set the allowed orientation and create an `ARWorldTrackingConfiguration` class that states that we are only interested in horizontal planes. To respond to the addition, updating, and removal of planes, we attach the event handlers we created earlier.

We instruct the ARKit component to delay calling the callbacks to allow ARKit to initialize properly. Note the spelling error in the `RunEngineFramesInARKitCallbakcs` property. This is a good example of why you need to carry out a review of your code, since it will be hard to change this name without breaking backward compatibility. Naming is hard.

The last thing is to tell ARKit to start running. We do this by calling the `arkitComponent.Run()` method.

Writing ARCore-specific code

It's now time to do the same for Android with ARCore. Just as with iOS, we are going to put all Android-specific code in a file of its own. This file is the `Game.Android.cs` that we created earlier.

Defining the ARCoreComponent

First, we are going to add a field that stores a reference to the `ARCoreComponent`. This wraps most of the interaction with ARCore. The `ARCoreComponent` is defined in the UrhoSharp.ARCore NuGet package that we installed at the beginning of the chapter.

Let's add some `using` statements and the field by going through the following steps:

1. In the `WhackABox` project, open the `Game.Android.cs` file.
2. Add the `arCore` private field, as described in the following code. Also, make sure that you add the `using` statements marked in bold:

```
#if __ANDROID__
using Com.Google.AR.Core;
using Urho;
using Urho.Droid;

namespace WhackABox
{
    public partial class Game
    {
        private ARCoreComponent arCore;
    }
}
#endif
```

The `using` statements will allow us to resolve the types that we need in this file and the `arCore` property will be a shorthand when we want to access ARCore functions.

We'll continue by adding some methods to this class.

SetPositionAndRotation

We need to add or update a `PlaneNode` whenever a plane is detected or updated. The `SetPositionAndRotation()` method updates the passed `PlaneNode` and sets properties on that node based on the content of the `AR.Core.Plane` object. Let's set this up by going through the following steps:

1. In the `WhackABox` project, open the `Game.Android.cs` file.
2. Add the `SetPositionAndRotation()` method to the class, as shown in the following code:

```
private void SetPositionAndRotation(Com.Google.AR.Core.Plane plane,
                                    PlaneNode node)
{
    node.ExtentX = plane.ExtentX;
    node.ExtentZ = plane.ExtentZ;
    node.Rotation = new Quaternion(plane.CenterPose.Qx(),
                                   plane.CenterPose.Qy(),
                                   plane.CenterPose.Qz(),
                                   -plane.CenterPose.Qw());

    node.Position = new Vector3(plane.CenterPose.Tx(),
                                plane.CenterPose.Ty(),
                                -plane.CenterPose.Tz());
}
```

The previous code updates the extent of the plane for the node and creates a rotation, `Quaternion`. Don't worry if you don't know what a `Quaternion` is—few people do—but they seem to magically hold the rotation information of the model in a very flexible way. The `plane.CenterPose` property is a matrix that holds the position and orientation of the plane. Finally, we update the position of the node from the `CenterPose` property.

The next step is to create a method that handles frame updates from ARCore.

Writing a handler for ARFrame updates

Android handles updates from ARCore a little bit differently than ARKit, which exposes three different events for added, updated, and removed nodes. When using ARCore, we get called whenever any changes occur, and the handler that will take care of this is the one we are about to add.

Let's add the method by going through the following steps:

1. In the WhackABox project, open the Game.Android.cs file.
2. Add the OnARFrameUpdated() method anywhere in the class, as shown in the following code:

```
private void OnARFrameUpdated(Frame arFrame)
{
    var all = arCore.Session.GetAllTrackables(
                 Java.Lang.Class.FromType(
                 typeof(Com.Google.AR.Core.Plane)));

    foreach (Com.Google.AR.Core.Plane plane in all)
    {
        var node =
        FindNodeByPlaneId(plane.GetHashCode().ToString());

        if (node == null)
        {
            node = new PlaneNode
            {
                PlaneId = plane.GetHashCode().ToString(),
                Name = $"plane{plane.GetHashCode()}"
            };

            CreateSubPlane(node);
            scene.AddChild(node);
        }

        SetPositionAndRotation(plane, node);
        UpdateSubPlane(node, Vector3.Zero);
    }
}
```

We start by querying the arCore component for all the planes that it keeps track of. We then iterate through this list and see whether we have any nodes in the scene by calling the FindNodeByPlaneId() method, using the hash code of the plane as the identifier. If we can't find any, we create a new PlaneNode and assign the hash code as the PlaneId. We then create a subplane that contains the Box component to visualize the plane, and, finally, we add it to the scene. We then update the position and the rotation of the plane and make a call to update the subplane as well. Now that we have the handler written, we need to hook it up.

Initializing ARCore

To initialize ARCore, we will add two methods. The first one is a method that will take care of the configuration of ARCore, called `OnConfigRequested()`. The second one is the `InitializeAR()` method that will be called from the shared `Game` class later on. This method is also defined in the iOS-specific code, but, as we talked about earlier, this method in iOS will never be compiled when we compile for Android, since we are using conditional compiling, which filters out code from the platform that isn't selected.

OnConfigRequested

ARCore needs to know a few things, just like iOS. In Android, this is done by defining a method that the ARCore component will call upon initialization. To create the method, go through the following steps:

1. In the `WhackABox` project, open the `Game.Android.cs` file.
2. Add the `OnConfigRequested()` method anywhere in the class, as shown in the following code:

```
private void OnConfigRequested(Config config)
{
    config.SetPlaneFindingMode(Config.PlaneFindingMode.Horizontal);
    config.SetLightEstimationMode

    (Config.LightEstimationMode.AmbientIntensity);
    config.SetUpdateMode(Config.UpdateMode.LatestCameraImage);
}
```

The method takes a `Config` object, which will store any configuration you make in this method. First, we set which type of plane we want to find. We are interested in `Horizontal` planes for this game. We define which kind of light-estimation mode we want to use and, finally, we select which update mode we want. In this case, we want to use the latest camera image available. You can do a lot of fine-tuning during configuration, but this is out of the scope of this book. Be sure to check out the documentation for ARCore to learn more about its awesome power.

We now have all the code we need to initialize ARCore.

InitializeAR

As mentioned previously, the `InitializeAR()` method shares the same name as the iOS-specific code, but the compiler will only include one of them in the build because of the use of conditional compiling. Let's set this up by going through the following steps:

1. In the `WhackABox` project, open the `Game.Android.cs` file.
2. Add the `InitializeAR()` method anywhere in the class, as shown in the following code:

```
private void InitializeAR()
{
    arCore = scene.CreateComponent<ARCoreComponent>();
    arCore.ARFrameUpdated += OnARFrameUpdated;
    arCore.ConfigRequested += OnConfigRequested;
    arCore.Run();
}
```

The first step is to create the `ARCoreComponent` provided by UrhoSharp. This component wraps the initialization of the native ARCore classes. We then add two event handlers: one for taking care of frame updates and one that will be called during initialization. The last thing we do is call the `Run()` method on the `ARCoreComponent` to start tracking the world.

Now that we have both ARKit and ARCore configured and ready to go, it's time to write the actual game.

Writing the game

In this section, we will initialize `Urho` by setting up the camera, lighting, and a renderer. The camera is the object that determines where objects will be rendered. The AR components take care of updating the position of the camera to virtually track your phone so that any object we render will be in the same coordinate space as what you are looking at. First, we need a camera that will be the viewing point of the scene.

Adding a camera

Adding a camera is a straightforward process, as shown in the following steps:

1. In the `WhackABox` project, open the `Game.cs` file.
2. Add the `camera` property to the class, as shown in the following code. You should place it right after the declaration of the class itself, but placing it anywhere within the class will work.

3. Add the `InitializeCamera()` method anywhere in the class, as shown in the following code:

```
private Camera camera;

private void InitializeCamera()
{
    var cameraNode = scene.CreateChild("Camera");
    camera = cameraNode.CreateComponent<Camera>();
}
```

In UrhoSharp, everything is a node just like everything is a GameObject in Unity, including the `camera`. We create a new node, which we call `camera`, and then we create a `Camera` component on that node and keep the reference to it for later use.

Configuring a renderer

UrhoSharp needs to render the scene to a `viewport`. A game can have multiple viewports, based on multiple cameras. Think of a game where you drive a car. The main `viewport` will be the game from the perspective of the driver. Another `viewport` might be the rear-view mirrors, which would actually be cameras themselves that render what they see on to the main `viewport`. Let's set this up by going through the following steps:

1. In the `WhackABox` project, open the `Game.cs` file.
2. Add the `viewport` property to the class, as shown in the following code. You should place it right after the declaration of the class itself, but placing it anywhere within the class will work.
3. Add the `InitializeRenderer()` method anywhere in the class, as shown in the following code:

```
private Viewport viewport;

private void InitializeRenderer()
{
    viewport = new Viewport(Context, scene, camera, null);
    Renderer.SetViewport(0, viewport);
}
```

The `viewport` property will hold a reference to the `viewport` for later use. The `viewport` is created by instantiating a new `viewport` class. The constructor of that class needs a `Context` provided by the base class, the `scene` that we will create while initializing the game, a camera to know which point in space to render from, and a render path, which we default to `null`. A render path allows for post-processing of the frame created while rendering. This is also outside the scope of this book, but it is worth checking out as well.

Now, let there be light.

Adding lights

To make objects visible, we need to define some lighting. We do this by creating a method that defines which type of lighting we want in the game. Let's set this up by going through the following steps:

1. In the `WhackABox` project, open the `Game.cs` file.
2. Add the `InitializeLights()` method anywhere in the class, as shown in the following code:

```
private void InitializeLights()
{
    var lightNode = camera.Node.CreateChild();
    lightNode.SetDirection(new Vector3(1f, -1.0f, 1f));
    var light = lightNode.CreateComponent<Light>();
    light.Range = 10;
    light.LightType = LightType.Directional;
    light.CastShadows = true;
    Renderer.ShadowMapSize *= 4;
}
```

Again, everything in UrhoSharp is a node, and lights are no exception to that rule. We create a generic node on the camera node by accessing the stored camera component and accessing the node it belongs to. We then set a direction of that node and create a `Light` component to define a light. The range of the light will be 10 units in length. The type is directional, meaning that it will shine from the position of the node in its defined direction. It will also cast shadows. We set the `ShadowMapSize` to four times the default value to give the shadow map some more resolution.

At this point, we have all we need to initialize UrhoSharp and the AR components.

Implementing the game startup

The base class of the `Game` class provides some virtual methods that we can override. One of these is `Start()`, which will be called shortly after the custom renderer has set up the `UrhoSurface`.

Add the method by going through the following steps:

1. In the `WhackABox` project, open the `Game.cs` file.
2. Add the `Start()` method anywhere in the class, as shown in the following code:

```
protected override void Start()
{
    scene = new Scene(Context);
    var octree = scene.CreateComponent<Octree>();

    InitializeCamera();
    InitializeLights();
    InitializeRenderer();

    InitializeAR();
}
```

The scene that we have been talking about is created here in the first line of the method. This is the scene that we look at when UrhoSharp is running. It keeps track of all nodes that we add to it. All 3D games in UrhoSharp need an `Octree`, which is a component that implements spatial partitioning. It is used by the 3D engine to quickly find objects in a 3D space without having to query every single one in each frame. The second line of the method creates this component directly on the scene.

Following this, we have the four methods that initialize the camera, the lights, and the renderer, and that make a call to one of the two `InitializeAR()` methods, based on which platform we are compiling for. If you start the app at this point, you should see that it finds planes and renders them, but that nothing more happens. It's time to add something to interact with.

Adding boxes

We are now going to focus on adding virtual boxes to our augmented world. We are going to write two methods. The first one is the AddBox() method, which will add a new box at a random position on a plane. The second is an override of the OnUpdate() method that UrhoSharp calls with each frame to perform game logic.

AddBox()

To add boxes to a plane, we need to add a method to do so. This method is called AddBox(). Let's set this up by going through the following steps:

1. In the WhackABox project, open the Game.cs file.
2. Add the random property to the class (preferably at the top, but anywhere in the class will work).
3. Add the AddBox() method anywhere in the class, as shown in the following code:

```
private static Random random = new Random();

private void AddBox(PlaneNode planeNode)
{
    var subPlaneNode = planeNode.GetChild("subplane");

    var boxNode = planeNode.CreateChild("Box");
    boxNode.SetScale(0.1f);

    var x = planeNode.ExtentX * (float)(random.NextDouble() -
0.5f);
    var z = planeNode.ExtentZ * (float)(random.NextDouble() -
0.5f);

    boxNode.Position = new Vector3(x, 0.1f, z) +
    subPlaneNode.Position;

    var box = boxNode.CreateComponent<Box>();
    box.Color = Color.Blue;
}
```

The static `random` object that we create will be used for randomizing the location of a box on a plane. We want to use a static `Random` instance, since we don't want to risk creating multiple instances that may be seeded with the same value, and that therefore return the exact same sequence of random numbers. The method starts by finding the subplane child of the `PlaneNode` instance that we pass in by calling `planeNode.GetChild("subplane")`. We then create a node that will render the box. To make the box fit the world, we need to set the scale to `0.1`, which will make it 10 cm in size.

We then randomize the position of the box using the `ExtentX` and `ExtentZ` properties, multiplied by a new random value between `0` and `1` that we first subtract `0.5` from. This is to center the position, since the position of the parent node is the center of the plane. Then, we set the position of the box node at the randomized position and 0.1 units above the plane. We also need to add the subplanes position, since it might be a little bit offset from the parent node. Finally, we add the actual box to be rendered and set the color to blue.

Let's now add code to call the `AddBox()` method, based on some game logic.

OnUpdate()

Most games use a game loop. This calls an `Update()` method, which takes an input and calculates the state of the game. UrhoSharp is no exception. The base class of our game has a virtual `OnUpdate()` method that we can override so that we can write code that will be executed with each frame. This method is called frequently, usually about 50 times per second.

We will now override the `Update()` method to add game logic that adds a new box every other second. Let's set this up by going through the following steps:

1. In the `WhackABox` project, open the `Game.cs` file.
2. Add the `newBoxTtl` field and the `newBoxIntervalInSeconds` field to the class at the top of the code.
3. Add the `OnUpdate()` method anywhere in the class, as shown in the following code:

```
private float newBoxTtl;
private readonly float newBoxIntervalInSeconds = 2;

protected override void OnUpdate(float timeStep)
{
    base.OnUpdate(timeStep);

    newBoxTtl -= timeStep;
```

```
if (newBoxTtl < 0)
{
    foreach (var node in scene.Children.OfType<PlaneNode>())
    {
        AddBox(node);
    }

    newBoxTtl += newBoxIntervalInSeconds;
}
}
```

The first field, `newBoxTtl` where `Ttl` is **time to live** (**TTL**), is an internal counter that will be reduced by the number of milliseconds that have passed since the last frame. When it fall below 0, we will add a new box to each plane of the scene. We find all instances of `PlaneNode` by querying the `Children` collection of the scene and returning only the children of the `PlaneNode` type. The second field, `newBoxIntervalInSeconds`, indicates how many seconds we will add to the `newBoxTtl` once it reaches 0. To know how much time has passed since the last frame, we use the `timeStep` parameter that is passed into the `OnUpdate()` method by UrhoSharp. The value of this parameter is the number of seconds since the last frame. It's usually a small value, which will be something like `0.016` if the update loop runs at 50 frames per second. It could vary though, which is why you will want to use this value to carry out the subtraction from `newBoxTtl`.

If you run the game now, you will see that boxes appear on the detected planes. We still cannot interact with them, however, and they look pretty boring. Let's continue by making them rotate.

Making boxes rotate

You can add your own components to UrhoSharp by creating a class that inherits from `Urho.Component`. We will be creating a component that will make the boxes spin around all three axes.

Creating the rotate component

As we mentioned, a component is a class that inherits from `Urho.Component`. This base class defines a virtual method called `OnUpdate()` that behaves the same way as the `Update()` method on the `Game` class itself. This allows us to add logic to the component so that it can modify the state of the node it belongs to.

Let's create the `rotate` component by going through the following steps:

1. In the `WhackABox` project, create a new class called `Rotator.cs` in the root of the project.
2. Add the following code:

```
using Urho;

namespace WhackABox
{
    public class Rotator : Component
    {
        public Vector3 RotationSpeed { get; set; }

        public Rotator()
        {
            ReceiveSceneUpdates = true;
        }

        protected override void OnUpdate(float timeStep)
        {
            Node.Rotate(new Quaternion(
                RotationSpeed.X * timeStep,
                RotationSpeed.Y * timeStep,
                RotationSpeed.Z * timeStep),
                TransformSpace.Local);
        }
    }
}
```

The `RotationSpeed` property will be used to determine the speed of rotation around any specific axis. It will be set when we assign the component to the box node in the next step. To enable the component to receive calls to the `OnUpdate()` method on each frame, we need to set the `ReceiveSceneUpdates` property to `true`. If we don't do this, the component will not be called by UrhoSharp at each update. It's set to `false` by default for performance reasons.

All the fun happens in the `override` of the `OnUpdate()` method. We create a new quaternion to represent a new rotation state. Again, we don't need to know how this works in detail, only that quaternions belong to the mystical world of advanced mathematics. We multiply each axis in the `RotationSpeed` vector by the `timeStep` to generate a new value. The `timeStep` parameter is the number of seconds that have passed since the last frame. We also define the rotation as being around the local coordinate space of this box.

Now that the component is created, we need to add it to the boxes.

Assigning the Rotator component

Adding the `Rotator` component is as simple as adding any other component. Let's set this up by going through the following steps:

1. In the `WhackABox` project, open the `Game.cs` file.
2. Update the `AddBox()` method by adding the code marked in bold in the following code:

```
private void AddBox(PlaneNode planeNode)
{
    var subPlaneNode = planeNode.GetChild("subplane");

    var boxNode = planeNode.CreateChild("Box");
    boxNode.SetScale(0.1f);

    var x = planeNode.ExtentX * (float)(random.NextDouble() -
0.5f);
    var z = planeNode.ExtentZ * (float)(random.NextDouble() -
0.5f);

    boxNode.Position = new Vector3(x, 0.1f, z) +
    subPlaneNode.Position;

    var box = boxNode.CreateComponent<Box>();
    box.Color = Color.Blue;

    var rotationSpeed = new Vector3(10.0f, 20.0f, 30.0f);
    var rotator = new Rotator() { RotationSpeed = rotationSpeed };
    boxNode.AddComponent(rotator);
}
```

We begin by defining how we want the box to rotate by creating a new `Vector3` struct and assigning it to a new variable called `rotationSpeed`. In this case, we want it to rotate 10 units around the *x* axis, 20 units around the *y* axis, and 30 units around the *z* axis. We use the `rotationSpeed` variable to set the `RotationSpeed` property of the `Rotator` component that we instantiate in the second row of the code we added.

Finally, we add the component to the `box` node. The boxes should now rotate in an interesting way.

Adding box hit-test

We now have rotating boxes that keep piling up. We need to add a way to remove boxes. The simplest thing would be to add a feature that removes boxes when we touch them, but we are going to make it a little fancier than that: whenever we touch a box, we want it to shrink and disappear before we remove it from the scene. To do this, we are going to use our newly acquired knowledge of components and then add some code to determine whether we are touching a box.

Adding a death animation

The `Death` component that we are about to add has the same template as the `Rotator` component that we created in the last section. Let's add it by going through the following steps and taking a look at the code:

1. In the `WhackABox` project, create a new class called `Death.cs`.
2. Replace the code in the class with the following code:

```
using Urho;
using System;

namespace WhackABox
{
    public class Death : Component
    {
        private float deathTtl = 1f;
        private float initialScale = 1;

        public Action OnDeath { get; set; }

        public Death()
        {
            ReceiveSceneUpdates = true;
        }

        public override void OnAttachedToNode(Node node)
        {
            initialScale = node.Scale.X;
        }

        protected override void OnUpdate(float timeStep)
        {
            Node.SetScale(deathTtl * initialScale);

            if (deathTtl < 0)
            {
```

```
                        Node.Remove();
            }

            deathTtl -= timeStep;
        }
    }
}
```

We first define two fields. The `deathTtl` field determines how long the animation will be in seconds. The `initialScale` field keeps track of the scale of the node when the component is attached to the node. To receive updates, we need to set `ReceiveSceneUpdates` to `true` in the constructor. The overridden `OnAttachedToNode()` method is called when the component is attached to a node. We use this method to set the `initialScale` field. After the component is attached, we start getting calls on each frame to `OnUpdate()`. On each call, we set a new scale of the node based on the `deathTtl` field multiplied by the `initialScale` field. When the `deathTtl` field reaches zero, we remove the node from the scene. If we don't reach zero, then we subtract the amount of time since the last frame was called, which is given to us by the `timeStep` parameter. All we need to do now is figure out when to add the `Death` component to a box.

DetermineHit()

We need a method that can interpret a touch on the 2D surface of the screen and figure out which boxes we are hitting using an imaginary ray travelling from the camera toward the scene we are looking at. This method is called `DetemineHit`. Let's set this up by going through the following steps:

1. In the `WhackABox` project, open the `Game.cs` file.
2. Add the `DetemineHit()` method anywhere in the class, as shown in the following code:

```
private void DetermineHit(float x, float y)
{
    var cameraRay = camera.GetScreenRay(x, y);
    var result = scene.GetComponent<Octree>
    ().RaycastSingle(cameraRay);

    if (result?.Node?.Name?.StartsWith("Box") == true)
    {
        var node = result?.Node;

        if (node.Components.OfType<Death>().Any())
        {
            return;
```

```
        }
            node.CreateComponent<Death>();
        }
    }
```

The x and y parameters that are passed into the method range from 0 to 1, where 0 represents the left edge or top edge of the screen and 1 represents the right edge or bottom edge of the screen. The exact center of the screen would be x=0.5 and y=0.5. Since we want to get a ray from the camera, we can use a method directly on the camera component called GetScreenRay(). It returns a ray from the camera in the scene in the same direction that the camera is set to. We use this ray and pass it to the Octree component's RaycastSingle() method, which returns a result that will contain a single node, if one is hit.

We examine the results, perform multiple null checks, and finally check whether the name of the node starts with Box. If this is true, we check to see whether the box we hit is already doomed by examining whether there is a Death component attached. If there is, we return. If there isn't, we create a Death component and leave the box to die.

This all looks good so far. We now need something to call the DetermineHit() method.

OnTouchBegin()

Touches are handled as events in UrhoSharp, and this means that they require event handlers. Let's create a handler for the TouchBegin event by going through the following steps:

1. In the WhackABox project, open the Game.cs file.
2. Add the OnTouchBegin() method anywhere in the code, as shown in the following:

```
private void OnTouchBegin(TouchBeginEventArgs e)
{
    var x = (float)e.X / Graphics.Width;
    var y = (float)e.Y / Graphics.Height;

    DetermineHit(x, y);
}
```

When a touch is registered, this method will be called and information about that touch event will be sent as a parameter. This parameter has an X and a Y property, which represent the point on the screen that we have touched. Since the DetermineHit() method wants the values in the range of 0 to 1, we need to divide the X and Y coordinates by the width and height of the screen.

Once that is done, we call the DetermineHit() method. To complete this section, we just have to wire up the event.

Wiring up input

All that's left now is to wire up the event to the Input subsystem of UrhoSharp. This is done by adding a single line of code to the Start() method, as shown in the following steps:

1. In the WhackABox project, open the Game.cs file.
2. In the Start() method, add the code highlighted in bold in the following code fragment:

```
protected override void Start()
{
  scene = new Scene(Context);
  var octree = scene.CreateComponent<Octree>();

  InitializeCamera();
  InitializeLights();
  InitializeRenderer();

  Input.TouchBegin += OnTouchBegin;

  InitializeAR();
}
```

This wires up the TouchBegin event to our OnTouchBegin event handler.

If you run the game now, the boxes should animate and disappear when you tap on them. What we need now is some kind of statistic that shows how many planes there are and how many boxes are still alive.

Updating statistics

At the beginning of the chapter, we added some controls to the XAML that displayed the number of planes and boxes that were present in the game. It's now time to add some code to update those numbers. We will be using internal messaging to decouple the game from the Xamarin.Forms page that we use to display this information.

The game will send a message to the main page that will contain a class that has all the information we need. The main page will receive this message and update the labels.

Defining a statistics class

We are going to use `MessagingCenter` in Xamarin.Forms, which allows us to send an object along with the message. We need to create a class that can carry the information we want to pass. Let's set this up by going through the following steps:

1. In the `WhackABox` project, create a new class called `GameStats.cs`.
2. Add the following code to the class:

```
public class GameStats
{
    public int NumberOfPlanes { get; set; }
    public int NumberOfBoxes { get; set; }
}
```

The class will be a simple data carrier that indicates how many planes and boxes we have.

Sending updates via MessagingCenter

When a node is created or removed, we need to send statistics to anything that is listening. To do this, we need a new method that will go through the scene and count how many planes and boxes we have, and then send a message. Let's set this up by going through the following steps:

1. In the `WhackABox` project, open the `Game.cs` file.
2. Add a method called `SendStats()` anywhere in the class, as shown in the following code:

```
private void SendStats()
{
    var planes = scene.Children.OfType<PlaneNode>();
    var boxCount = 0;
```

```
        foreach (var plane in planes)
        {
            boxCount += plane.Children.Count(e => e.Name == "Box");
        }

        var stats = new GameStats()
        {
            NumberOfBoxes = boxCount,
            NumberOfPlanes = planes.Count()
        };

        Xamarin.Forms.Device.BeginInvokeOnMainThread(() =>
        {
            Xamarin.Forms.MessagingCenter.Send(this, "stats_updated",
                stats);
        });
    }
```

The method checks all children of the `scene` object to find nodes of the `PlaneNode` type. We iterate through all of these nodes and count how many of the node's children have the name `Box`, and then indicate this number in a variable called `boxCount`. When we have this information, we create a `GameStats` object and initialize it with the box count and the plane count.

The last step is to send the message. We have to make sure that we are using the UI thread (the `MainThread`) since we are going to update the GUI. Only the UI thread is allowed to touch the GUI. This is done by wrapping the `MessagingCenter.Send()` call in `BeginInvokeOnMainThread()`.

The message that is sent is `stats_updated`. It contains the stats information as an argument. Let's now make use of the `SendStats()` method.

Wiring up events

The scene has a lot of events that we can wire up. We will hook up to `NodeAdded` and `NodeRemoved` to determine when we need to send statistics information. Let's set this up by going through the following steps:

1. In the `WhackABox` project, open the `Game.cs` file.
2. In the `Start()` method, add the code that is highlighted in bold in the following fragment:

```
protected override void Start()
{
```

```
scene = new Scene(Context);
scene.NodeAdded += (e) => SendStats();
scene.NodeRemoved += (e) => SendStats();
var octree = scene.CreateComponent<Octree>();

InitializeCamera();
InitializeLights();
InitializeRenderer();

Input.TouchEnd += OnTouchEnd;

InitializeAR();
    }
```

Each time a node is either added or removed, a new message will be sent to the GUI.

Updating the GUI

This will be the last method we add to the game. It handles the information updates and also updates the labels in the GUI. Let's add it by going through the following steps:

1. In the WhackABox project, open the MainPage.xaml.cs file.
2. Add a method called StatsUpdated() anywhere in the code, as shown in the following fragment:

```
private void StatsUpdated(Game sender, GameStats stats)
{
    boxCountLabel.Text = stats.NumberOfBoxes.ToString();
    planeCountLabel.Text = stats.NumberOfPlanes.ToString();
}
```

The method receives the GameStats object that we sent and updates the two labels in the GUI.

Subscribing to the updates in the MainForm

The last line of code to add will wire up the StatsUpdated handler to an incoming message. Let's set this up by going through the following steps:

1. In the WhackABox project, open the MainPage.xaml.cs file.

2. In the constructor, add the line of code that is highlighted in bold in the following fragment:

```
public MainPage()
{
    InitializeComponent();
    MessagingCenter.Subscribe<Game, GameStats>(this,
    "stats_updated", StatsUpdated);
}
```

This line of code hooks up an incoming message with the content `stats_updated` to the `StatsUpdated` method. Now run the game and go out into the world to hunt down those boxes!

The completed app looks something like the following screenshot, with spinning boxes popping up at random locations:

Summary

In this chapter, we learned how to integrate AR into Xamarin.Forms by using custom renderers. We took advantage of UrhoSharp to use cross-platform rendering, components, and input management to interact with the world. We also learned a bit about `MessagingCenter`, which can be used to send internal in-process messages between different parts of an application to reduce coupling.

Next up, we are going to dive into machine learning and create an app that can recognize a hotdog in an image.

Hot Dog or Not Hot Dog Using Machine Learning

9

In this chapter, we will learn how to use machine learning to create a model that we can use for image classification. We will export the model as a TensorFlow model that we can use on Android devices and a CoreML model that we can use on iOS devices. In order to train and export models, we will use Azure Cognitive Services and the Custom Vision service.

Once we have exported the models, we will learn how to use them for Android and iOS apps.

The following topics will be covered in this chapter:

- Training a model with Azure Cognitive Service Custom Vision
- How to use TensorFlow models for image classification on an Android device
- How to use CoreML models for image classification on an iOS device

Technical requirements

To be able to complete this project, you need to have Visual Studio for Mac or PC installed, as well as the Xamarin components. See `Chapter 1`, *Introduction to Xamarin*, for more details on how to set up your environment. To use Azure Cognitive Services, you need a Microsoft account. The source code for this chapter is available at the GitHub repository at `https://github.com/PacktPublishing/Xamarin.Forms-Projects/tree/master/Chapter-9`.

Machine learning

The term machine learning was coined in 1959 by Arthur Samuel, an American pioneer in artificial intelligence. Tom M. Mitchell, an American computer scientist, provided a more formal definition of machine learning later:

> *A computer program is said to learn from experience E with respect to some class of tasks T and performance measure P if its performance at tasks in T, as measured by P, improves with experience E.*

In simpler terms, this quote describes a computer program that has the ability to learn without being explicitly programmed. In machine learning, algorithms are used to build a mathematical model of sample data or training data. The models are used for computer programs to make predictions and decisions without being explicitly programmed for the task in question.

Azure Cognitive Services – Custom Vision

Custom Vision is a tool or service that can be used for training models for image classification and for detecting objects in images. In Custom Vision, we are able to upload our own images and tag them so that they can be trained for image classification. If we train a model for object detection, we can also tag specific areas of an image. Because models are already pretrained for basic image recognition, we don't need a large amount of data to get a great result. The recommendation is to have at least 30 images per tag.

When we have trained a model, we can use it with an API that is part of the Custom Vision service. We can also, however, export models for CoreML (iOS), TensorFlow (Android), ONNX (Windows), and Dockerfile (Azure IoT Edge, Azure Functions, and AzureML). These models can be used to carry out classification or object detection without having a connection to the Custom Vision service.

CoreML

CoreML is a framework that was introduced in iOS 11. CoreML makes it possible to integrate Machine Learning models into iOS apps. On top of CoreML, we have three high-level APIs—Vision APIs for image analysis, natural language APIs for natural language processing, and Gameplay Kit for evaluating learned decision trees. More information about CoreML can be found in the official documentation from Apple at `https://developer.apple.com/documentation/coreml`.

TensorFlow

TensorFlow is an open source machine learning framework, which can be found at `https://www.tensorflow.org/`. TensorFlow can be used for more than simply running models on mobile devices—it can also be used for training models. For running it on mobile devices, we have TensorFlow Mobile and TensorFlow Lite. The models that are exported from Azure Cognitive Services are for TensorFlow Mobile. There are also Xamarin bindings for both TensorFlow Mobile and TensorFlow Lite, which are available as NuGet packages. However, bear in mind that plans have been made to depreciate TensorFlow Mobile during 2019. This does not mean that we can't use it after that, but it does mean that it is unlikely to get any more updates after they have depreciated it, and as long as Custom Vision still exports models for TensorFlow Mobile, we will continue to use it. The concepts will be the same, even if the APIs look a bit different.

Project overview

If you have seen the TV series *Silicon Valley*, you have probably heard of the *Not Hotdog* application. In this chapter, we will learn how to build that app. The first part of this chapter will involve collecting the data that we will use for creating a machine learning model that can detect whether or not a photo has a hot dog.

In the second part of the chapter, we will build an app for iOS and an app for Android where the user can pick a photo in the photo library in order to analyze it to see whether it has a hot dog. The estimated time for completing this project is 120 minutes.

Getting started

We can use either Visual Studio 2017 on a PC or Visual Studio for Mac to do this project. To build an iOS app using Visual Studio for PC, you must have a Mac connected. If you don't have access to a Mac at all, you can choose to just do the Android parts of this project. Similarly, if you only have a Mac, you can choose to just do the iOS or Android parts of this project.

Building the Hot Dog or Not Hot Dog application using machine learning

Let's get started! We will first train a model for image classification that we can use later in the chapter to decide whether a photo has a hot dog.

Training a model

To train a model for image classification, we need to collect photos of hot dogs and photos that aren't of hot dogs. Because most items in the world are not hot dogs, we need more photos that don't contain hot dogs. It's better if the photos of hot dogs cover a lot of different hot-dog scenarios—with bread, with ketchup, or with mustard, such as. This is so the model will be able to recognize hot dogs in different situations. When we are collecting photos that aren't of hot dogs, we also need to have a big variety of photos that are both of items that are similar to hot dogs and that are completely different to hot dogs.

The model that is in the solution on GitHub was trained with 240 photos, 60 of which were of hot dogs and 180 of which were not.

Once we have collected all the photos, we will be ready to start training the model by going through the following steps:

1. Go to `https://customvision.ai`.
2. Log in and create a new project.
3. Give the project a name—in our case, `HotDogOrNot`.
4. The project type should be **Classification**.
5. Select **General (compact)** as the domain. We use a compact domain if we want to export models and run them on a mobile device.

7. Click **Create project** to continue, as shown in the following screenshot:

Tagging images

Once we have created a project, we can start to upload images and tag them. We will start by adding photos of hot dogs by going through the following steps:

1. Click **Add images**.
2. Select the photos of hot dogs that should be uploaded.

3. Tag the photos with **hotdog,** as shown in the following screenshot:

Once we have uploaded all the photos of hot dogs, it is time to upload photos that aren't of hot dogs by going through the following steps. For best results, we should also include photos of objects that look similar to hot dogs but are not:

1. Click **Add images**.
2. Select the photos that aren't of hot dogs.

3. Tag the photos with **not-hotdog**, as shown in the following screenshot. Set this tag as a negative tag. A negative tag is used for photos that don't contain any objects that we have created other tags for. In this case, none of the photos we will upload contain hot dogs:

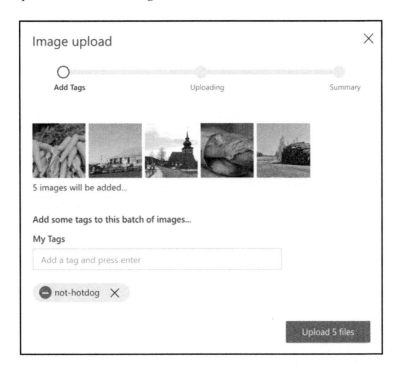

Training a model

Once we have uploaded the photos, it is time to train a model. Not all the photos that we are uploading will be used for training; some will be used for verification, to give us a score about how good the model is. If we upload photos in chunks and train the model after each chunk, we will be able to see our scores improving. To train a model, click the green **Train** button at the top of the page.

The following screenshot shows the result of a training iteration, where the precision of the model is **93.4%**:

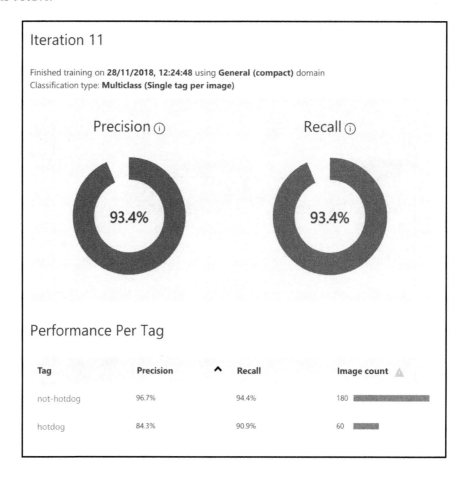

Exporting a model

Once we have trained a model, we will be able to export it so that it can be used on a device. We can use the APIs if we want to, but to make fast classifications, and to be able to do this offline, we will add the models to the app packages. Export and download the **CoreML** model and the **TensorFlow** model, as shown in the following screenshot:

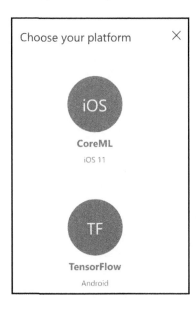

Building the app

Once we have one CoreML model and one TensorFlow model, it is time to build the app. Our app will use the trained models to classify photos according to whether they are photos of hot dogs. The CoreML model that we exported from the Custom Vision service will be used for iOS and the TensorFlow model for Android.

Create a new project with the template for **Mobile App (Xamarin.Forms)**. The template can be found under the **Cross-Platform** tab. Use `HotDotOrNot` as the name of the project, as shown in the following screenshot:

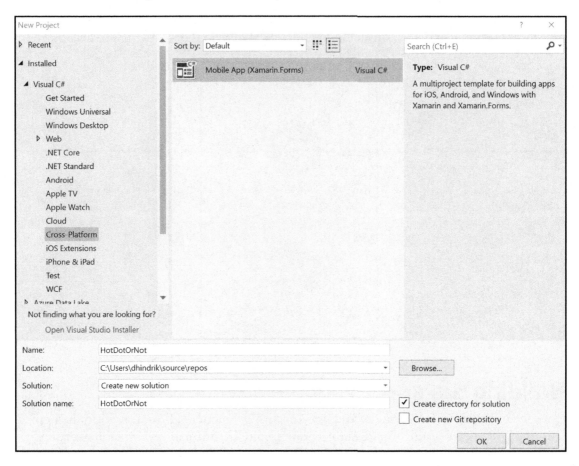

In the next step, we will select what Xamarin.Forms template we should use. For our project, select **Blank**. For this project, we will target Android and iOS as the platforms and use **.NET Standard** as the code-sharing strategy, as shown in the following screenshot:

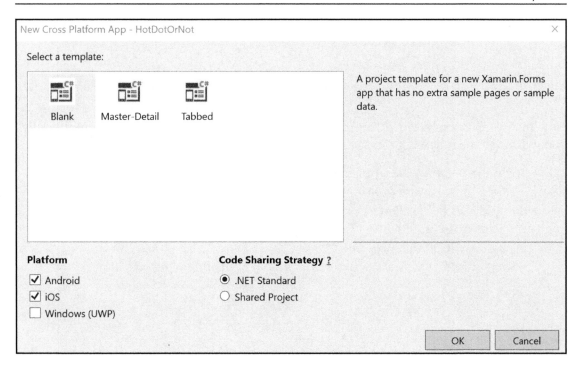

Before doing anything else we will update the Xamarin.Forms NuGet package to make sure that we have the latest version of it.

Classifying images with machine learning

The code that we will use for image classification cannot be shared between the iOS and the Android projects. However, to be able to carry out classifications from shared code (the HotDogOrNot project), we will create an interface. First, however, we will create a class for the EventArgs that we will use in the interface by going through the following steps:

1. In the HotDogOrNot project, create a new class called ClassificationEventArgs.

2. Add EventArgs as a base class, as shown in the following code:

```
using System;
using System.Collections.Generic;

public class ClassificationEventArgs : EventArgs
{
    public Dictionary<string, float> Classifications { get; private
    set; }
```

```
public ClassificationEventArgs(Dictionary<string, float>
classifications)
{
    Classifications = classifications;
}
}
```

Now that we have created the `ClassificationEventArgs`, we can create the interface by going through the following steps:

1. In the `HotdogOrNot` project, create a new interface called `IClassifier` in the `HotdogOrNot` project.
2. Add a method called `Classify` that doesn't return anything but takes a byte array as an argument.
3. Add an event that uses the `ClassificationEventArgs` and call it `ClassificationCompleted`, as shown in the following code:

```
using System;
using System.Collections.Generic;

public interface IClassifier
{
    void Classify(byte[] bytes);
    event EventHandler<ClassificationEventArgs>
    ClassificationCompleted;
}
```

Using CoreML for image classification

The first thing we will do is add the CoreML model to the `HotDogOrNot.iOS` project by going through the following steps:

1. Extract the ZIP file that we get from the Custom Vision service.
2. Find the `.mlmodel` file and rename it as `hotdog-or-not.mlmodel`.
3. Add it to the `Resources` folder in the iOS project.
4. Make sure that the build action is `BundleResource`. If you are using Visual Studio on a Mac, a `.cs` file will be created. Remove this file, because it will be easier to use the model without the code.

When we have added the file to the iOS project, we will be ready to create the iOS implementation of the `IClassifier` interface by going through the following steps:

1. Create a new class called `CoreMLClassifier` in the `HotDogOrNotDog.iOS` project.
2. Add the `IClassifier` interface.
3. Implement the `ClassificationCompleted` event and the `Classify` method from the interface, as shown in the following code:

```
using System;
using System.Linq;
using CoreML;
using Foundation;
using ImageIO;
using Vision;
using System.Collections.Generic;

namespace HotDogOrNot.iOS
{
    public class CoreMLClassifier : IClassifier
    {
        public event EventHandler<ClassificationEventArgs>
        ClassificationCompleted;
        public void Classify(byte[] bytes)
        {
            //Code will be added here
        }
    }
}
```

The first thing we will do in the `Classify` method is compile the CoreML model by going through the following steps:

1. Get the path of the model with the `NSBundle.MainBundle.GetUrlForResource` method.
2. Compile the model with the `MLModel.CompileModel` method. Pass the model's URL and an error object that will indicate whether one or more errors occurred during the compilation of the model.
3. Use the URL from the `CompileModel` method and pass it to `MLModel.Create` to create a model object that we can work with, as shown in the following code:

```
var modelUrl = NSBundle.MainBundle.GetUrlForResource("hotdog-or-
not", "mlmodel");
var compiledUrl = MLModel.CompileModel(modelUrl, out var error);
var compiledModel = MLModel.Create(compiledUrl, out error);
```

Because we are going to use a photo for the CoreML model, we can use the Vision APIs that are built on top of the CoreML. To do this, we will use `VNCoreMLRequest`. Before creating the request, however, we will create a callback that will handle when the request is completed by going through the following steps:

1. Open the `CoreMLClassifier.cs`.
2. Create a new private method called `HandleVNRequest` with two parameters, one of the `VNRequst` type and one of the `NSError` type.
3. If the error is `null`, invoke the `ClassificationCompleted` event with `ClassificationEventArgs`, which contains an empty `Dictionary`.
4. If the error is not null, get the result with the `GetResults` method on the `VNRequest` object.
5. Order the classifications by `Confidence` so that the classification with the highest confidence is first.
6. Convert the result to a `Dictionary` using the `ToDictionary` method.
7. Invoke the `ClassificationCompleted` event with `ClassificationEventArgs`, which contains the sorted dictionary. This is shown in the following code:

```
private void HandleVNRequest(VNRequest request, NSError error)
{
    if (error != null)
    {
    ClassificationCompleted?.Invoke(this, new
    ClassificationEventArgs(new Dictionary<string, float>()));
    }

    var result = request.GetResults<VNClassificationObservation>();
    var classifications = result.OrderByDescending(x =>
    x.Confidence).ToDictionary(x => x.Identifier, x =>
    x.Confidence);

    ClassificationCompleted?.Invoke(this, new
    ClassificationEventArgs(classifications));
}
```

When we have created the callback, we will go back to the `Classify` method and perform the classification by going through the following steps:

1. Convert the model to a `VNCoreMLModel`, because we need this to use the Vision APIs. Use the `VNCoreMLModel.FromMLModel` method to convert the model.

2. Create a new `VNCoreMLRequest` object and pass the `VNCoreMLModel` and the callback we created as arguments to the constructor.

3. Convert the input data to an `NSData` object using the `NSData.FromArray` method.

4. Create a new `VNImageRequestHandler` object and pass the data object, `CGImagePropertyOrientation.Up`, and a new `VNImageOptions` object to the constructor.

5. Use the `Perform` method on the `VNImageRequestHandler` and pass the `VNCoreMLRequest` in an array and an error object as an argument, as shown in the following code:

```
public void Classify(byte[] bytes)
{
    var modelUrl = NSBundle.MainBundle.GetUrlForResource("hotdog-or-
not", "mlmodel");
    var compiledUrl = MLModel.CompileModel(modelUrl, out var error);
    var compiledModel = MLModel.Create(compiledUrl, out error);

    var vnCoreModel = VNCoreMLModel.FromMLModel(compiledModel, out error);

    var classificationRequest = new VNCoreMLRequest(vnCoreModel, HandleVNRequest);

    var data = NSData.FromArray(bytes);
    var handler = new VNImageRequestHandler(data, CGImagePropertyOrientation.Up, new VNImageOptions());

    handler.Perform(new[] { classificationRequest }, out error);
}
```

Using TensorFlow for image classification

Now that we have written the code in iOS to recognize hot dogs, it is now time to write the code for Android. The first things to do is to add the files we exported from the Custom Vision to the Android project. For TensorFlow, the actual model and the labels (the tags) are separated into two files. Let's set this up by going through the following steps:

1. Extract the ZIP file that we got from the Custom Vision service.
2. Find the `model.pb` file and rename it as `hotdog-or-not-model.pb`.

3. Find the `labels.txt` file and rename it as `hotdog-or-not-labels.txt`.

4. Import the files to the `Assets` folder in the Android project. Make sure that the build action is Android Asset.

When we have imported the files into the Android project, we can start to write code. To get the libraries we need for TensorFlow, we also need to install a NuGet package by going through the following steps:

1. In the `HotDogOrNotDog.Android` project, install the `Xam.Android.Tensorflow` NuGet package.

2. Then, create a new class called `TensorflowClassifier` in the `HotDogOrNotDog.Android` project.

3. Add the `IClassifier` interface to the `TensorflowClassifier` class.

4. Implement the `ClassificationCompleted` event and the `Classify` method from the interface, as shown in the following code:

```
using System;
using System.Collections.Generic;
using System.IO;
using System.Linq;
using Android.App;
using Android.Graphics;
using Org.Tensorflow.Contrib.Android;

public class TensorflowClassifier : IClassifier
{
        public event EventHandler<ClassificationEventArgs>
        ClassificationCompleted;

        public void Classify(byte[] bytes)
        {
            //Code will be added here
        }
}
```

The first thing we will do in the `Classify` method is read the model and the label files from the `Assets` folder by going through the following steps:

1. Use the `TensorFlowInferenceInterface` class to import the model. After that, use the path to the asset folder and the name of the model file as arguments for the constructor.

2. Use `StreamReader` to read the labels.

3. Read the whole text file, split by line breaks (`'/n'`), and trim the text on each row to remove whitespaces. We will also filter away items that are empty or null and convert the result to a list of strings, as shown in the following code:

```
public void Classify(byte[] bytes)
{
    var assets = Application.Context.Assets;

    var inferenceInterface = new
    TensorFlowInferenceInterface(assets, "hotdog-or-not-model.pb");

    var sr = new StreamReader(assets.Open("hotdog-or-not-
    labels.txt"));
    var labels = sr.ReadToEnd().Split('\n').Select(s => s.Trim())
    .Where(s => !string.IsNullOrEmpty(s)).ToList();
}
```

`TensorFlow` models do not understand images, so we need to convert them to binary data. The images need to be converted to a float array of point values, one per red, green, and blue value for each pixel. Some adjustments to the color values are also necessary. As well as this, we need to resize the images so that they are 227 x 227 pixels. To do this, write the following code:

```
var bitmap = BitmapFactory.DecodeByteArray(bytes, 0, bytes.Length);
var resizedBitmap = Bitmap.CreateScaledBitmap(bitmap, 227, 227, false)
                            .Copy(Bitmap.Config.Argb8888, false);

var floatValues = new float[227 * 227 * 3];
var intValues = new int[227 * 227];

resizedBitmap.GetPixels(intValues, 0, 227, 0, 0, 227, 227);

for (int i = 0; i < intValues.Length; ++i)
{
    var val = intValues[i];
    floatValues[i * 3 + 0] = ((val & 0xFF) - 104);
    floatValues[i * 3 + 1] = (((val >> 8) & 0xFF) - 117);
    floatValues[i * 3 + 2] = (((val >> 16) & 0xFF) - 123);
}
```

We are now ready to run the model by going through the following steps:

1. Create a new array of floats with the same size as the list of labels. The output of the model will be fetched into this array. An item in the array will represent the confidence for a tag. The matching label will have the same position in the labels list as the confidence result in the float array.

2. Run the `Feed` method of the `TensorFlowInferenceInterface` and pass `"Placeholder"` as the first argument, the binary data as the second argument, and the dimensions of the image as the third argument.

3. Run the `Run` method of `TensorFlowInferenceInterface` and pass an array that contains a string with the value `"loss"`.

4. Run the `Fetch` method of the `TensorFlowInferenceInterface`. Pass `"loss"` as the first argument and the float arrays for the outputs as the second argument.

5. Create a `Dictionary <string, float>` and fill it with the labels and the confidence for each label.

6. Invoke the `ClassificationCompleted` event with `ClassificationEventArgs`, which contains the dictionary, as shown in the following code:

```
var outputs = new float[labels.Count];
inferenceInterface.Feed("Placeholder", floatValues, 1, 227, 227,
3);
inferenceInterface.Run(new[] { "loss" });
inferenceInterface.Fetch("loss", outputs);

var result = new Dictionary<string, float>();

for (var i = 0; i < labels.Count; i++)
{
    var label = labels[i];
    result.Add(label, outputs[i]);
}

ClassificationCompleted?.Invoke(this, new
ClassificationEventArgs(result));
```

Creating a base ViewModel

Before we initialize the app, we will create a base ViewModel so that we can use it when we are registering the other ViewModels. In this, we will put the code that can be shared between all the ViewModels of the app. Let's set this up by going through the following steps:

1. In the `HotDogOrNot` project, create a new folder called `ViewModels`.
2. Create a new class called `ViewModel` in the `ViewModels` folder we created.
3. Make the new class public and abstract.

4. Add and implement the `INotifiedPropertyChanged` interface. This is necessary because we want to use data bindings.

5. Add a `Set` method that will make it easier for us to raise the `PropertyChanged` event from the `INotifiedPropertyChanged` interface. The method will check whether the value has changed. If it has, it will raise the event.

6. Add a static property of the `INavigation` type called `Navigation`, as shown in the following code:

```
using System;
using System.Collections.Generic;
using System.ComponentModel;
using System.Runtime.CompilerServices;
using Xamarin.Forms;

namespace HotDogOrNot
{
    public abstract class ViewModel : INotifyPropertyChanged
    {
        public event PropertyChangedEventHandler PropertyChanged;
        protected void Set<T>(ref T field, T newValue,
        [CallerMemberName] string propertyName = null)
        {
            if (!EqualityComparer<T>.Default.Equals(field,
                newValue))
            {
                field = newValue;
                PropertyChanged?.Invoke(this, new
                PropertyChangedEventArgs(propertyName));
            }
        }

        public static INavigation Navigation { get; set; }
    }
}
```

Initializing the app

We are now ready to write the initialization code for the app. We will set up **inversion of control (IoC)** and carry out the necessary configuration.

Creating a Resolver

We will now create a helper class that will ease the process of resolving object graphs through `Autofac`. This will help us to create types based on a configured IoC container. In this project, we will use `Autofac` as the IoC library by going through the following steps:

1. In the `HotDogOrNot` project, install the NuGet package `Autofac` to the `HotDogOrNot` project.

2. Create a new class called `Resolver` in the root.

3. Add a private static field of the `IContainer` type called `container` (from `Autofac`).

4. Add a public static method called `Initialize` with `IContainer` as a parameter. Set the value of the parameter to the container field.

5. Add a generic `static public` method called `Resolve`, which will return an instance that is based on the type argument with the `Resolve` method of `IContainer`, as shown in the following code:

```
using System;
using Autofac;

namespace HotDogOrNot
{
    public class Resolver
    {
        private static IContainer container;

        public static void Initialize(IContainer container)
        {
            Resolver.container = container;
        }

        public static T Resolve<T>()
        {
            return container.Resolve<T>();
        }
    }
}
```

Creating a Bootstrapper

To configure the dependency injection and initialize the Resolver, we will create a
bootstrapper. We will have one shared bootstrapper and one bootstrapper for each
platform to match their specific configurations. We will have different implementations of
the IClassifier in iOS and Android. To create a bootstrapper, go through the following
steps:

1. Create a new class in the HotDogOrNot project and name it Bootstrapper.
2. Write the following code in the new class, as shown in the following code:

```
using System.Linq;
using System.Reflection;
using Autofac;
using HotdogOrNot.ViewModels;
using Xamarin.Forms;
namespace HotDogOrNot
{
    public class Bootstrapper
    {
        protected ContainerBuilder ContainerBuilder { get; private
        set; }

        public Bootstrapper()
        {
            Initialize();
            FinishInitialization();
        }

        protected virtual void Initialize()
        {
            ContainerBuilder = new ContainerBuilder();

            var currentAssembly = Assembly.GetExecutingAssembly();

            foreach (var type in
            currentAssembly.DefinedTypes.Where(e =>
            e.IsSubclassOf(typeof(Page))))
            {
                ContainerBuilder.RegisterType(type.AsType());
            }

            foreach (var type in
            currentAssembly.DefinedTypes.Where(e =>
            e.IsSubclassOf(typeof(ViewModel))))
            {
                ContainerBuilder.RegisterType(type.AsType());
```

```
        }
    }

    private void FinishInitialization()
    {
        var container = ContainerBuilder.Build();

        Resolver.Initialize(container);
    }
  }
}
```

Creating the iOS bootstrapper

In the iOS bootstrapper, we will have configurations that are specific to the iOS app. To create an iOS app, we go through the following steps:

1. In the `HotDogOrNot.iOS` project, create a new class and name it `Bootstrapper`.

2. Make the new class inherit from `HotDogOrNot.Bootstrapper`.

3. Write the following code and resolve all the references:

```
using System;
using Autofac;

public class Bootstrapper : HotdogOrNot.Bootstrapper
{
    public static void Init()
    {
        var instance = new Bootstrapper();
    }

    protected override void Initialize()
    {
        base.Initialize();

        ContainerBuilder.RegisterType<CoreMLClassifier>
        ().As<IClassifier>();
    }
}
```

4. Go to `AppDelegate.cs` in the iOS project.

5. Before the call to `LoadApplication`, in the `FinishedLaunching` method, call the `Init` method of the platform-specific bootstrapper, as shown in the following code:

```
public override bool FinishedLaunching(UIApplication app,
NSDictionary options)
{
        global::Xamarin.Forms.Forms.Init();
        Bootstrapper.Init();

        LoadApplication(new App());

        return base.FinishedLaunching(app, options);
}
```

Creating the Android bootstrapper

In the Android bootstrapper, we will have configurations that are specific to the Android app. To create bootstrapper in Android, we go through the following steps:

1. In the Android project, create a new class and name it `Bootstrapper`.
2. Make the new class inherit from `HotDogOrNot.Bootstrapper`.
3. Write the following code and resolve all the references:

```
using System;
using Autofac;

public class Bootstrapper : HotDogOrNot.Bootstrapper
{
        public static void Init()
        {
            var instance = new Bootstrapper();
        }

        protected override void Initialize()
        {
            base.Initialize();

            ContainerBuilder.RegisterType<TensorflowClassifier>
            ().As<IClassifier>().SingleInstance();
        }
}
```

4. Go to the `MainActivity.cs` file in the Android project.
5. Before the call to `LoadApplication,` in the `OnCreate` method, call the `Execute` method of the platform-specific bootstrapper, as shown in the following code:

```
protected override void OnCreate(Bundle savedInstanceState)
{
    TabLayoutResource = Resource.Layout.Tabbar;
    ToolbarResource = Resource.Layout.Toolbar;

    base.OnCreate(savedInstanceState);
    global::Xamarin.Forms.Forms.Init(this, savedInstanceState);

    Bootstrapper.Init();

    LoadApplication(new App());
}
```

Building the first view

The first view in this app will be a simple view with two buttons. One button will be for starting the camera so the users can take a photo of something to determine whether it is a hot dog. The other button will be for picking a photo from the photo library of the device.

Building the ViewModel

We will start by creating the `ViewModel`, which will handle what will happen when a user taps one of the buttons. Let's set this up by going through the following steps:

1. Create a new class called `MainViewModel` in the `ViewModels` folder.
2. Add `ViewModel` as a base class for `MainViewModel`.
3. Create a private field of the `IClassifier` type and call it `classifier`.
4. Create a constructor that has the `IClassifier` as a parameter.
5. Set the value of the classifier field to the value of the parameter in the constructor, as shown in the following code:

```
using System.IO;
using System.Linq;
using System.Windows.Input;
using HotdogOrNot.Models;
using HotdogOrNot.Views;
using Xamarin.Forms;
```

```
public class MainViewModel : ViewModel
{
    private IClassifier classifier;

    public MainViewModel(IClassifier classifier)
    {
        this.classifier = classifier;
    }
}
```

We will use the `Xam.Plugin.Media` NuGet package for taking the photo and accessing the photo library of the device. We need to install the package for all projects in the solution by using the NuGet package manager. Before we can use the package, however, we need to do some configuration for each platform. We will start with Android. Let's set this up by going through the following steps:

1. The plugin needs the `WRITE_EXTERNAL_STORAGE` and `READ_EXTERNAL_STORAGE` permissions. The plugin will add these for us, but we need to override the `OnRequestPermissionResult` in the `MainActivity.cs`.

2. Call the `OnRequestPermissionsResult` method, as shown in the following code.

3. Add `CrossCurrentActivity.Current.Init(this, savedInstanceState)` after initializing Xamarin.Forms in the `OnCreate` method in the `MainActivity.cs` file, as shown in the following code:

```
public override void OnRequestPermissionsResult(int requestCode,
string[] permissions, Android.Content.PM.Permission[] grantResults)
{
Plugin.Permissions.PermissionsImplementation.Current.OnRequestPermi
ssionsResult(requestCode, permissions, grantResults);
}
```

We also need to add some configuration about the file paths from which the users can pick photos. Let's set this up by going through the following steps:

1. In the `HotDogOrNot.Android` project, add a folder called `xml` to the `Resources` folder

2. Create a new XML file called `file_paths.xml` in the new folder.

3. Add the following code to `file_paths.xml`:

```xml
<?xml version="1.0" encoding="utf-8"?>
<paths xmlns:android="http://schemas.android.com/apk/res/android">
    <external-files-path name="my_images" path="Pictures" />
    <external-files-path name="my_movies" path="Movies" />
</paths>
```

The last thing we need to do to set up the plugin for the Android project is add the following code in the `AndroidManifest.xml` (it can be found in the `Properties` folder of the Android project) inside the application element:

```xml
<manifest xmlns:android="http://schemas.android.com/apk/res/android"
  android:versionCode="1" android:versionName="1.0"
  package="xfb.HotdogOrNot">
    <uses-sdk android:minSdkVersion="21" android:targetSdkVersion="27"
     />
    <application android:label="HotdogOrNot.Android">
    <provider android:name="android.support.v4.content.FileProvider"
    android:authorities="${applicationId}.fileprovider"
    android:exported="false" android:grantUriPermissions="true">
    <meta-data android:name="android.support.FILE_PROVIDER_PATHS"
    android:resource="@xml/file_paths"></meta-data>
    </provider>
    </application>
</manifest>
```

For the iOS project, the only thing we need to do is add the following four usage descriptions to the `info.plist`:

```xml
<key>NSCameraUsageDescription</key>
<string>This app needs access to the camera to take photos.</string>
<key>NSPhotoLibraryUsageDescription</key>
<string>This app needs access to photos.</string>
<key>NSMicrophoneUsageDescription</key>
<string>This app needs access to microphone.</string>
<key>NSPhotoLibraryAddUsageDescription</key>
<string>This app needs access to the photo gallery.</string>
```

Once we have finished with the configuration for the plugin, we can start using it. We will start by creating a method that will handle the media file that we will get both when the user is taking a photo and when the user is picking a photo.

Let's set this up by going through the following steps:

1. Open the `MainViewModel.cs` file.

2. Create a private method called `HandlePhoto` that has a parameter of the `MediaFile` type.

3. Add an `if` statement to check whether the `MediaFile` parameter is null. If so, perform an empty return.

4. Get the stream of the photo using the `GetStream` method of the `MediaFile` class.

5. Add a private field of the `byte []` type called `bytes`.

6. Convert the stream into a byte array with the `ReadFully` method that we will create in the next step.

7. Add an event handler to the `ClassificationCompleted` event of the classifier. We will create the event handler later in this chapter.

8. Finally, add a call to the `Classify` method of the classifier and use the byte array as the argument, as shown in the following code:

```
private void HandlePhoto(MediaFile photo)
{
    if(photo == null)
    {
        return;
    }

    var stream = photo.GetStream();
    bytes = ReadFully(stream);

    classifier.ClassificationCompleted +=
    Classifier_ClassificationCompleted;
    classifier.Classify(bytes);
}
```

We will now create the `ReadFully` method that we called in the preceding code. We will use this to read the full stream into a byte array. The code will look as follows:

```
private byte[] ReadFully(Stream input)
{
    byte[] buffer = new byte[16 * 1024];
    using (MemoryStream memoryStream = new MemoryStream())
    {
        int read;
        while ((read = input.Read(buffer, 0, buffer.Length)) > 0)
```

```
    {
        memoryStream.Write(buffer, 0, read);
    }
    return memoryStream.ToArray();
  }

}
```

Before we create the event handler, we will create a model that we will use inside the event handler by going through the following steps:

1. In the `HotDogOrNot` project, create a new folder called `Models` in the `HotDogOrNot` project.
2. Create a new class in the `Models` folder called `Result`.
3. Add a property of the `bool` type called `IsHotdog`.
4. Add a property of the `float` type called `Confidence`.
5. Add a property of the `byte[]` type called `PhotoBytes`, as shown in the following code:

```
public class Result
{
    public bool IsHotdog { get; set; }
    public float Confidence { get; set; }
    public byte[] PhotoBytes { get; set; }
}
```

We can now add an event handler to the ViewModel by going through the following steps:

1. Create a method called `Classifier_ClassificationCompleted` that has an `object` and a `ClassificationEventArgs` parameter.
2. Remove the event handler from the classifier so that we don't allocate unnecessary memory.
3. Check whether the classifications dictionary contains any items. If it does, order the dictionary so that the classifications with the highest confidence (values) will be first.
4. Create a new `Result` object and set the properties as shown in the following code:

```
void Classifier_ClassificationCompleted(object sender,
ClassificationEventArgs e)
{
    classifier.ClassificationCompleted -=
    Classifier_ClassificationCompleted;
```

```
        Result result = null;

        if (e.Classifications.Any())
        {
            var classificationResult =
            e.Classifications.OrderByDescending(x => x.Value).First();

            result = new Result()
            {
                IsHotdog = classificationResult.Key == "hotdog",
                Confidence = classificationResult.Value,
                PhotoBytes = bytes
            };
        }
        else
        {
            result = new Result()
            {
                IsHotDog = false,
                Confidence = 1.0f,
                PhotoBytes = bytes
            };
        }
    }
```

When we have created the result view, we will go back to the event handler to add the navigation to the result view. The last thing we will do in this `ViewModel` is create a `Command` property for the buttons that we have in the view. Let's start by setting up the **take photo** button by going through the following steps:

1. Create a new property of the `ICommand` type called `TakePhoto` in the `MainViewModel.cs` file.

2. Use an expression to return a new `Command`.

3. Pass an `Action` as an expression to the constructor of the `Command`.

4. In the `Action`, use the `CrossMedia.Current.TakePhotoAsync` method and pass a `StoreCameraMediaOptions` object to it.

5. In `StoreCameraMediaOptions`, set the default camera as the rear camera using the `DefaultCamera` property.

6. Pass the result of the call to the `TakePhotoAsync` method to the `HandlePhoto` method, as shown in the following code:

```
public ICommand TakePhoto => new Command(async() =>
{
    var photo = await CrossMedia.Current.TakePhotoAsync(new
```

```
StoreCameraMediaOptions()
{
  DefaultCamera = CameraDevice.Rear
});

HandlePhoto(photo);
});
```

The final thing we will do in the `MainViewModel` for now is to handle what happens when the **pick photo from library** button is tapped. Let's set this up by going through the following steps:

1. Create a new property of the `ICommand` type called `PickPhoto`.
2. Use an expression to return a new `Command`.
3. Pass an `Action` as an expression to the constructor of the `Command`.
4. In the `Action`, use the `CrossMedia.Current.PickPhotoAsync` to open the default photo picker of the operating system.
5. Pass the result of the call to the `TakePhotoAsync` method of the `HandlePhoto` method, as shown in the following code:

```
public ICommand PickPhoto => new Command(async () =>
{
    var photo = await CrossMedia.Current.PickPhotoAsync();

    HandlePhoto(photo);
});
```

Building the view

Now, once we have created the `ViewModel`, it is time to create the code for the GUI. Go through the following steps to create the GUI for the `MainView`:

1. Create a new folder called `Views` in the `HotDogOrNot` project.
2. Add a new `XAML` `ContentPage` called `MainView`.
3. Set the `Title` property of the `ContentPage` to `Hotdog or Not hotdog`.
4. Add a `StackLayout` to the page and set its `VerticalOptions` property to `Center`.
5. Add a `Button` to the `StackLayout` with the text `Take Photo`. For the `Command` property, add a binding to the `TakePhoto` property in the `ViewModel`.

6. Add a `Button` to the `StackLayout` with the text `Pick Photo`. For the `Command` property, add a binding to the `PickPhoto` property in the `ViewModel`, as shown in the following code:

```
<ContentPage xmlns="http://xamarin.com/schemas/2014/forms"
             xmlns:x="http://schemas.microsoft.com/winfx/2009/xaml"
             x:Class="HotDogOrNot.Views.MainView"
             Title="Hot dog or Not hot dog">
    <ContentPage.Content>
        <StackLayout VerticalOptions="Center">
            <Button Text="Take Photo" Command="{Binding TakePhoto}" />
            <Button Text="Pick Photo" Command="{Binding PickPhoto}" />
        </StackLayout>
    </ContentPage.Content>
</ContentPage>
```

In the code behind the `MainView`, we will set the binding context of the view by going through the following steps:

1. Add `MainViewModel` as a parameter of the constructor.
2. After the `InitialComponent` method call, set the `BindingContext` property of the view to the `MainViewModel` parameter.
3. Use the static method `SetBackButtonTitle` on the `NavigationPage` class so that an arrow for navigation back to this view will be shown in the navigation bar on the result view, as shown in the following code:

```
public MainView(MainViewModel viewModel)
{
    InitializeComponent();

    BindingContext = viewModel;
    NavigationPage.SetBackButtonTitle(this, string.Empty);
}
```

Now we can go to `App.xaml.cs` and set the `MainPage` to `MainView` by going through the following steps:

1. In the `HotDogOrNot` project, go to `App.xaml.cs`.
2. Create an instance of `MainView` using the `Resolve` method on the `Resolver`.
3. Create a `NavigationPage` and pass the `MainView` to the constructor.
4. Set the static `Navigation` property on the `ViewModel` to the value of the `Navigation` property on the `NavigationPage`.

5. Set the `MainPage` property to the instance of the `NavigationPage` that we created in step 3.

6. Delete `MainPage.xaml`, because we no longer need it. You should be left with the following code:

```
public App()
{
    InitializeComponent();

    var mainView = Resolver.Resolve<MainView>();
    var navigationPage = new NavigationPage(mainView);

    ViewModel.Navigation = navigationPage.Navigation;

    MainPage = navigationPage;
}
```

Building the result view

The last thing we need to do in this project is to create the result view. This view will show the input photo, and whether or not it is a hot dog.

Building the ViewModel

Before we create the view, we will create a `ViewModel` that will handle all the logic for the view by going through the following steps:

1. Create a class called `ResultViewModel` in the `ViewModels` folder in the `HotdogOrNot` project.
2. Add `ViewModel` as a base class to the `ResultViewModel`.
3. Create a property of the `string` type called `Title`. Add a private field for the property.
4. Create a property of the `string` type called `Description`. Add a private field for the property.
5. Create a property of the `byte[]` type called `PhotoBytes`. Add a private field for the property, as shown in the following code:

```
using HotdogOrNot.Models;

namespace HotDogOrNot.ViewModels
{
    public class ResultViewModel : ViewModel
```

```
    {
        private string title;
        public string Title
        {
            get => title;
            set => Set(ref title, value);
        }

        private string description;
        public string Description
        {
            get => description;
            set => Set(ref description, value);
        }

        private byte[] photoBytes;
        public byte[] PhotoBytes
        {
            get => photoBytes;
            set => Set(ref photoBytes, value);
        }
    }
}
```

The final thing we will do in the `ViewModel` is to create an `Initialize` method that will have the result as a parameter. Let's set this up by going through the following steps:

1. In the `Initialize` method, set the `PhotoBytes` property to the value of the `PhotoBytes` property of the `result` parameter.

2. Add an `if` statement that checks whether the `IsHotDog` property of the `result` parameter is `true` and whether the `Confidence` is higher than 90%. If this is the case, set the `Title` to `"Hot dog"` and the `Description` to `"This is for sure a hotdog"`.

3. Add an `else if` statement to check whether the `IsHotdog` property of the `result` parameter is `true`. If this is the case, set the `Title` to `"Maybe"` and the `Description` to `"This is maybe a hotdog"`.

4. Add an `else` statement that sets the `Title` to `"Not a hot dog"` and the `Description` to `"This is not a hot dog"`, as shown in the following code:

```
public void Initialize(Result result)
{
    PhotoBytes = result.PhotoBytes;

    if (result.IsHotdog && result.Confidence > 0.9)
    {
```

```
                Title = "Hot dog";
                Description = "This is for sure a hot dog";
            }
            else if (result.IsHotdog)
            {
                Title = "Maybe";
                Description = "This is maybe a hot dog";
            }
            else
            {
                Title = "Not a hot dog";
                Description = "This is not a hot dog";
            }
    }
```

Building the view

Because we want to show the input photo in the input view, we need to convert it from `byte[]` to `Xamarin.Forms.ImageSource`. We will do this in a value converter that we can use together with the binding in the XAML by going through the following steps:

1. Create a new folder called `Converters` in the `HotDogOrNot` project.
2. Create a new class called `BytesToImageConverter`.
3. Add and implement the `IValueConverter` interface, as shown in the following code:

```
using System;
using System.Globalization;
using System.IO;
using Xamarin.Forms;
public class BytesToImageConverter : IValueConverter
{
    public object Convert(object value, Type targetType, object
    parameter, CultureInfo culture)
    {
        throw new NotImplementedException();
    }

    public object ConvertBack(object value, Type targetType, object
    parameter, CultureInfo culture)
    {
        throw new NotImplementedException();
    }
}
```

The `Convert` method will be used when a `ViewModel` updates a view. The `ConvertBack` method will be used in two-way bindings when the `View` updates the `ViewModel`. In this case, we only need to write code for the `Convert` method by going through the following steps:

1. First, check whether the `value` parameter is `null`. If so, we should return `null`.
2. If the value not is `null`, cast it as `byte[]`.
3. Create a `MemoryStream` from the byte array.
4. Return the result of the `ImageSource.FromStream` method to which we will pass the stream to, as shown in the following code:

```
public object Convert(object value, Type targetType, object
parameter, CultureInfo culture)
{
    if(value == null)
    {
        return null;
    }
    var bytes = (byte[])value;
    var stream = new MemoryStream(bytes);

    return ImageSource.FromStream(() => stream);
}
```

The view will contain the photo, which will take up two-thirds of the screen. Under the photo, we will add a description of the result. Let's set this up by going through the following steps:

1. In the `Views` folder, create a new XAML `ContentPage` and name it `ResultView`.
2. Import the namespace for the converter.
3. Add the `BytesToImageConverter` to the `Resources` for the page and give it the key `"ToImage"`.
4. Bind the `Title` property of the `ContentPage` to the `Title` property of the `ViewModel`.
5. Add a `Grid` to the page with two rows. The `Height` value for the first `RowDefinition` should be `2*`. The height of the second row should be `*`. These are relative values that mean that the first row will take up two-thirds of the `Grid`, while the second row will take up one-third of the `Grid`.
6. Add an `Image` to the `Grid` and bind the `Source` property to the `PhotoBytes` property in the `ViewModel`. Use the converter to convert the bytes to the `ImageSource` of the `Source` property.

7. Add a `Label` and bind the `Text` property to the `Description` property of the `ViewModel`, as shown in the following code:

```
<ContentPage xmlns="http://xamarin.com/schemas/2014/forms"
             xmlns:x="http://schemas.microsoft.com/winfx/2009/xaml"
             xmlns:converters="clr-
namespace:HotdogOrNot.Converters"
             x:Class="HotdogOrNot.Views.ResultView"
             Title="{Binding Title}">
<ContentPage.Resources>
        <converters:BytesToImageConverter x:Key="ToImage" />
</ContentPage.Resources>
    <Grid>
        <Grid.RowDefinitions>
            <RowDefinition Height="2*" />
            <RowDefinition Height="*" />
        </Grid.RowDefinitions>

        <Image Source="{Binding PhotoBytes, Converter=
        {StaticResource ToImage}}" Aspect="AspectFill" />
        <Label Grid.Row="1" HorizontalOptions="Center"
        FontAttributes="Bold" Margin="10" Text="{Binding
        Description}" />
    </Grid>
</ContentPage>
```

We also need to set the `BindingContext` of the view. We will do this in the same way as we did in the `MainView`—in the code-behind file (`ResultView.xaml.cs`), as shown in the following code:

```
public ResultView (ResultViewModel viewModel)
{
    InitializeComponent ();
    BindingContext = viewModel;
}
```

The very last thing we need to do is add navigation from the `MainView` to the `ResultView`. We will do this by adding the following code at the end of the `Classifier_ClassificationCompleted` method in the `MainViewModel`:

```
var view = Resolver.Resolve<ResultView>();
((ResultViewModel)view.BindingContext).Initialize(result);

Navigation.PushAsync(view);
```

Below could you see how the app will look if we upload a photo of a hot dog:

Summary

In this chapter, we built an app that can recognize whether or not a photo has a hot dog. We accomplished this by training a machine learning model for image classification using Azure Cognitive Services and the Custom Vision service.

We exported models for CoreML and TensorFlow and we learned how to use them in apps for both iOS and Android. In these apps, a user can take a photo or pick a photo from their photo library. This photo will be sent to the model to be classified, and we will get a result that tells us whether or not the photo is of a hot dog.

Other Books You May Enjoy

If you enjoyed this book, you may be interested in these other books by Packt:

Mastering Xamarin UI Development - Second Edition
Steven F. Daniel

ISBN: 9781788995511

- Build native and cross-platform apps for both iOS and Android using the Xamarin and Xamarin.Forms platform using C# 7.
- Implement and customize different user-interface layouts and Animations within your application and use the PlatFormEffects API to change appearance of control elements.
- Understand the MVVM architectural pattern and how to implement this with your apps.
- Build a NavigationService class to enable. navigation between your ViewModels as well as Implementing Data-Binding to control elements within your XAML pages and ViewModels.
- Work with the Razor Templating Engine to create Models and Razor Pages that communicate with an SQLite database.
- Build a LocationService class to incorporate location-based features within your cross-platform apps to display the user's current location by creating a custom cross-platform map control and handle location tracking updates.
- Work with the Microsoft Azure App Services Platform and Implement Social networking features within your app using the Twitter API.
- Unit Testing your Xamarin.Forms apps using the NUnit and UITest Frameworks

React and React Native - Second Edition
Adam Boduch

ISBN: 9781789346794

- Learn what has changed in React 16 and how you stand to benefit
- Craft reusable components using the React virtual DOM
- Learn how to use the new create-react-native-app command line tool
- Augment React components with GraphQL for data using Relay
- Handle state for architectural patterns using Flux
- Build an application for web UIs using Relay

Leave a review - let other readers know what you think

Please share your thoughts on this book with others by leaving a review on the site that you bought it from. If you purchased the book from Amazon, please leave us an honest review on this book's Amazon page. This is vital so that other potential readers can see and use your unbiased opinion to make purchasing decisions, we can understand what our customers think about our products, and our authors can see your feedback on the title that they have worked with Packt to create. It will only take a few minutes of your time, but is valuable to other potential customers, our authors, and Packt. Thank you!

Index

Printed in Great Britain
by Amazon

12581274R10237